Critical Perspectives on Migration in the Twenty-First Century

EDITED BY

MARIANNA KARAKOULAKI, LAURA SOUTHGATE
& JAKOB STEINER

E-INTERNATIONAL
RELATIONS
PUBLISHING

E-International Relations
www.E-IR.info
Bristol, England
2018

ISBN 978-1-910814-41-3 (paperback)
ISBN 978-1-910814-42-0 (e-book)

Production: Michael Tang
Cover Image: Dimitris Tosidis

A catalogue record for this book is available from the British Library.

E-IR Edited Collections

Series Editors: Stephen McGlinchey, Marianna Karakoulaki and Agnieszka Pikulicka-Wilczewska

Books Editor: Cameran Clayton

Editorial assistance: Matt Harker, Majer Ma, Xolisile Ntuli, Max Nurnus and Farah Saleem

E-IR's Edited Collections are open access scholarly books presented in a format that preferences brevity and accessibility while retaining academic conventions. Each book is available in print and digital versions, and is published under a Creative Commons license. As E-International Relations is committed to open access in the fullest sense, free electronic versions of all of our books, including this one, are available on our website.

Find out more at: http://www.e-ir.info/publications

About the E-International Relations website

E-International Relations (www.E-IR.info) is the world's leading open access website for students and scholars of international politics, reaching over 3 million unique readers. E-IR's daily publications feature expert articles, blogs, reviews and interviews – as well as student learning resources. The website is run by a registered non-profit organisation based in Bristol, UK and staffed with an all-volunteer team of students and scholars.

Abstract

Thousands of people risk their lives daily by crossing borders in search of a better life. During 2015, over one million of these people arrived in Europe. Images of refugees in distress became headline news in what was considered to be the worst humanitarian crisis in Europe since 1945. This book provides a critical overview of recent migration flows and offers answers as to why people flee, what happens during their flight and investigates the various responses to mass migratory movements. Divided in two parts, the book addresses long-running academic, policy and domestic debates, drawing on case studies of migration in Europe, the Middle East and the Asia Pacific. Coming from a variety of different fields, the contributors provide an interdisciplinary approach and open the discussion on the reasons why migration should be examined critically.

Acknowledgements

First of all, we would like to thank all the contributors to this book. We tried to gather scholars and practitioners from different academic fields and from different stages in their careers in order to provide a more interdisciplinary narrative to this book. We are thankful for their trust and patience. Finally, we would like to dedicate this book to all those who risk their lives in order to reach safe shores and yet remain unknown to most of us whilst making a huge difference in these uncertain times and spaces.

Editors

Marianna Karakoulaki is Articles Editor and a Director of E-International Relations. She is an award winning journalist and foreign correspondent. She regularly reports as a freelance foreign correspondent for Deutsche Welle and has worked with IRIN, The Telegraph, Middle East Eye, CBC Radio, Voice of America, BBC Radio, Channel 4 News, Radio Television Suisse, Human Rights Watch and Refugees International among others.

Laura Southgate is a Lecturer in Politics and International Relations at Aston University. She is a regular contributor for Global Risk Insights and a Senior Commissioning Editor for E-International Relations. Her research focuses on regional intervention and state resistance to sovereignty violation in Southeast Asia. Her work has been published in *International Politics*, *Intelligence and National Security*, and *Journal of Asian Security and International Affairs*.

Jakob Steiner is a PhD student at the Department of Physical Geography at Universiteit Utrecht, the Netherlands and a Senior Commissioning Editor for E-International Relations. He has conducted field research on drivers of local migration and rural development in rural Pakistan and on the paths of Pakistani men leaving along the common refugee routes for Europe.

Contributors

Sally Clark attained her doctorate from Swinburne University in 2016. Her PhD, titled 'Navigating Asylum: Journeys from Indonesia to Australia' charts the precarious nature of life in transit for Hazara asylum seekers undergoing refugee status determination and explores the connection between conditions in transit and irregular migration. She is currently lecturing in international politics and conducting research on displacement and exceptionality in marginalised groups.

Kamel Doraï is a researcher at the French National Centre for Scientific Research currently based at IFPO, Jordan and research associate at MIGRINTER, University of Poitiers. His work focuses mainly on asylum seekers and refugees in the Middle East. He is currently conducting research on Syrian and Palestinian refugees from Syria in Jordan and Lebanon as well as on the urbanization process of Palestinian refugee camps in Lebanon.

Susana Ferreira holds a PhD in International Relations and International Security from the NOVA University of Lisbon and the Instituto Universitario General Gutiérrez Mellado. She is a researcher with the Instituto Português de Relações Internacionais (IPRI), NOVA University and the Centro de Investigação de Segurança e Defesa do IUM (CISDI). She has been a visiting scholar at the Instituto Universitario General Gutiérrez Mellado and at the Institute for the Study of International Migration, Georgetown University.

Andriani Fili is part of the interdisciplinary research group of Border Criminologies as managing editor of the blog and social media, and a Research Associate at the University of Oxford Centre for Criminology. She is a PhD candidate at the University of Lancaster. Her research focuses on resistance in women's immigration detention centres in Greece. She has published on immigration detention in Greece and is currently co-editing a book on criminal justice research in an era of mass mobility.

Benjamin Hulme is a PhD candidate in EU Law at the University of Warwick. His primary research interest is EU migration and asylum law, in particular, returns and readmission. His wider interests include EU constitutional, human rights and external relations law and policy. He holds an LL.B. Law degree and an LL.M. in International Human Rights Law from the University of York.

Amadu Wurie Khan is an independent researcher and consultant on forced migration, international development, the news media and social policy. He has contributed to teaching and research at the University of Edinburgh and Njala University. Amadu Khan is a human rights journalist and storyteller-performer artist. He is currently a Senior Research Fellow at the Nomoli Media Group.

Dora Kostakopoulou is Professor of European Union Law, European Integration and Public Policy at Warwick Law School. She was Co-director of the Institute of Law, Economy and Global Governance at the University of Manchester (2005–2011) and Director of the Centre for European Law at the University of Southampton (2011–2012). She was British Academy, Thank Offering to Britain Fellow (2003–2004) and recipient of an Innovation Award by the Arts and Humanities Research Council (2004–2005).

Anitta Kynsilehto holds an Academy of Finland Postdoctoral Fellowship (2015–2018) for a project titled 'Everyday politics of solidarity: Undocumented Mobilities in Europe and the Mediterranean'. She works at the Tampere Peace Research Institute and is the author of *Choreographies of Resistance: Mobile Bodies and Relational Politics* (with Tarja Väyrynen, Eeva Puumala, Samu Pehkonen and Tiina Vaittinen; Rowman & Littlefield, 2017) and *Gender and Mobility: A Critical Introduction* (with Elina Penttinen; Rowman & Littlefield, 2017). She serves as board member to the EuroMed Rights network.

Nicola Langdon researches and lectures in International Relations and sustainability issues at the University of Plymouth. Her research interests lie predominantly in the realms of security studies and foreign policy, with a specific focus upon the interplay between the media and interventionism. Her PhD, from the University of Plymouth, focused upon morality framing during conflict. More recently she has applied this methodology to look at issues of sustainability, including green energy production.

Emma Larking is currently a Visiting Fellow at the Australian National University's School of Regulation and Global Governance RegNet, where her research focuses on political mobilisations for social justice, especially anti-poverty campaigns and the global food sovereignty movement. She has published widely on the concept and status of human rights, and on refugees and forced migration. She is the author of *Refugees and the Myth of Human Rights: Life Outside the Pale of the Law* (Ashgate, 2014) and co-editor with Hilary Charlesworth of *Human Rights and the Universal Periodic Review: Rituals and Ritualism* (Cambridge University Press, 2014).

Valsamis Mitsilegas is Professor of European Criminal Law, Dean for Research (Humanities and Social Sciences) and Head of the Department of Law at Queen Mary University of London (QMUL). He is currently serving as Academic Lead for Internationalisation for the University. He is the Inaugural

Director of the Queen Mary Institute for the Humanities and Social Sciences (IHSS) and has been the Director of the Queen Mary Criminal Justice Centre since 2011. His latest books are *The Criminalisation of Migration in Europe* (Springer, 2015) and *EU Criminal Law after Lisbon* (Hart, 2016).

Thomas Nail is an Associate Professor of Philosophy at the University of Denver. He is the author of *Returning to Revolution: Deleuze, Guattari and Zapatismo* (Edinburgh University Press, 2012), *The Figure of the Migrant* (Stanford University Press, 2015), *Theory of the Border* (Oxford University Press, 2016) and co-editor of *Between Deleuze and Foucault* (Edinburgh University Press, 2016). His work has appeared in publications such as *Angelaki, Theory & Event, Philosophy Today, Parrhesia, SubStance, Deleuze Studies, Foucault Studies*.

Özlem Özdemir works for The Gendarmerie General Command in Turkey. She received her PhD from Akdeniz University, Institute of Social Sciences, Faculty of Communication in 2014. She was an academic visitor at Swansea University College of Arts and Humanities in 2013–2014, and a post-doctoral academic visitor at Swansea University College of Science, Department of Geography between 2014–2016.

Jenny Poon is a PhD Candidate at the Faculty of Law of the University of Western Ontario, a qualified Barrister & Solicitor in Ontario, as well as a Visiting Study Fellow at the University of Oxford Refugee Studies Centre, Trinity Term 2017. Jenny's research focuses on examining the principle of non-refoulement as a norm in international and European law and comparative analysis of the United Kingdom and Germany.

Contents

I

Introduction

Critical Perspectives on Migration in the Twenty-First Century

MARIANNA KARAKOULAKI, LAURA SOUTHGATE
& JAKOB STEINER

In the summer of 2015 the island of Lesbos in Greece, located just a few miles from the shores of Turkey, became a symbol of the so-called migration crisis in Europe. In an island of less than 87,000 residents, thousands of people were arriving on a daily basis. In some ways, Lesbos represented the European dream: the first step to safety and prosperity for thousands of people, far from the conflicts of the Middle East. That summer the 'migration crisis', so dubbed by the media, had just reached its climax. Two years later, Lesbos still struggles to cope with overcrowded camps, and has become the symbol of Europe's mismanagement of migration (Broderick 2017; Holland 2017; Sallet 2017; Stone 2017). How did we get here? How can we place this in a wider debate on migration? And what is missing to lead that debate?

The Century of the Migrant: A Fractious Debate

Central to this edited collection is the individual plight of millions of displaced peoples in what has been referred to as the 'century of the migrant' (Nail 2015, 1). Since the start of the twenty-first century, the number of international migrants has grown rapidly, from 173 million in 2000, to 244 million in 2015, and to 258 million in 2017 (UN 2015, 1; 2017). Of those, 65.6 million were forced to flee their countries due to conflict and persecution in 2016, leading the United Nations High Commissioner for Refugees (UNHCR) to conclude that forced displacement was at its highest peak in decades (UNHCR 2017). The routes taken are often dangerous, putting refugees at continuous risk even after they have left a war zone. On 9 November 2017, an article listed the names of 33,293 migrants who died on their way to reach Europe. That list was an attempt to 'identify thousands of dead as human beings, with an origin, a past, a life' (Casdorff and Maroldt 2017).

Domestic debate as to the relative costs and benefits of migration is extensive and fractious. As of 2008, more than 30 million foreign citizens were living in the 27 Member States of the European Union (Spencer 2011, 1). In the United Kingdom, a 2012 poll showed that 68% of the British public believed that migration had a negative effect on Britain (YouGov 2012). Germany, which accepted 890,000 migrants in 2015, held pro- and anti-migration marches following the European migration crisis (Amnesty International 2016). In France, which declared it would accept 24,000 refugees in the wake of the migrant crisis, public opinion was split, with at least half opposing the arrival of more refugees (Chrisafis 2016). What these figures show is both the degree to which migration dominates domestic policy, particularly during election periods and in the wake of specific crises, and the mixed feelings citizens hold towards the issue. Indeed, recent studies suggest that the United Kingdom's decision to leave the European Union (EU) following the controversial 'Brexit' campaign held in 2016, was due in part to anti-migrant prejudice and fears of uncontrolled migration (Meleady et al., 2017).

Current academic debate on the subject of migration is equally varied and contested. Whilst some scholars focus on the economic and cultural impact of migration (Eckstein and Najam 2013), others focus on political borders and boundaries (De Genova 2017; Bacas and Kavanagh 2013), state and institution migration policies (Boswell and Geddes 2011), human rights (Gammeltoft-Hansen and Vedsted-Hansen 2017) and gender (Yucesahin and Yazgan 2017) to name but a few. Acknowledging the importance of these contributions to the study of migration, this edited collection seeks to build on their work by providing an inter-disciplinary analysis of migration in the twenty-first century. Straddling the political, legal and humanitarian disciplines, this collection shines a light on underlying perspectives and drivers of migration, and critically appraises current international and regional responses. It addresses the long-running academic, policy and domestic debate, drawing on case studies of migration in Europe, the Middle East and the Asia Pacific.

Before moving forward with the structure of the book, this chapter will briefly examine migrant terminology, followed by an overview of classical theories of migration more commonly used in the previous century.

Debating Terminology: Migrant, Refugee or Asylum Seeker?

The media's sudden focus on migration and the rising number of people arriving on Europe's shores has sparked a debate on terminology. If one looks at a variety of reports from 2015 and before, the terms migrant, refugee and asylum seeker were used interchangeably, as the debate over terminology became heated. In August 2015, Al Jazeera decided to stop using the word 'migrant' in an attempt to avoid any negative connotations with that term, and substituted it with the word 'refugee' (Malone, 2015). Other media outlets published articles explaining these terms in more detail, with reasons why people needed to take care when using them due to the potential legal implications of using the wrong term (Sengupta 2015; Spencer 2015; Travis 2015; UNHCR 2016b).

The way a migrant is defined, however, is a complex issue. For the International Organisation of Migration (IOM), a migrant is someone who is moving across borders or within a state, despite their legal status, the reasons and causes of the movement, or the length of the stay in the host country (IOM n.d.). The UNHCR, on the other hand, defines a migrant as someone who chooses to move mainly to improve his or her life (2016b). One of the reasons why the definition of 'migrant' is so complex is that it includes a wide range of people who are all in a different situation, who cross borders because of different reasons, yet all have their movement as a common factor (Koser 2007).

A 'refugee', on the other hand, is strictly defined by legal texts and international conventions. According to the Convention Relating to the Status of Refugees (1951) defines a refugee as someone who:

> owing to a well-founded fear of being persecuted for reasons of race, religion, nationality, membership of a particular social group or political opinion, is outside the country of his nationality and is unable or, owing to such fear, is unwilling to avail himself of the protection of that country; or who, not having a nationality and being outside the country of his former habitual residence as a result of such events, is unable or, owing to such fear, is unwilling to return to it.

Finally, an 'asylum seeker' is someone who has fled their country of origin and has made a claim for asylum under the 1951 Refugee Convention, and their status has not yet been determined (O' Neil 2010, 6; UNHCR 2011).

In his book 'The Figure of the Migrant' (2015), Thomas Nail adopts the use of the word 'migrant'. He explains, however, that whilst everyone who crosses borders is a migrant, their movement differs as '[f]or some movement offers opportunity, recreation, and profit with only a temporary expulsion. For others, movement is dangerous and constrained, and their social expulsions are much more severe and permanent' (2015, 2). While this book's contributors use the terms interchangeably, Thomas Nail provides a history of the theory of the migrant in the first chapter of the book, providing an important guideline to this underlying challenge of terminology.

Theorising Migration in the Twentieth Century

During the twentieth century, those who studied migration mainly focused on its economic aspects. Thus, the theories that developed during that period were mostly of an economic nature. The type of migration that characterises the most recent migratory flow – and the one that most contributors of this book focus on – is different, with a majority appearing to flee from conflict-affected areas.

An attempt to explain the reasons why people migrate was made by Ernest Ravenstein in 1885, when he published the 'Laws of Migration'. Ravenstein came to the conclusion that migration is the result of a push and pull process that makes people cross borders, either by being *pushed* by their unfavourable countries' conditions, or *pulled* by the host countries' favourable conditions. The following suppositions are central to Ravenstein's Laws: that migrants are less likely to move long distances; there is a process of absorption in which people who surround a rapidly growing town are drawn to it, thus leaving rural areas to migrants from distant areas; there is an inverse process of absorption with similar characteristics; each migration flow produces a counter-flow; migrants who move long distances usually prefer large centres with economic growth; those who live in a town are less likely to migrate than those in rural areas; and that women migrate more than men (Ravenstein 1885).

Migration theories of the twentieth century draw upon Ravenstein's Laws of Migration, whilst focusing on the economics of migration (either internal migration or international migration). Everett Lee (1966) attempted to provide a Theory of Migration by emphasising push and pull factors, the difficulties migrants face, and migrant profiling (age, gender, class, education). The Neoclassical Economic Theory, which is mainly used to describe migration between two countries, suggests that there is a correlation between the global supply and demand for labour and the reason people migrate, effectively driven by a wage gap among geographical areas (Sjaastad 1962; Todaro 1969; Jennissen 2007). The Dual Labour Market Theory suggests that it is pull factors that lead people to migrate, because there is always demand for migrant workers in developed countries – something that is inherent in their economic structure (Piore 1979; Massey et al. 1993, 440–1; Jennissen 2007). Additionally, the World Systems Theory focuses on a more sociological examination of migration, suggesting that due to the interaction among global societies, migration is influenced by the capitalist development of the global market (Massey et al. 1993).

These dominant theories have been subjected to criticism (Arango 2000; Massey et al. 1998), notably that they are overtly focused on why some people move whilst ignoring why others do not, as well as a lack of attention to state policies as influencers of migration. As Arango (2000) notes, migration is 'both very complex and straightforward'. General explanations are therefore bound to be 'reductionistic'. However, the basic unequal distribution of resources (including a 'safe living environment') lies convincingly at the basis of many migration patterns. In any case, in order to adequately describe migration in the twenty-first century these commonly applied theories need to be expanded to include a number of other dimensions beyond the economic 'push and pull'. These should include societal factors and broader social processes and changes. Recent attempts to expand the theoretical debate have led to more interdisciplinary approaches to theorising migration (Massey et al. 1993; Favell 2008; Bretell and Hollifield 2000; Castles 2008). This book seeks to contribute to this growing interdisciplinary debate.

One critical dimension is evident from recent developments: the inclusion of refugees in the larger debate. And while the development of an actual theory to describe current developments may be too farfetched – and considering the complexity of the problem also not necessarily desirable – a collection of critical approaches to discuss the topic should provide a guide to what is relevant in this increasingly complex field.

Structure of the Book

The chapters that follow are presented in two parts: 'Perspectives of Migration' and 'Drivers and Responses to Migration'. Our attempt here is to move beyond one single perspective; be it forced migration, the economics of migration, or refugee studies – among others – to draw on under-theorised perspectives on migration. The chapters in this collection are therefore underpinned by a critical theoretical analysis. By considering in greater detail the philosophical history of the migrant, the language and framing of migration, and narratives of security, sovereignty and identity, the collected authors critique current approaches and offer new and innovative ways to address migration in the twenty-first century.

Perspectives

As an entry point into the book, Thomas Nail uses a theoretical lens to discuss the modern philosophical history of the political centrality of the migrant. Through his examination of the works of Marx, Nietzsche, Arendt, Deleuze and Guattari, Badiou, Agamben, Balibar, and Hardt and Negri, Nail reveals the existence of a common figure defined by movement. With this theoretical history, Nail claims we are now in a position to move forward with the consequences and political history of this figure for the twenty-first century. For Nail, this is a century at a crossroads, where migration has reached a critical threshold, and new theories are required that favour the figure of the migrant. Nail's chapter provides an answer to the most divisive debate of the past couple of years by discussing the history and theory of the migrant.

Following the theoretical debate on the migrant, Amadu Wurie Khan looks into the identity of migrants and argues that they can have multiple identities and are not restricted to a 'singular' national identity. He considers the United Kingdom (UK) government's formulation of restrictive and assimilationist citizenship policies, and the impact of such policies on aspiring UK citizens. Khan explores this internalisation of cultures and identities through examination of the experiences and views of 23 asylum seekers and refugees residing in Edinburgh and Glasgow in Scotland, with interview questions covering a range of topics from naturalisation and statelessness, participation in 'British' citizenship classes, and transnational cultural practices.

Emma Larking's chapter opens the discussion on migration and human rights. Larking examines the universality of human rights, which she seeks to expose as a false premise. According to this argument, the universal enjoyment of human rights is in fact heavily circumscribed, with access to rights linked to citizenship of just a few states. For Larking, structural impediments to universalising human rights, most notably the principle of sovereignty, have been downplayed by many international law scholars and human rights practitioners. As Larking seeks to show, re-casting human rights along recommended lines is possible, and can do more for self-determination than continuing to uphold an outdated conception of sovereignty.

The next chapter by Susana S. Ferreira looks into the European Union (EU) and the current migratory crisis, and examines the securitisation narratives of European leaders. Through an analysis of EU security practices and narratives, Ferreira argues that the EU has entered a crisis mode, with increasingly negative and xenophobic statements leading to the securitisation of the migration crisis. Going one step further, Ferreira explores perceptions of European citizens, and the growing support for nationalist and populist parties in Europe, to claim that there has been an acceptance of this securitisation by the public. For Ferreira, if the EU does not move beyond a securitisation approach, security, stability and the free movement of people are at risk.

Chapter five sees Marianna Karakoulaki's attempt to shed light on the refugee crisis in Greece. By using ethnography as a methodology, Karakoulaki tells five different stories that took place in five different periods between 2015 and 2017. These stories are an attempt to examine the way in which borders create violence, the kinds of violence they create and how this violence can be fought. Karakoulaki concludes that the violence of the borders can be eliminated with a no borders politics.

The final chapter of the 'Perspectives' section, by Nicola Langdon, examines the Syrian refugee crisis through the lens of the British press. Through a discursive construction of the crisis, Langdon focuses her attention on British media 'threat' framing, 'othering' and cosmopolitan framing, which she argues, have impacted upon public understandings and perceptions of refugees. For Langdon, by framing the refugee movement as a threat and manipulating the proximity of the event, the British media has shaped our compassion for those suffering from violence and insecurity, and our support for policy formation in the wake of the Syrian crisis.

The second part of the book – 'Drivers and Responses' – starts by examining what drives people to migrate, focusing specifically on the current migratory flows from the Middle East, how these drivers are framed and what happens when refugees stop moving. In the first chapter of this section, Kamel Doraï examines the movement of Syrian refugees towards neighbouring countries and consequently assesses the socio-political consequences of the mass arrival of Syrian refugees in Lebanon and Jordan since 2011. More specifically, Doraï focuses on the gradual changes of migration policies in both countries and its consequences on migration patterns, with special attention placed on Palestinian refugees from Syria, and the forms of settlement of the Syrian refugees. For Doraï, the large influx of refugees from Syria has had a significant local impact on host societies, and has led to the development of restrictive migration policies in neighbouring countries.

Remaining on the topic of Syrian refugees, Özlem Özdemir's chapter examines an often-ignored issue; women refugees during the flight. Özdemir claims neither the migratory route is safe nor transit camps are safe for women refugees. Through a gender and human security analysis Özdemir looks into the specifics of women's displacement by placing her focus on Syrian women refugees during the recent refugee crisis. Özdemir showcases the gendered nature of migration and concludes human security during migration needs to be examined through a gendered lens.

A book on migration would not have been complete if it did not assess the way migration is dealt with on a larger political, legal and social level. Sally Clark examines Australia's asylum policies and its transit camps as she explores the effects of developed nation-states' aggressive border security policies on forced migrants and the transit countries that host them. For Clark, these practices are designed to exclude forced migrants from territories where the rights of asylum are enshrined. In her examination of the Australia-Indonesia relationship, Clark ascertains that Australia, in a bid to protect itself from unwanted migration, has implemented border security policies that have had an instrumental role in reconfiguring the search for asylum in Southeast Asia. In so doing, migrants have been left desperately searching for ways to seek protection.

On the same topic, Andriani Fili provides an in-depth examination of containment practices in Greece. Fili argues that Greece's policies towards irregular migration have increasingly relied upon detention and deportation, to the detriment of human lives. Driven by an interest in the Greek notion of hospitality, Fili considers the primary characteristics of the Greek detention system. In doing so, Fili claims that Greek detention practices have been legitimised through a narrative of deterrence, the rationalisation of deportation and the denial of both policies' racialised nature. As a result, Greece's humanitarian and leftist ideals have been abandoned, and its migrants are left at risk and unaccounted for.

The following chapter by Anitta Kynsilehto examines different types of migrant solidarity action, both those with a humanitarian orientation, and those geared towards advocacy. For Kynsilehto, the distinctions in solidarity action are becoming increasingly difficult to uphold. This is due to inequalities that actors at all levels regularly witness, and the radical undermining of human rights frameworks. Drawing on insights from her own ongoing multi-sited ethnographic research at different borders around the Mediterranean Sea, Kynsilehto addresses the spatialities and temporalities of solidarity activism, and the critical practices and politics of movements, before addressing the tendency of criminalising solidarity action and the long-term impact on actions of solidarity.

Remaining on the topic of solidarity but from a different perspective, Valsamis Mitsilegas assesses its legal meaning in the Common European Asylum System. Mitsilegas seeks to demonstrate the limits of a state-centred approach to solidarity. In this view, claims of solidarity have been advanced with states as beneficiaries and reference points. Instead, Mitsilegas advocates for a concept of solidarity centred on the individual, achievable by the application of the principle of mutual recognition in the field of positive asylum decisions. Looking forward, Mitsilegas argues for a uniform refugee status across the European Union, which can act as a catalyst for a strengthened refugee-centred solidarity.

The next chapter by Benjamin Hulme and Dora Kostakopoulou analyses the European Union's migration policy. Hulme and Kostakopoulou examine a number of historical developments in the European Union's migration policy, before moving on to focus on more recent developments in EU policy. These recent developments include the creation of a new European Coast Guard, and new forms of 'third country' agreements and the harmonisation of 'third country' information. The authors highlight a number of concerns with regards to these developments, including the need to respect human rights and provide effective protection to those in need. However, for Hulme and Kostakopoulou, these developments are a significant step in the development of a truly Common European Asylum System.

The final chapter of the book by Jenny Poon is an in-depth examination of the legal responses to the refugee crisis. Poon argues that the international and regional legal responses to the refugee crisis have been inadequate and much too late. At the international level, Poon claims that guidelines imposed by the UNHCR permit group recognition of refugee status, rather than the processing of applications on a case-by-case basis. At the regional level, it is argued that the European Union's process of swapping one asylum claimant for another promotes violation of the principle of non-refoulement. For Poon, change should be implemented at both levels in order to properly safeguard the rights of asylum claimants and refugees.

The topic of migration is one that has no end. Whilst it is difficult to grasp all aspects of migration fully, this book tries to bridge the gap between different fields and frameworks and provide an insight into the current migration crisis. The ultimate goal of the editors is to encourage discussion on the utility of the critical perspective as a theoretical tool of analysis, and the interdisciplinary nature of migration and refugee studies.

References

Amnesty International. 2016. *Germany 2016/2017*. https://www.amnesty.org/ en/countries/europe-and-central-asia/germany/report-germany/.

Arango, Joachin. 2000. "Explaining Migration: A Critical View." *International Social Science Journal* 52, no 165: 283–296.

Bacas, Jutta Lauth and William Kavanagh, eds. 2013. *Border Encounters: Asymmetry and Proximity at Europe's Frontiers*. Oxford: Berghahn Books.

Boswell, Christina and Andrew Geddes. 2011. *Migration and Mobility in the European Union*. New York: Palgrave Macmillan.

Brettell, Caroline and James F. Hollifield. 2000. *Migration Theory*. New York: Routledge.

Broderick, Ryan. 2017. "These Shocking WhatsApp Videos Show The Conditions Inside One Of Europe's Worst Refugee Camps." *Buzzfeed*, 18 December 2017. https://www.buzzfeed.com/ryanhatesthis/these-shocking-whatsapp-videos-show-the-conditions-from?utm_term=.xtn5bWb4L#.luAwpkpID.

Casdorff, Stephan-Andreas and Lorenz Maroldt. 2017. "Künstlerin dokumentiert das Sterben von 33.293 Geflüchteten" [Artist Documents the Deaths of 33,293 Refugees]. *Der Tagesspiegel*, 09 November 2017. http://www.tagesspiegel.de/politik/die-liste-von-banu-cennetoglu-kuenstlerin-dokumentiert-das-sterben-von-33-293-gefluechteten/20558658.html.

Castels, Stephen. 2008. "Development and Migration – Migration and Development: What comes first?" Paper presented at Social Science Research Council Conference Migration and Development: Future Directions for Research and Policy, New York City, 28 February–1 March 2008.

Chrisafis, Angelique. 2016. "French PM Manuel Valls Says Refugee Crisis Is Destabilising Europe." *The Guardian*. 22 January 2016. https://www.theguardian.com/world/2016/jan/22/french-pm-manuel-valls-says-refugee-crisis-is-destabilising-europe.

De Genova, Nicholas, ed. 2017. *The Borders of "Europe": Autonomy of Migration, Tactics of Bordering*. Durham: Duke University Press.

Eckstein, Susan and Adil Najam. 2013. *How Immigrants Impact Their Homelands*. Durham: Duke University Press.

Favell, Adrian. 2008. "The New Face of East-West migration in Europe." *Journal of Ethnic and Migration Studies* 34, no. 5: 701–716.

Frontex. n.d. "Migratory Routes Map." http://frontex.europa.eu/trends-and-routes/migratory-routes-map/.

Gammeltoft-Hansen, Thomas and Jens Vedsted-Hansen, eds. 2017. *Human Rights and the Dark Side of Globalisation: Transnational Law Enforcement and Migration Control*. London: Routledge.

Holland, Lisa. 2017. "Migrants 'Stuck and Forgotten' in Notorious Camp on Lesbos." *Sky News*, 10 July 2017. https://news.sky.com/story/migrants-stuck-and-forgotten-in-notorious-camp-on-lesbos-10944205.

International Organisation of Migration (IOM). n.d. "Who is a Migrant?" Accessed 28 October 2017. https://www.iom.int/who-is-a-migrant.

Jennissen, Roel. 2007. "Causality Chains in the International Migration Systems Approach." *Population Research and Policy Review* 26, 411–36.

Koser, Khalid. 2007. *International Migration: A Very Short Introduction*. Oxford, New York: Oxford University Press.

Lee, Everett. 1966. "A Theory of Migration." *Demography* 3, 47–57.

Massey, Douglas, Joaquin Arango, Graeme Hugo, Ali Kouaouci, Adela Pellegrino and J. Edward Taylor. 1993. "Theories of International Migration: A Review and Appraisal." *Population and Development Review* 19, no. 3.

Massey, Douglass S., Joaquin Arango, Graeme Hugo, Ali Kouaouci, Adela Pellegrino and J. Edward Taylor. 1998. *Worlds in Motion: Understanding International Migration at the End of the Millennium*. Oxford University Press.

Malone, Barry. 2015. "Why Al Jazeera Will Not Say Mediterranean 'Migrants'." *Al Jazeera*, 20 August 2015. http://www.aljazeera.com/blogs/editors-blog/2015/08/al-jazeera-mediterranean-migrants-150820082226309.html.

Meleady, Rose, Charles R. Seger and Marieke Vermue. 2017. "Examining the Role of Positive and Negative Intergroup Contact and Anti-Immigrant Prejudice in Brexit." *British Journal of Social Psychology* 53, no. 4.

Nail, Thomas. 2015. *The Figure of the Migrant*. Stanford: Stanford University Press.

Piore, Michael. 1979. *Birds of Passage: Migrant Labor and Industrial Societies*. Cambridge: Cambridge University Press.

Ravenstein, Ernest G. 1885. "The Laws of Migration." *Journal of the Royal Statistical Society* 48: 167–235. https://cla.umn.edu/sites/cla.umn.edu/files/the_laws_of_migration.pdf.

Sallet, Oliver. 2017. "Refugees Living in Dire Conditions on Lesbos." *Deutsche Welle*, 18 December 2017. http://www.dw.com/en/refugees-living-in-dire-conditions-on-lesbos/av-41837591?maca=en-Twitter-sharing.

Singleton, Ann. 2015. "Speaking Truth to Power? Why Civil Society, Beyond Academia, Remains Marginal in EU Migration Policy." In *Integrating Immigrants in Europe*, edited by Peter Scholten, Han Entzinger, Rinus Penninx, Stijn Verbeek. Springer.

Sjaastad, Larry. 1962. "The Costs and Returns of Human Migration." *Journal of Political Economy* 70: 80–93.

Spencer, Sarah. 2011. *The Migration Debate*. Bristol: Policy Press.

Spencer, Richard. 2015. "What Is the Difference between a Refugee, a Migrant and an Asylum Seeker?" *The Telegraph,* 22 September 2015. http://www.telegraph.co.uk/news/worldnews/europe/eu/11883027/What-is-the-difference-between-a-refugee-a-migrant-and-an-asylum-seeker.html.

Stone, Mark. 2017. "The Refugee Families Living Among Filth and Faeces in Camp in Greece." *Sky News*, 20 December 2017. https://news.sky.com/story/the-refugee-families-living-among-filth-and-faeces-in-camp-in-greece-11177872.

Todaro, Michael. 1969. "A Model of Labor Migration and Urban Unemployment in Less Developed Countries." *The American Economic Review* 59: 138–148.

Travis, Alan. 2015. "Migrants, Refugees and Asylum Seekers: What's the Difference?" *The Guardian*. https://www.theguardian.com/world/2015/aug/28/migrants-refugees-and-asylum-seekers-whats-the-difference.

United Nations Department for Economic and Social Affairs. 2015. *International Migration Report 2015: Highlights*. ST/ESA/SER.A/375. http://www.un.org/en/development/desa/population/migration/publications/migrationreport/docs/MigrationReport2015_Highlights.pdf.

United Nations Department of Economic and Social Affairs. 2017. "The International Migration Report [Highlights]." New York: United Nations. https:// www.un.org/development/desa/publications/international-migration-report-2017.html.

United Nations High Commissioner for Refugees (UNHCR). 2007. "Statistics on Displaced Iraqis around the World: Global Overview." http://www.unhcr. org/461f7cb92.pdf.

United Nations High Commissioner for Refugees (UNHCR). 2010. *Conventions and Protocol Regarding the Status of Refugees*. http://www. unhcr.org/3b66c2aa10.pdf.

United Nations High Commissioner for Refugees (UNHCR). 2011. "UNHCR Resettlement Handbook. Divisions of International Protection." http://www. unhcr.org/46f7c0ee2.pdf.

United Nations High Commissioner for Refugees (UNHCR). 2016a. "Mixed Movements in South-East Asia." https://unhcr.atavist.com/mm2016.

United Nations High Commissioner for Refugees (UNHCR). 2016b. "UNHCR viewpoint: 'Refugee' or 'migrant' – Which is right?" http://www.unhcr.org/news/ latest/2016/7/55df0e556/unhcr-viewpoint-refugee-migrant-right.html.

United Nations High Commissioner for Refugees (UNHCR). 2017. "Global Trends: Forced Discplacement in 2016." http://www.unhcr.org/5943e8a34.pdf.

YouGov. 2012. *Sunday Times Survey Results*. 6 January. http://cdn.yougov. com/cumulus_uploads/document/d51j2t3jzl/YG-Archives-Pol-ST-results-06-080112.pdf.

Yucesahin, Murat and Pinar Yazgan, eds. 2017. *Revisiting Gender and Migration*. London: Transnational Press.

Part One

Perspectives

1

The Political Centrality of the Migrant

THOMAS NAIL

Political theory from Plato to Rawls has largely treated the migrant as a secondary or derived political figure of relatively little importance. Political theory has tended to privilege citizens and states over migrants and their circulations.

This chapter, however, shows for the first time that within this dominant history is also a subterranean or minor history of political theory that grants the figure of the migrant a certain degree of centrality or importance. If we want to rethink migration in the twenty-first century, we must be able to rethink the basic assumptions that we have inherited from a certain dominant history of political theory. One of the best ways to do this is to begin with the subterranean history that has been buried below it from Marx to Badiou. Any future theory of the migrant must begin from the previous attempts to think about the nature of its centrality and importance in political theory. Since this history has nowhere else been elaborated, this chapter presents it here for others to build on.

The Age of Mass Migration

The modern philosophical history of the thesis of the centrality of the migrant begins alongside what is commonly referred to as the 'age of mass migration' that took place between 1840 and 1914 (Hatton and Williamson 1998).

Karl Marx

The first historical expression of the centrality of the migrant occurs in *Capital*

Vol. I published in 1867 by a migrant in exile, Karl Marx. This is perhaps the first work of philosophy to explicitly valorise the revolutionary potential and political-economic centrality of the figure of the migrant, or what Marx calls the 'relative surplus population' (Marx 1976, 781). Marx (1976, 784) goes as far as to say that the relative surplus population is:

> the lever of capitalist accumulation, indeed it becomes a condition for the existence of the capitalist mode of production. It forms a disposable industrial reserve army, which belongs to capital just as absolutely as if the latter had bread it at its own cost.

As capitalist markets expand, contract, and multiply 'by fits and starts', Marx says, capital requires the possibility of suddenly adding and subtracting 'great masses of men into decisive areas without doing any damage to the scale of production. The surplus population supplies these masses' (Marx 1976, 785). If there were 100% employment in all markets then where would a new and expanding market get its labour? If there was total employment, then workers would not be easily replaced and their strikes would have substantial force over production.

Capitalist production thus requires a mass of workers which is superfluous to its requirements for two reasons: 1) so that when expansion or multiplication of markets occurs there will be a surplus of workers ready at hand and 2) so that this surplus of unemployed workers will make the current workers highly replaceable and thus over-workable, thus requiring less active workers (thus increasing surplus population further), and making active workers available at a cheaper wage. 'Modern industry's whole form of motion,' Marx claims, 'therefore depends on the constant transformation of a part of the working population into unemployed or semi-employed "hands"' (Marx 1976, 786).

The proletariat is always already a migrant proletariat. At any moment an employed worker could be unemployed and forced to relocate according to the demands of capitalist valorisation. In fact, its mobility is *the condition of modern industry's whole form of motion*. Without the migration of surplus population to new markets, from the rural to the city, from city to city, from country to country (what Marx calls the 'floating population') capitalist accumulation would *not be possible at all*. As the most mobile and deterritorialised part of the proletariat, however, the surplus population also has the greatest potential for revolutionary transformation. Unemployed workers have the least to lose and the most to gain from revolution. They also have more time to educate, organise, and motivate others. Also, as the most mobile, the surplus population is always on the brink of deterritorialising capitalism itself insofar as it is capitalism that relies on their existence. In this way the strikes of the unemployed might be more powerful than the strikes of the actively employed. Or, said in another way, the surplus population is also the lever which allows for the success of an active workers' strike. Without the solidarity of their potential replacements, the striking workers cannot win: they will be replaced by the mobile surplus population. Thus, as the most mobile figure of Marx's thought, the surplus population is both the conditions of mobility for modern industry and the conditions of the proletariat's emancipation from the bonds of territorial immobility.

Friedrich Nietzsche

The second major work of philosophy during this time to valorise the transformative power and centrality of the migrant is *The Gay Science* published in 1882 by the stateless migrant, Friedrich Nietzsche. Eighteen years after *Capital Vol. 1* was published, 1882 was the highest year of annual migration in Europe in the entire age of mass migration (Hatton and Williamson 1998). In aphorism 377, titled 'We who are homeless', Nietzsche writes *as* a migrant *to* migrants as the 'children of the future' (Nietzsche 1974, 338). Here, there is a dual sense of subject and temporality in his address. Nietzsche addresses the present and empirical migrants of his time, who are moving around Europe and the world by the millions, but does so by addressing them in the future and collective unifying sense of an 'untimely we'. 'We' are both now-here and nowhere. 'We' are a people which is here but whose time is also yet to come. The use of the word 'we' and the amount of political content gives this relatively long aphorism a strong political tone even as Nietzsche clearly rejects traditional political categories.

For Nietzsche, these migratory children of the future occupy a special place in *The Gay Science*. Not because they appear often, but because it is to them 'especially' that Nietzsche 'commends [his] secret wisdom and', the book's title, the *'gaya sciensza'* (Nietzsche 1974, 338).The number of such unequivocally valorised figures in Nietzsche's works are few (i.e. the Übermensch, barbarians, etc.). To these figures we should add another: the homeless migrants of Europe. According to Nietzsche, it is migrants who have pushed the farthest by rejecting all the 'ideals that might lead one to feel at home even in this fragile, broken time of transition' (Nietzsche 1974, 338). It is they who 'constitute a force that breaks open ice and other all too thin "realities"'. 'We homeless', Nietzsche says, reject both conservatism, liberalism, 'progress,' as well as a 'return to any past periods' (Nietzsche 1974, 338). 'We homeless' migrants, Nietzsche says, are fleeing capitalism just as much as the humanist notions of 'equal rights,' and 'a free society' which mask their weakness with virtue. 'We homeless,' Nietzsche continues, are too 'well travelled' and too 'racially mixed' to fall prey to 'the European system of a lot of petty states' (Nietzsche 1974, 340).

In these rapid sentences Nietzsche identifies and clearly valorises a figure of the migrant who abandons or was perhaps abandoned by the political parties of left and right, historical progress, humanism, nostalgia, nationalism, racism, capitalism, socialism, and religion. The migrants' being out-of-place and out-of-time, is not only the conditions for their marginalisation but the conditions under which their movement can create a new place and a new time.

For Nietzsche, this new migrant figure expresses a radical exodus from all the diseases of its age. But in the final lines of this aphorism the figure of the homeless migrant also offers the possibility of a new world. 'The hidden Yes in you is stronger than all Nos and Maybes that afflict you and your age like a disease; and when you have to embark on the sea, you emigrants, you, too, are compelled to this by – a faith!' (Nietzsche 1974, 340) Despite Nietzsche's emphasis on all the migrants are leaving behind, there is also an even more powerful capacity to create something new that they can say yes to. But the hope in such a new world is already a kind of faith. It is a strange faith: the faith of the faithless.

The Age of Displacement

Migration, displacement, and statelessness during the period of 1914 to 1970 easily rivals 'the age of mass migration' at more than 60 million displaced people.

Hannah Arendt

In 1951, another exiled migrant philosopher, Hannah Arendt, wrote one of the most well-known articulations of the philosophical dilemma posed by these events. 'The Decline of the Nation-State and the Ends of the Rights of Man', in *The Origins of Totalitarianism* describes this group of European migrants, refugees and stateless people as 'the most symptomatic group in contemporary politics' (Arendt 1951, 277). This is the case because they expose the internal paradox of the modern nation-state and the idea of natural rights. 'Only with a completely organized humanity', she writes, 'could the loss of home and political status become identical with expulsion from humanity altogether' (Arendt 1951, 297). Only when the entire world has been divided into nation-states that define the rights of man as the rights of the citizen, do we see the truly exclusionary nature of nation-states. Political rights exist only when protected by a political community. It is thus with the emergence of stateless migrants, a people who are truly in-between places, without a legal origin or destination, that the universal pretensions of the supposedly 'inalienable' human rights show themselves to be false.

According to Arendt, the stateless migrant was not suffering the 'loss of any specific rights, but the loss of a community willing and able to guarantee any rights whatsoever': the loss of the 'right to have rights' (Arendt 1951, 297). Arendt writes,

> No paradox of contemporary politics is filled with a more poignant irony than the discrepancy between the efforts of well-meaning idealists who stubbornly insist on regarding as 'inalienable' those human rights, which are enjoyed only by citizens of the most prosperous and civilized countries, and the situation of the rightless themselves (Arendt 1951, 297).

Thus, the centrality of the figure of the displaced migrant lies in two things for Arendt: 1) the displaced migrant demonstrates a division internal to the dominant political philosophy of the time, between the citizen and the human; and 2) if societies are going to change, they must begin by including this increasingly large number of displaced migrants who have been pushed outside public life (the sphere of equality) into private life (the sphere of difference), which is undermining public, political life. For Arendt, displaced migrants are 'the most symptomatic group in contemporary politics', not because they are the most numerous or powerful, but because their displacement most reveals to us the condition of modern politics and its future: not right, but the right to have rights.

The Age of Globalisation

Today, with currently over 214 million international migrants world-wide, the contemporary age of migration ('the second wave') is the largest yet, with no signs of decreasing.[1]

Gilles Deleuze and Félix Guattari

Directly following Virilio's insight five years later (Deleuze and Guattari 1987, 65)[2], French philosophers Gilles Deleuze and Félix Guattari place the figure of the nomad (defined by speed) at the heart of their political philosophy of

---

[1]   As of 2010, there were 215 million international migrants and 740 million internal migrants according to the United Nations Human Development Report (2009, 21).

[2]   'Virilio's texts are of great importance and originality in every respect' (Deleuze and Guattari, 1987 fn 65).

revolution in *A Thousand Plateaus* (1982/1987). 'If the nomad', Deleuze and Guattari say, 'can be called the Deterritorialised par excellence, it is precisely because there is no reterritorialisation afterward as with the migrant, or upon something else as with the sedentary (Deleuze and Guattari 1987, 381). Thus, it is not the nomad who is a type of proletariat, as defined by Marx, Virilio, and others, but rather the 'proletariat [who is] the heir to the nomad' (Deleuze and Guattari 1987, 558 fn 61).

However, Deleuze and Guattari also introduce three novel distinctions into the history of the philosophy of the migrant with their concept of the nomad. First, they distinguish between three types of speed which Virilio conflates: '1) speeds of nomadic, or revolutionary, tendency (riot, guerrilla warfare); 2) speeds that are regulated, converted, appropriated by the State apparatus (management of the public ways); and 3) speeds that are reinstated by a worldwide organisation of total way, or planetary over-armament' (Deleuze and Guattari 1987, fn 65). Second, they distinguish between speed, which is intensive, and movement, which is extensive. 'Movement designates the relative character of a body considered as "one" and which goes from point to point; speed, on the contrary...can spring up at any point' (Deleuze and Guattari 1987, 381). Third, they distinguish between the migrant, which they define by the extensive movement from one point to another and the nomad, defined by the 'path that is between two points', whose stopping points are only relays or consequences of the nomad's principle trajectory (Deleuze and Guattari 1987, 380).

The first distinction Deleuze and Guattari make between different types of speed is crucial. Part II of the present chapter develops this in more depth. The second distinction is significant, but only insofar as one understands movement and speed (extensive and intensive) as absolutely coexistent in every situation. They are absolutely distinct and yet every movement has a degree of speed, and every speed has a degree of movement: like a cartography with 'a latitude and a longitude', as Deleuze and Guattari say elsewhere.[3] Thus, the migrant and the nomad coexist in the same figure. In fact, Deleuze and Guattari define both migrant and nomad in exactly the same way: 'as the movement between points' (Deleuze and Guattari 1987, 380). The two even 'mix and form a common aggregate', they say (Deleuze and Guattari 1987, 380). The difference is that the migrant is defined by the

---

[3]   Deleuze and Guattari make this clear when they say, 'On the plane of consistency, a body is defined only by a longitude and a latitude: in other words the sum total of the material elements belonging to it under given relations of movement and rest, speed and slowness (longitude); the sum total of the intensive affects it is capable of at a given power or degree of potential (latitude). Nothing but affects and local movements, differential speeds. The credit goes to Spinoza for calling attention to these two dimensions of the Body (Deleuze and Guattari 1987, 260).

fact that it will settle permanently and the nomad will move on.

However, there are thus three ways in which a migrant is also a nomad. The first is practical: the majority of empirical migrants move multiple times in their life, even if it is within the same country. 'Settlement' is thus not an adequate way to describe their 'arrival', since this arrival is almost always a partial one (partial status, precarity, possible deportation, etc.). The second way is conceptual: there are already two words that define the migrant by its departure from a settlement or its arrival and resettlement: the emigrant and the immigrant. The word 'migrant' is literally the one in-between, intermezzo, in-transit: not defined by settlement. If one defines the migrant by settlement, then one is merely duplicating the definition of emigrant or immigrant. The third way is etymological: the French and English word migration comes from the Latin word *migrātiō*, which means 'a change of abode, move' (Oxford Latin Dictionary 1982). This word, and the similar Greek one, μέτοικος (*métoikos*), from *metá*, indicating change, and *oîkos* 'dwelling', both come from the proto-Indo-European root *Mei,* meaning 'change'. There is nothing in the etymology of the word migrant that indicates *permanent* settlement.

Thus the real distinction that should be upheld is between the migrant-nomad on one side and the emigrant-immigrant on the other. The first is defined by change and movement (in-between), the second is defined by settlement (departure from, or arrival to).

Alain Badiou

Two years after the book *A Thousand Plateaus* was published (1980), French philosopher Alain Badiou published *Theory of the Subject,* where he too granted the migrant a central role in his political philosophy. With respect to politics, Badiou argues that 'the immigrated workers are at the centre of the current process of political subjectivity' (Badiou 2009, 263). Since, for Badiou, 'our society – imperialist society – is defined as a whole by the declaration that immigrant workers are not of this society, that it is impossible that they ever be', then 'the immigrant proletarians are the inexistent proper to the national totality' (Badiou 2009, 263). The 'immigrated proletarians' are those whose marginalisation and (inclusive) exclusion is required for France to identify itself as a unity, which excludes some and includes others. Thus,

> a protest struggle in which the immigrants, represented as a particular social force, demand the same political rights as the French, forces the inexistent whose national multiplicity determines its closure as imperialist, that is, it forces the immanent popular internationalism (Badiou 2009, 263–264).

For Badiou, proletarian migrants are central to the current process of political subjectivity for two reasons: 1) through their marginalisation and exclusion they provide the condition for the unity of national identity. Without the internal exclusion of the migrant, the national totality would lose its identity, and; 2) the demand for the political unity of nationals and immigrants is thus the key point for the transformation of the whole of politics and a new form of international revolutionary subjectivity.

Badiou was so committed to the centrality of this figure that he founded a political action group with Natacha Michel and Sylvain Lazarus called *L'Organisation Politique,* which was particularly committed to helping organise and support undocumented migrants (*les sans-papiers*). The group (active 1985–2007) often worked with migrants staying in French hostels and aided their demonstrations for equal rights.

Despite the group's dissolution, Badiou remains committed to the thesis of the centrality of the migrant. This is evidenced in his more recent book, *The Meaning of Sarkozy* (2008). In this book Badiou claims that 'the intimate link between politics and the question of foreigners is...absolutely central today' (Badiou 2008, 69). And further, that 'the concrete articulation of [the demands of thousands of foreigners in our countries] defines what is most important in politics today' (Badiou 2008, 68–69).

Giorgio Agamben

Closer to the turn of the century, Italian philosopher Giorgio Agamben argues a radical version of this thesis in his essay 'Beyond Human Rights', published in a short collection of essays titled *Means Without End: Notes on Politics* (1996/2000). It is important to note that while he frames his argument in terms of the refugee, which is a type of migrant, much of what he says is equally applicable to non-refugee migrants as well. Before expanding on this point it is worth quoting him at length:

> The refugee is perhaps the only thinkable figure for the people of our time and the only category in which one may see today – at least until the process of dissolution of the Nation-State and its sovereignty has achieved full completion – the forms and limits of a coming political community. It is even possible that, if we want to be equal to the absolutely new tasks ahead, we will have to abandon decidedly, without reserve, the funda-mental concepts through which we have so far represented the subjects of the political (Man, the Citizen and its rights, but also the sovereign people, the worker, and so forth) and build

> our political philosophy anew starting from the one and only figure of the refugee (Agamben 2000, 16).

Taking Arendt as the historical point of reference for this thesis, Agamben argues that what is new in our time is that unprecedented numbers of people are no longer representable inside the nation-state (Agamben 2000, 21–22). Industrialised countries today face 'a permanently resident mass of noncitizens who do not want to be and cannot be either naturalized or repatriated. These noncitizens often have nationalities of origin, but, in as much as they prefer not to benefit from their own states' protection, they find themselves, as refugees, in a condition of *de facto* statelessness' (Agamben 2000, 23). Insofar as the refugee, according to Agamben, is the figure who unhinges the universality promised by the nation-state-territory, 'it deserves instead to be regarded as the central figure of our political history' (Agamben 2000, 21–22).

This is an important philosophical continuation of the thesis of the centrality of the migrant in the following sense: If the novel issue of our time, according to Agamben, is truly the 'permanently resident mass of noncitizens' living inside industrial countries and threatening the unity and universality of the nation-state-territory trinity, then it does not follow that the refugee *alone* is the central figure of our political history. Refugees alone are only about 7% of these global non-citizen masses. Among non-citizen masses 15.4 million are refugees and 214 million are international migrants (25–32 million of whom are undocumented). Agamben's thesis is important, and thus should be expanded accordingly. Thus, this chapter follows Agamben in arguing that we must build our political philosophy anew, not only from the limited figure of the refugee, but the larger figure of the migrant.

Étienne Balibar

At the turn of the century, French philosopher Étienne Balibar wrote two short articles succinctly articulating the centrality of the migrant (the non-status migrant, in particular) for political philosophy: 'Le droit de cité ou l'apartheid?' [The Right to the City or Apartheid], published in *Sans-Papiers: l'archaïsme fatal* [Undocumented: the Fatal Archaism] (1999) and a modified version of the last section of this text titled 'What We Owe to the Sans-Papiers', published in 2000. In these texts, Balibar names three central contributions of the *sans-papiers*: 1) They have rejected their 'illegality' by daring to make themselves seen and heard as real people 'with their particularities and the universality of their condition as modern proletarians'. 'As a result, we understand better what democracy is: an institution of collective debate, the conditions of which are never handed down from above', but must be fought for and demanded from below; 2) 'They have also brought to light one of the principle mechanisms of the extension of institutional racism, which tends toward a sort of European apartheid by associating the legislation of "exceptions" with the diffusion of discriminatory ideologies'; and 3) 'Finally, we owe them for having (among others – like those of the strike of December 1995, recreated citizenship among us, in as much as it is not an institution or a statute but a collective practice'. Through their activism 'they have given political activity the transnational dimension which we so greatly require in order to open up perspectives of social transformation and of civility in the era of globalization' (Balibar 2000, 42–43).

The *sans-papiers*, 'the excluded among the excluded', reveal to us the universal condition of the modern proletariat, the racism inherent in national exclusion, and a new form of transnational political subjectivity unrestricted by national citizenship. But it is not their battle to fight alone. Balibar thus concludes these contributions with a final call to action, to 'commit ourselves ever more numerously at their side, until right and justice are repaid them' (Balibar 2000, 43). Aiming to make good on this claim, both Balibar and Badiou became members of the *Collectif Malgré Tout* [Despite it all Collective], an anti-capitalist political organisation dedicated to, among other causes, the struggle for the rights of migrants in France.

Michael Hardt and Antonio Negri

The final text I would like to flag in the history of this thesis is also from 2000 and also places the figure of the migrant at the heart of political philosophy: Michael Hardt and Antonio Negri's book *Empire* (2000). In an 'Intermezzo' entitled 'Counter-Empire', they introduce the figure of the migrant as the source of a coming communist revolution against capitalist empire. 'A specter haunts the world', they say, 'and it is the specter of migration' (Hardt and Negri 2000, 213). Unlike Deleuze and Guattari, Hardt and Negri quite clearly (and rightly) identify the concept of nomadism with migration. It is worth quoting them at length:

> Whereas in the disciplinary era sabotage was the fundamental notion of resistance, in the era of imperial control it may be desertion. Whereas being-against in modernity often meant a direct and/or dialectical opposition of forces, in postmodernity being-against might well be most effective in an oblique or diagonal stance. Battles against the Empire might be won through subtraction and defection. This desertion does not have a place; it is the evacuation of the places of power (Hardt and Negri 2000, 212).

Rather than arguing that the mobility of the worker follows the accumulation of capital, Hardt and Negri argue that it is capital that follows the workers desire for resistance and exodus. 'Mobility and mass worker nomadism', they say, 'always express a refusal and a search for liberation: the resistance against the horrible conditions of exploitation and the search for freedom and new conditions of life' (Hardt and Negri 2000, 212). Thus, desertion and exodus are the new forces of anti-capitalist resistance in post-modernity (Hardt and Negri 2000, 213). Their desertion is out-of-place and thus is the condition for the creation of something new.

Hardt and Negri draw on the two ancestors of this thesis: Marx and Nietzsche. Following Nietzsche, Hardt and Negri equate this vast and mobile group of revolutionary migrants to 'New Barbarians' (Hardt and Negri 2000, 214). Quoting Nietzsche, they ask 'where are the barbarians of the twentieth century? Obviously they will come into view and consolidate themselves only after tremendous socialist crises' (Hardt and Negri 2000, 213). But this 'barbarian' force is not merely a force of destruction or exodus, it is also the capacity to create an alternative, as we read in *The Gay Science*. 'The counter-Empire', Hardt and Negri say, 'must also be a new global vision, a new way of living in the world' (Hardt and Negri 2000, 214). A further expansion of this thesis, they say, would be 'to write a general history of the modes of production from the standpoint of the workers' desire for mobility' (Hardt and Negri 2000, 212). That is, a philosophical history of the power of mobility from the standpoint of the proletarian migrant. This is precisely what this chapter offers: the next step in the political philosophy of migration and the defence of the political centrality of the migrant.

Conclusion

The history of the political theory of migration reveals the existence of a common figure defined by movement – what we can call the figure of the migrant. Now that we have a theoretical history of this common figure defined by political movement, we are prepared to move forward with the conse-quences and political history of this figure for the twenty-first century. The above theories of the migrant are only the beginning. Today we need a whole new theory and history that inverts the political primacy of the citizen in favour of the figure of the migrant.

This means developing new theories of citizenship, sovereignty, borders, rights and nations – all from the perspective of the migrant. This means returning to political history and identifying all the old figures of the migrant and regimes of expulsion like the nomad, the barbarian, the vagabond and the proletariat that remain continuous with and inform the present. The present is still defined by the history of these techniques.

This is the century of the migrant because the return of all the old techniques of expulsion now make it clear for the first time that the migrant has always been a constitutive social figure. In other words, migrants are not marginal or exceptional figures, as they have so often been treated, but rather the essential lever by which all hitherto existing societies have sustained and expanded their social form. Territorial societies, states, juridical systems and economies all required the social expulsion of migrants in order to expand. The recent explosion in migrant mobility is only a provocation to finally see what has always been happening – and do something about it.

Political theory in the twenty-first century is at an interesting crossroads where migration has reached such a critical threshold that what seemed to be an exception has now become the rule. The question now is how to understand the rules of this game in a much more adequate way.[4]

References

Agamben, Giorgio. 2000. *Means without End: Notes on Politics*. Translated by Vincenzo Binetti and Cesare Casarino. Minneapolis: University of Minnesota Press.

Arendt, Hannah. 1951. *The Origins of Totalitarianism*. New York: Harcourt.

Badiou, Alain. 2008. *The Meaning of Sarkozy*. Translated by David Fernbach. New York: Verso.

Badiou, Alain. 2009. *Theory of the Subject*. Translated by Bruno Bosteels. London: Continuum.

Balibar, Étienne. 2000. "What we Owe to the *Sans-Papiers*." In *Social Insecurity: Alphabet City.* Edited by Len Guenther, and Cornelius Heesters. Toronto: Anansi.

Deleuze, Gilles and Félix Guattari. 1987. *A Thousand Plateaus: Capitalism and Schizophrenia*. Translated by Brian Massumi. Minneapolis: University of Minnesota Press.

---

[4]   For the beginning of such a theoretical effort see: Thomas Nail, *The Figure of the Migrant* (Stanford University Press, 2015) and Thomas Nail, *Theory of the Border* (Oxford University Press, 2016).

Hardt, Michael and Antonio Negri. 2000. *Empire*. Cambridge: Harvard University Press.

Hatton, Timothy J. and Jeffrey G. Williamson. 1998. *The Age of Mass Migration: Causes and Economic Impact*. New York: Oxford University Press.

International Organization for Migration. 2015. "Global Migration Trends FactSheet." http://gmdac.iom.int/global-migration-trends-factsheet.

Marx, Karl. 1976 [1867]. *Capital: A Critique of Political Economy Vol. 1*. Translated by Ben Fowkes. London: Penguin: New Left Review.

Nietzsche, Friedrich. 1974 [1882]. *The Gay Science: With a Prelude in Rhymes and an Appendix of Songs*. Translated by Walter Kaufmann. New York: Vintage Books.

Oxford Latin Dictionary. 1982. Oxford: Oxford Press.

United Nations Development Programme. 2009. *United Nations Human Development Report.* "Overcoming Barriers: Human Mobility and Development." http://oppenheimer.mcgill.ca/IMG/pdf/HDR_2009_EN_Complete.pdf.

2

The Cultural 'Therapeutics' of Sovereignty in the Context of Forced Migration

AMADU WURIE KHAN

Anti-asylum policies continue to be characteristic of contemporary European Union (EU) countries, as politicians attempt to placate public anxiety and hostility against perceptions of an asylum 'influx' (Chandler 2006, 71). This hostile treatment of asylum seekers and refugees has fallen short of the EU's commitment to 'universalising the political subject' and duty of care to victims of political repression who are not their citizens (Chandler 2006). As the recent United Kingdom (UK) election and EU referendum have shown, anti-asylum and immigration rhetoric tends to heighten as political elites seek to present a 'fortress Britain' immigration stance to win political campaigns. There is a presumption that electorates tend to be anti-immigration and anti-asylum, and to win a mandate to govern, political elites make attempts to resonate with the anti-asylum sentiments of their citizens (Nolan 1998, 241). Consequently, successful UK governments have formulated restrictive and assimilationist policies like 'citizenship classes and tests', deportation and reduced welfare provision for certain immigrants, such as asylum seekers and refugees. The intention is to convey a message that the government has the capacity to control the asylum-migration 'crisis' (Rudolph 2005), and the 'influx' does not pose a threat to an 'imagined' Britishness and state sovereignty (Dwyer 2010). In this sense, policy-making has evolved into a therapeutic process of state legitimisation by which political elites demonstrate that they are in sync with the electorates' beliefs about immigration (Nolan 1998, 20).

Notwithstanding the hostile asylum policies and cultural assimilation, asylum seekers and refugees, as immigrants and aspiring UK citizens, continue to retain and express multiple identities, and are not restricted to a singular 'imagined' British national identity. This paper explores this internation-alisation of cultures and identities through the experiences and views of asylum seekers and refugees in Edinburgh and Glasgow in Scotland, UK across a range of topics including naturalisation and statelessness, particip-ation in 'British' citizenship classes, and transnational cultural practices. The chapter considers the futility of UK governments' formulations of restrictive and assimilationist policies (on immigration and citizenship) to assert British cultural homogeneity and state sovereignty (Dwyer 2010). In addition, the paper draws from Nolan's 'therapeutic state' to explore the tensions between the UK state's mandatory citizenship classes and tests, and asylum-seeking migrants' identity formations (Nolan 1998).

The Cohort, Citizenship Classes and the 'Therapeutic' State

The research for this chapter is drawn from fieldwork among asylum seekers and refugees residing in Edinburgh and Glasgow in Scotland on the topic of media communication, asylum-seeking migration and citizenship. The evidence for the chapter is based on in-depth, semi-structured, individual face-to-face interviews with twenty-three asylum-seeking and refugee migrants. The sample is composed of twelve males and eleven females, aged between 26 and 65 years. Eight of the participants, four men and four women, self-describe themselves as Muslims. Each individual describes their experiences as asylum seekers/refugees in terms of fleeing persecution from countries in Africa, Asia, the Middle-East and South America. Each person had been dispersed as an asylum seeker to Edinburgh or Glasgow, where they became aware of the UK's citizenship policy involving citizenship classes, tests and oath. The citizenship classes and tests were introduced into UK law in 2002, and have since been repeatedly amended. The citizenship classes and tests incorporate knowledge of life in the UK and language classes and tests. The designated main language is English, although immigrants can choose Scottish Gaelic or Welsh, which are national languages of UK territories of Scotland and Wales respectively. The content of citizenship consists of British history and accomplishments, politics, geography and civic life, although such content may reflect the realities of the UK homeland territories (Scotland, Wales and Northern Ireland) where it is administered. The oath element occurs at a citizenship ceremony, usually taken upon successful completion of the language and citizenship tests. Oath-taking involves swearing or affirming a citizenship oath of allegiance to Her Majesty the Queen at a citizenship ceremony. The oath swearing is to God, while affirming the oath does not have any religious context.

The sample of participants was generated by 'snowballing', 'convenience' and non-random techniques. This means participants were selected for ease of access and ability to speak English. Additionally, participants were either known by the researcher or were asked to recommend others to participate in the study. This sampling method also entailed opportunistic recruitment of participants through accidental or off-chance encounters. Employing snow-balling, non-random and convenience techniques enabled the recruitment of participants to be on-going throughout the research. However, I used different networks for accessing participants including attending public and private meetings, social functions and other activities organised for asylum seekers and refugees by gatekeeper agencies, including Refugee Community Organ-isations (RCOs). Four participants were known by the researcher prior to interviewing through common participation in IKAZE, a theatre group run by asylum seekers and refugees in Edinburgh. One participant was known in advance of the interview through common membership of the then Exiled Journalists' Network (EJN), a UK wide organisation for exiled journalists.

All 23 participants were informed of the researcher's refugee status prior to being interviewed. In order to control potential researcher bias in collecting and analysing the interview data, measures employed included 'respondent validation' and note-taking of contextual information to cross-check the accuracy of views and to inform the analysis (Creswell 1998; Beresford and Evans 1999; Arthur and Nazroo 2003; Small and Uttal 2005; Kezar 2005). Note-taking involves recording background information, emotional accounts and practices that are relevant in understanding the issue being investigated. For example, I sometimes gleaned information from 'back-stage' chats, including whilst travelling with participants on the bus to and from an interview session. Through 'respondent validation', I got feedback on the accuracy of participants' views, and asked them to provide their own definitions of concepts or words to mitigate misunderstanding. Note-taking of contextual information was, therefore, useful to inform the analysis, and mitigated against bias.

Participants were guaranteed confidentiality and anonymity to facilitate part-icipation (Powles 2004). Verbal consent was sought to use recordings and take notes, and to let me know of any issue they would not like to be recorded (Powles 2004). Seeking consent was not only done before interviews, but was also reiterative (Mackenzie et al. 2007, 308).

'Cultural Therapy' as Locus for Sovereignty

Nolan's (1998) book *The Therapeutic State* is a US case study that provides interesting insights on government (and allied institutions) attempts to connect with society at the individual level. He argues that policy-making has a therapeutic basis in which political elites seek legitimacy from their electorates and citizens. In order to respond to citizens' concerns, political elites resort to formulating policies that acquire symbolic significance but yield less or no material impact on the issue of concern (La Fond 1992). The ensuing 'therapeutic culture' becomes an institutionalised practice of formulating laws aimed at averting or stopping a perceived problem whilst communicating to the public that political elites are responsive to the concerns of citizens. By so doing, 'therapeutic culture' is a symbol of political power with ambiguous outcomes; whilst individuals embrace the therapeutic culture, it could also be incapable of solving the perceived problem (Jones 2009; Nolan 1998).

However, Nolan's analysis of cultural therapy as a political tool for social control of citizens by political elites is silent on its relevance for non-citizens like asylum-seeking migrants residing in liberal democracies. Yet, the concept of 'therapeutic culture' has explanatory value for understanding governments' assimilationist citizenship policies in countries like the UK. This is because policies like citizenship classes are a manifestation of the visible assertion of state authority on non-citizens in two respects: the imposition of a 'pathological identity' and controlling access to citizenship, and moral panics on asylum. Cohen (1987) observed that a 'moral panic' can occur when 'a condition, episode, person or group of persons emerges to become defined as a threat to societal values or interests' (Cohen 1987, 9). The moral panic generates a state of impending crisis emanating from uncontrollable asylum-seeking migration, resulting in portraying asylum seekers as 'folk devils' or as 'bad citizens', and an embodiment of 'evil' (Rothe and Muzzati 2004; Ejarvec 2003; Hall 1997; Cohen 2002). The 'folk devils', in this case asylum seekers and refugees, are perceived as bereft of responsible social actions, and blamed for the breakdown of social cohesion, and a threat to an 'imagined' Britishness and the national citizenship order (Gifford 2004,148; Bruter 2004; ICAR 2004; Ejarvec 2003; Speers 2001; Bloch 2000; Anderson 1991). The 'pathological identity' ascribed to asylum seekers and refugees is further reinforced by the citizenship classes policy in prescribing 'cultural competence' in and 'normative commitment' to an 'imagined' Britishness, as a prerequisite for admission into national citizenship (see Nolan 1998). By so doing, the policy pathologises non-citizen immigrants as afflicted with a 'disease': that of not being British enough (Veit-Brause 1995).

In the context of Nolan's 'cultural therapeutics', the citizenship classes become the 'technocratic' treatment of this disease. This is because they are used to ground into the psyche of immigrants, the language, histories, values, traditions and achievements of the British nation-state (Camilleri 1995, 220; Crick 2000). As the current Prime Minister, Teresa May argued when she was the coalition government's Home Secretary, content of citizenship that prioritises the learning of British history and traditions would instil 'British patriotism' among immigrants (Jones 2011). Through this, the state aims to control the behaviour, and social and cultural values of minority populations in line with those prescribed by policymakers. Citizenship classes, therefore, constitute what Tyler referred to as a 'biopolitics', meaning a set of legal, moral and social strategies to control and shape the behaviour of individuals (2010, 62). More importantly, the prescribed behaviour and values are predominantly those of the mainstream or the majority white population (Byrne 2007; Gillespie 2007; Fortier 2010; Lentin and Titley 2011; Khan 2012).

At the same time, in legislating the citizenship classes and tests, political elites signify that they are responsive to citizens' concerns and the moral panic over the perceived perils of uncontrollable asylum-seeking migration. In this regard, citizenship classes, as a cultural therapeutic intervention, are intended to manage public unease about a perceived asylum seeker 'influx' posing a threat to an 'imagined' Britishness. Yet, as the UK referendum on leaving the EU reminded us, we know that migration into the UK continues unabated because under its international humanitarian obligation, the UK cannot gratuitously refuse to grant asylum. To do so would evoke a political backlash, as occurred with US President Donald Trump's ban on refugees and Muslims. In this sense, policymaking has involved a therapeutic process of state legitimisation by which political elites socially control non-citizens and show that they are accordant with citizens' beliefs about immigration (Nolan 1998, 20).

From the interviews, it is clear the participants' opinions of this policy are nuanced. On the one hand, participants perceived this policy as a practical opportunity to learn more about citizenship rights and responsibilities in a British context. Thus, the classes were viewed as protocols of life necessary for the migrants to manage everyday life in a new environment, for example by improving their communication skills and social interactions among both the linguistically diverse asylum-seeking migrant population and indigenous British citizens. The participants also perceived the classes in therapeutic terms similar to official policy: as a tool that would facilitate immigrants' social engagement, inclusion and integration (Home Office 2001).

On the other hand, participants felt coerced into accepting that, as non-British citizens, they lacked the language, values and histories of 'Britishness':

It [learning about citizenship and English] doesn't have to be a forced matter. They are putting pressure on people, if I may say so (110, Zimbabwean, Glasgow).

Since I have been in Zimbabwe, born and bred there, and colonised by the British, I speak fluent English. I didn't have to go to school to study their English' (110, Zimbabwean, Glasgow).

The participants raised serious questions relating to using citizenship classes to exert sovereignty. Although the policy excludes immigrants from selected English-speaking territories, participants, like *110*, from former British colonial territories where English is the official language of schooling, perceived the policy as discriminatory against the 'ex-colonial other'. Many participants attributed the perceived discrimination of the policy to a deliberate attempt by the state at differentiating newcomer non-UK citizens from UK citizens:

I have got friends, who are Scottish, Isabel that was here. She says: 'Some questions in that book [citizenship study material] you know them better than me'. They [policymakers] say to be a British citizen you have to know the geographical area of the UK, but the Scottish, they know nothing. We know more than they [Scottish friends] do. So [knowing about] the geographical area of the UK should apply to every citizen living in UK soil not just asylum seekers and refugees (121, Angolan, Glasgow).

This person's recounting of the views of a UK citizen, particularly a Scot, highlights the policy's discriminatory potential in mandating ethnic minority immigrants learning about British culture, history and geography whilst native-born UK residents are exempt. Others, like *102*, felt the policy typifies asymmetrical power relations in the West in dealing with non-Western states and their citizens:

Europe also had their troubles [wars]...millions were displaced and went all over the place: in Latin America, in Africa. And the governments there gave them land, gave them opportunities...to succeed...and the good thing about that was nobody was asked even for a passport, and they were just very welcomed in these places (102, Chilean, Edinburgh).

The post-colonial critique of the policy was based on the belief that UK citizens were not subjected to similar policies of cultural assimilation and sovereignty when they migrated to former colonial countries. Participants, therefore, perceived the compulsory element of the policy as an expression of coercive state authority:

You don't need to force people to become citizens, you know. It has to be natural; it has to be a natural process. I think, to some degree, it is coercive and it shouldn't be like that. Citizenship is a natural process...(112, Cameroonian, Glasgow).

Citizenship classes and tests were also viewed as part of a government hidden-agenda to control access to national citizenship:

I think behind it, there is a concern in the way it [classes and tests] is being applied. It could be used as a way to refuse people full integration. What about people who can't read and write? How are you going to integrate them into the citizenship programme? So, I think there are some anomalies with regards to the issue (112, Cameroonian, Glasgow).

Thus, one participant described the policy as a 'symbolic gesture' to communicate to UK citizens that something was being done to contain the threat posed by asylum-seeking migration to British values (*111, Cameroonian, Edinburgh*). In this case, as others have argued, immigration and citizenship policies are predicated on the assumption that native-born citizens will only tolerate and support immigration if they believe in their government's determination to control migration (Kofman 2005, 459; Rudolph 2005).

Participants' assessments could also be unpacked in Nolan's therapeutic terms. Firstly, the policy functioned in part as an antidote for public hostility and moral panics on asylum, and as a therapeutic form of state legitimation to socially control non-citizens (Nolan 1998, 293). In this case, immigrants felt that they were expected to prove that they have the knowledge, and values of an 'imagined' Britishness beyond that required of British citizens (McGhee 2009). Given that some Scots, as UK citizens, see themselves as ethnically and nationally different from other nationalities within the UK, such as English, Welsh or even British (Lord Goldsmith 2008), *121*'s experience suggests that citizenship classes construct ethnic minorities as the source of social problems afflicting communities. Secondly, immigrants often ascribe to a utilitarian pragmatic logic with respect to citizenship classes and tests that is different from the state's therapeutic logic. Although participants compre- hended the classes and tests as a cultural therapeutic intervention by the state, they nonetheless pragmatically subscribed to them to the extent that the classes were useful to their British citizenship formation, particularly in enabling their social inclusion and ending their 'refugee-hood' and statelessness. This area, and its relevance to challenging sovereignty, is discussed below.

Statelessness, Naturalisation and Sovereignty

All 23 participants described themselves as victims of social and political injustices in their homelands. Many were from so-called 'failed states' where their government was either unwilling or unable to protect them, or was itself responsible for oppressing them (Tickner 1995; Chandler 2006). Seeking asylum shows that challenges to state sovereignty include citizens' 'exit' to escape state repression (Moses 2005). At the same time, 'exit' constitutes making claims to human rights and international solidarity, and loyalties to political membership are not restricted to territorial borders (Joppke 1997). Asylum seekers' actions constitute an 'exit' from the oppressive sovereignty of their homelands (Hirschman 1970) and a challenge to the UK to exercise its sovereignty to uphold its responsibilities to protect international humanitarian norms (Joppke 1997). Although asylum is not a legal obligation under The Universal Declaration of Human Rights of 1948, and is therefore not prioritised over state sovereignty, participants perceived the UK as morally obligated to grant them asylum (Guiraudon and Lahav 2000; Chandler 2006, 55):

In fact, these countries, so-called developed countries, promote the problem. Like the British are responsible for the arms trading and promoting wars, like the Americans do. So they see this human disaster and they don't want to take responsibility for it (102, Chilean, Edinburgh).

All of the participants also partly blamed a protracted and often unsuccessful asylum process for their statelessness. Their general perception was that having rights to naturalisation would end their statelessness and attendant threat of deportation. More broadly, participants attributed their statelessness to their exclusion from rights of residency and naturalisation in the UK and threats of deportation:

At the moment, I just see myself as okay. Legally on paper, I am a Zimbabwean citizen. But personally I just see myself as a person in a dilemma. I don't know where to go. I can't go to the right. I can't go to the left (107, Zimbabwean, Glasgow).

If [the UK government] talked about bad things, deportation, I am not feeling good. Last year I remember in my work they take, early morning, they take about four or five ... a Kurdish family... they deport them.... (119, Eritrean, Glasgow)

You have to think about your home first, where you are coming from is not good for me, you understand me? So I just have to bear it (108, Nigerian, Glasgow).

These comments suggest the emotional consequences of exclusion from the rights of residency or statelessness. Consequently, asylum seekers choose to continue holding on to their homeland national citizenship. This embodies the problematic choice confronting many asylum seekers: to either continue being stateless, while anxiously awaiting the outcome of their asylum claim, or be deported to their homelands to face further persecution. All of the participants chose the former, as the lesser of two evils. Consequently, some chose to evade deportation either by legal challenge or by 'going underground', 'under the radar' or being 'illegal', which are metaphors for resisting the sovereign state's authority to exclude them from membership in the polity.

Some spoke of their homelands' policies that proscribed them from attaining dual citizenship. Four participants said they would forfeit their homeland's citizenship if they were to acquire any other citizenship including that of the UK. Three of these individuals were from Somalia and one from Sierra Leone (with the latter repealing its law prohibiting dual citizenship in 2007). In this case, the acceptance of dual citizenship policies by nation-states like the UK is an act of recognition of transnational citizenship rights, with attendant dual citizenship responsibilities for émigré nationals (Sales 2007, 234). As such, immigrants in these host and origin countries are allowed multiple national identities, while also submitting to multiple state sovereignties.

This has both internationalist and multicultural components. Morally, it is consistent with international human rights norms of free movement and an individual's freedom of choice with respect to country of residence. Culturally, it is an acknowledgement by host states like the UK that immigrants, as citizens of their homelands, continue to maintain emotional attachments and cultural ties to their countries of origin. In this sense, acceptance of an immigrant's dual citizenship is a practical government response to the ethnic and cultural diversity within contemporary Western states. Yet, this is at odds with the state's promulgation of assimilationist citizenship classes to assert sovereignty over an 'imagined' British cultural identity.

The next section further considers how the participants' opposition to the assimilationist citizenship policy was expressed through cultural and technological practices. It is another reminder that forced migrants do not succumb to the way they have been pathologised by the cultural therapeutics of officials.

Cultural Production and Sovereignty

The participants' opposition to the UK state's attempt to assert cultural homogeneity and 'Brito-centric' national identity through citizenship classes was more directly channelled through organising social, cultural and artistic events. Seven of the eight women participants were also involved in organising and delivering art and cultural activities facilitated by refugee advocacy networks such as Oxfam-Scotland and the British Red Cross. The activities were often targeted to grass-roots local residents and schools:

While we respect the [British] culture, the law of the land, we equally keep our own culture, and that in itself will make our children understand where we came from (112, Cameroonian, Glasgow).

These events served two identity functions that are relevant to appraising cultural sovereignty. First, the events represented the participants' acceptance of British cultural diversity; and second, the events were used to educate UK citizens about their plight and cultures (Khan 2008, 13). The events therefore embodied immigrants' expression of cultural attachment and identity with their homelands. In this regard, transnational identity expressions (Morrel 2008) constitute a challenge to the authority of the state to prescribe or impose its cultural and national identity preferences.

Further, the participants used the internet for a similar purpose, specifically as a technological instrument for political mobilisation, and engagement with other asylum seekers and their interlocutors including UK citizens. For instance, one participant stated that:

The computer has given me the opportunity to write and express myself and communicate with others in South America and the world over (102, Chilean, Edinburgh).

In this case, fifteen of the participants were either members of, or involved in running, internet-based networks, while three owned websites that were devoted to political, social and cultural participation in the UK and beyond.

One participant belonged to the Exiled Journalists' Network (EJN). The organisation was founded by asylum-seeking migrant journalists residing in the UK to respond to their exclusion from the mainstream UK media, and provide a 'voice' to counter the negative coverage of asylum seekers in the UK media. EJN also contests the repression of free speech and other human rights abuses perpetrated by states against their citizens around the world. Another participant participated in FABULA (Forum of Arts for Better Understanding of Latin American Culture), which contests misrepresentations of Latin-American cultures in UK media and cultural spaces.

Additionally, both EJN and FABULA aim to mobilise support among UK citizens to influence the UK government to act in support of their claims-making for cultural, political and social rights within and beyond the UK. This shows that the asylum-seeking migrants prefer to view the UK state in humanitarian terms, as a community of solidarity for persecuted individuals and a facilitator of rights and responsibilities at the international level (Joppke 1997; Murphy and Harty 2003, 187). It shows, too, that a number of the participants recognised that public support for non-citizen asylum seekers was crucial in influencing policy-makers to be more asylum-friendly. As such, these websites function as self-organising technological instruments and virtual spaces for political and cultural mobilisation, contestation and participation at cross-border levels. In this sense, they are spaces by which the participants make claims for recognition of asylum-seeking migrants' human and cultural rights and identities within and beyond the territorial borders of the UK.

Conclusion

This UK case study shows that asylum-seeking immigrants and their cross-border activities challenge the ability of the state to restrict territorial access and impose an 'imagined' identity (Veit-Brause 1995, 69). UK citizenship classes and tests assume a social contract in which non-citizen immigrants accept certain obligations of 'British' core values of the state. Yet, mandates on cultural assimilation are at odds with immigrants' expressions of an internationalisation of cultures which pushes their political and cultural identities beyond the nation-state (Kofman 2005, 464). The unintended effects of multiple identities and transnational political and cultural activities contradict the goal of the policy, which is aimed at asserting its authority to control immigrants' orientation to an 'imagined' Britishness.

It has also been discussed that immigrants seeking asylum challenge the UK state to honour its international humanitarian obligations to grant asylum, and question the potential excesses of its policies regulating inward asylum migration and deportation. Recent anti-immigrant legislation in the UK and other Western states highlights the exclusionary power of sovereignty. At the same time, by accepting the right of immigrants to have dual citizenship, the state compromises its sovereign authority to assert a Brito-centric national and cultural identity. The assumption by the sovereign states in the West that members of the polity should share a common national and cultural identity, and an 'ethnic' conception of formal membership, is therefore precarious. It is also precarious for the state to assume that all members of the state should have allegiance to a dominant cultural identity. As evidenced in this paper, the multiple identities and citizenship formations by and among immigrants are at odds with assimilationist policies. Immigrants could make claims to and contest official identities that are prescribed to accompany membership of the political community. These actions confront the territorial construction of citizenship and raise serious questions about the efficacy of using restrictive and assimilationist policies to include or exclude asylum seekers.

Yet, the way this cultural therapeutics is experienced by asylum seekers and refugees is nuanced. In one sense it is futile because asylum seekers and refugees, as aspiring UK citizens, would acquire knowledge of the language, and British cultural values and histories for pragmatic reasons of their own volition. On the other hand, as others reminded us, participants claimed that they are supportive of some aspects of this form of 'cultural therapeutics' insofar as it gives them knowledge of the cultural, social and linguistic resources to enable their social inclusion in the polity (La Fond 1992, Nolan 1998). Additionally, immigrants are opposed to the state's therapeutic conceptualisation of Britishness that is skewed towards the majority white population, and where exclusion on ethnic and religious basis is the locus for British citizenship and the rights enjoyed by British citizens. Immigrants construct Britishness as culturally and ethnically diverse, to which they aspire to orientate. State therapeutic apparatuses such as assimilationist citizenship classes are, therefore, based on a false premise that immigrants are incapable of acquiring the behaviours, language and cultural values of the host country (see Jones 2009).

References

Anderson, Benedict. 1991. *Imagined Communities: Reflections and the Origin and Spread of Nationalism*. London and New York: Verso.

Arthur, Sue and James Nazroo. 2003. "Designing Fieldwork Strategies and Materials." In *Qualitative Research Practice*, edited by Jane Ritchie and Jane Lewis. London: Sage.

Beresford, Peter and Clare Evans. 1999. "Research Note: Research and Empowerment." *British Journal of Social Work* 29: 671–677.

Bloch, Alice. 2000. "Refugee Settlement in Britain: The Impact of Policy on Participation." *Journal of Ethnic and Migration Studies*, no. 26: 75–88.

Bruter, Michael. 2004. "On What Citizen Mean by Feeling 'European': Perceptions of News, Symbols and Borderless-ness." *Journal of Ethnic and Migration Studies*, no. 30: 21–39.

Byrne, Bridget. 2007. "England – Whose England? Narratives of Nostalgia, Emptiness and Evasion in Imaginations of National Identity." *Sociological Review*, no 55: 509–530.

Christopher Bickerton, Philip Cunliffe and Alexander Gourevitch. 2007. "Introduction." In *Politics without Sovereignty*, edited by Christopher J. Bickerton, Philip Cunliffe and Alexander Gourevitch, 1–19. Abindon, Oxon: University College London.

Brown, Chris. 2007. "Foreword." In *Politics without Sovereignty*, edited by Christopher J. Bickerton, Philip Cunliffe and Alexander Gourevitch, xi–xii. Abindon, Oxon: University College London.

Brown, Wendy. 1993. "Wounded Attachment." *Political Theory* 21, no.3, (Summer): 390–410.

Bull, Hedley. 1977. *The Anarchical Society. A Study of Order in World Politics*. London: Macmillan.

Camilleri, Joseph. 1995. "State, Economy, and Civil Society." In *The State in Transition: Reimagining Political Space*, edited by Joseph A. Camilleri, Anthony P. Jarvis and Albert J. Paolini, 209–228. Boulder. CO: Lynne Rienner.

Cash, John D. 1995. "State, Civil Society, and the Political Subject in a Divided Society: Reimagining Political Relations in Northern Ireland." In *The State in Transition: Reimagining Political Space*, edited by Joseph A. Camilleri, Anthony P. Jarvis and Albert J. Paolini, 105–124. Boulder. CO: Lynne Rienner.

Chandler, David. 2006. *From Kosovo to Kabul: Human Rights and International Intervention*. London: Pluto.

Cohen, Stanley. 2002. *Folk Devils and Moral Panics. The Creation of Mods and Rockers*. London and New York: Routledge.

Creswell, John. 1998. *Qualitative Inquiry and Research Design: Choosing among Five Traditions*. Thousand Oaks, CA: Sage.

Crick, Bernard. 2000. "Meditation on Democracy, Politics and Citizenship." In *Social Inclusion: Possibilities and Tensions*, edited by Peter Askonas and Angus Stewart, 217–227. Basingstoke: Macmillan, 217–227.

Dwyer, Pete. 2010. *Understanding Social Citizenship*. Bristol: The Policy Press.

Erjavec, Karmen. 2003. "Media Construction of Identity through Moral Panics: discourses of immigration in Slovenia." *Journal of Ethnic and Migration Studies*, no. 29: 83–101.

Fortier, Anne-Marie. 2010. "Proximity by Design? Affective citizenship and the Management of Unease." *Citizenship Studies*, no. 14: 17–30.

Gifford, Christopher. 2004. "National and post-national dimensions of citizenship education in the UK." *Citizenship Studies*, no. 8: 145–158.

Gillespie, Marie. 2007. "Media, Security and Multicultural Citizenship: A Collaborative Ethnography." *European Journal of Cultural Studies*, no 10: 275–294.

Guiraudon, Virginie and Gallya Lahav. 2000. "A Reappraisal of the State Sovereignty Debate: The Case of Migration Control." *Comparative Political Studies* 33, no. 2: 163–195.

Gustafson, Per. 2002. "Globalisation, Multiculturalism and Individualism: The Swedish Debate on Dual Citizenship." *Journal of Ethnic and Migration Studies* 28, no. 3: 463–481.

Hall, Stuart. 1997. "Racist Ideologies and the Media." In *Media Studies: A Reader*, edited by Paul Marris, Sue Thornham and Caroline Basset. Edinburgh: Edinburgh University Press.

Hirschman, Albert. 1970. *Exit, Voice, and Loyalty*. Cambridge, MA: Harvard University Press.

Home Office. 2001. *Secure borders, Safe Haven: Integration with Diversity in Modern Britain*. London: HMSO.

The Information Centre about Asylum and Refugees in the UK (ICAR). 2004. *Media Image, Community Impact Executive Summary. Assessing the Impact of Media and Political Images of Refugees and Asylum seekers on Community Relations in London*. London: ICAR. https://goo.gl/KjvyMj.

Jarvis, Anthony P. and Albert J. Paolini. 1995." Locating the State." In *The State in Transition: Reimagining Political Space*, edited by Joseph A. Camilleri, Anthony P. Jarvis and Albert J. Paolini, 3–19. Boulder. CO: Lynne Rienner.

Jones, Jonathan. 2011. "How Britain Got Its Patriotism Back." *The Guardian,* 17 December 2011. https://www.theguardian.com/culture/2011/dec/17/ jonathan-jones-britain-new-patriotism.

Jones, Lee. 2009. "Resisting Emotional Education." Changing the Subject: Views from International Politics, Oxford Brookes University, 3 February 2008. *Culture Wars.* http://www.culturewars.org.uk/index.php/site/article/resisting_ emotional_education/.

Joppke, Christian. 1997. "Asylum and State Sovereignty: A Comparison of the United States, Germany, and Britain." *Comparative Political Studies* 30, no. 3 (Summer): 259–298.

Kezar, Adrianna. 2005. "Consequences of Radical Change in Governance: A Grounded Theory Approach." *The Journal of Higher Education* 76, no. 6: 634–668.

Khan, Amadu Wurie. 2008. "Countering Media Hegemony, Negative Representation, the 'Bad Citizen': Asylum Seekers Battle for the Hearts and Minds of Scotland." *eSharp* 11 (Spring). https://www.gla.ac.uk/research/az/ esharp/issues/11/.

Khan, Amadu Wurie. 2012. "UK Media's Pathology of the Asyum Seeker & the (mis)Representation of Asylum as a Humanitarian Issue." *eSharp,* 54–86. https://www.gla.ac.uk/media/media_237469_en.pdf

Kofman, Eleonore. 2005. "Citizenship, Migration and the Reassertion of National Identity." *Citizenship Studies* 9, no. 5: 453–467.

Kunz, Egon. 1981. "Exile and Resettlement: Refugee Theory." *The International Migration Review* 15, no. 1 (Spring–Summer): 42–51.

La Fond, John Q. 1992. "Washington's Sexually Violent Predator Law: A Deliberate Misuse of the Therapeutic State for Social Control." *Seattle University Law Review* 15.

Lentin, Alana and Gavan Titley. 2011. *The Crisis of Multiculturalism. Racism in a Neoliberal Age.* London: Zed Books.

Lord Goldsmith, QC. 2008. "Citizenship: Our Common Ground". Speech. http://image.guardian.co.uk/sys-files/Politics/documents/2008/03/11/

citizenship-report-full.pdf.

Mackenzie, Catriona, Christopher McDowell and Eileen Pittaway. 2007. "Beyond 'Do No Harm': The Challenge of Constructing Ethical Relationships in Refugee Research." *Journal of Refugee Studies* 20, no. 2: 299–319.

Morrell, Gareth. 2008. "Globalisation, Transnationalism and Diaspora." Information Centre about Asylum and Refugees. http://library.bsl.org.au/jspui/bitstream/1/993/1/Globalisation_transnationalism.pdf.

Moses, Jonathon W. 2005. "Exit, Vote and Sovereignty: Migration, States and Globalization." *Review of International Political Economy* 12, no. 1: 53–77.

Murphy, Michael and Siobhán Harty. 2003. "Post-Sovereign Citizenship." *Citizenship Studies* 7, no. 2: 181–197.

Nickels, Henri Charles. 2007. "Framing Asylum Discourse in Luxembourg." *Journal of Refugee Studies* 20, no. 1: 37–59.

Nolan, James L. 1998. *The Therapeutic State: Justifying Government at Century's End.* New York: New York University Press.

Phillips, David and Yitzhak Berman. 2003. "Social Equality and Ethnos Communities: Concepts and Indicators." *Community Development Journal* 38, no. 4: 344–357.

Powles, Julia. 2004. "Life Histories and Personal Narratives: Theoretical and Methodological Issues Relevant to Research and Evaluation in Refugee Context." New Issues in Refugee Research Working Paper No.106, UNHCR, September.

Rothe, Dawn and Stephen L. Muzzatti. 2004. "Enemies Everywhere: Terrorism, Moral Panic, and US Civil Society." *Critical Criminology,* no. 12: 327–350.

Rudolph, Christopher. 2005. "Sovereignty and Territorial Borders in a Global Age." *International Studies Review* 7, no. 1: 1–20.

Sales, Rosemary. 2007. *Understanding Immigration and Refugee Policy.* Bristol: Policy Press.

Small, Stephen and Lynet Uttal. 2005. "Action-Oriented Research: Strategies for Engaged." *Journal of Marriage and Family* 67: 936–948.

Speers, Tammy. 2001. *Welcome or Over Reaction? Refugees and Asylum Seekers in the Welsh Media*. Cardiff: Oxfam/Welsh Media Forum.

Tickner, J Ann. 1995. "Inadequate Provider? A Gendered Analysis of States and Security." In *The State in Transition: Reimagining Political Space*, edited by Joseph A. Camilleri, Anthony P. Jarvis and Albert J. Paolini, 125–137. Boulder, CO: Lynne Rienner.

Tyler, Imogen. 2010. "Designed to Fail: A Biopolitics of British Citizenship." *Citizenship Studies*, no. 14: 61–74.

Veit-Brause, Irmline. 1995. "Rethinking the State of the Nation." In *The State in Transition: Reimagining Political Space*, edited by Joseph A. Camilleri, Anthony P. Jarvis, and Albert J. Paolini, 59–75. Boulder, CO: Lynne Rienner.

3

Migration and Human Rights – Exposing the Universality of Human Rights as a False Premise

EMMA LARKING

In the twenty-first century, the ability to migrate to some country other than one's own, and to enjoy in that country legal status akin to that of a citizen, is a global marker of privilege. Such freedom is accorded only to a small class of people. For Bauman (1998, 9), international mobility is now the world's 'most powerful and most coveted stratifying factor' (as cited in Castles 2005, 217).

In Castles's account (2005), there exist hierarchies of citizenship based on how much international freedom of movement a country's passport provides and the degree to which the rights of its citizens are recognised at home and abroad. On this basis he identifies five tiers of citizenship, with citizens of the US occupying the first tier; citizens of other highly developed countries the second; citizens of transitional and newly industrialising countries the third; and citizens of less developed countries the fourth tier. In the fifth tier, Castles includes members of failed states, stateless people and a group he refers to as 'non-citizens', whose residence status where they live is irregular or unlawful. While we might quibble with the details – for example, placing citizens of the US in the top tier ignores the inability of the country's poorer citizens to access rights in their own country and material constraints on their ability to migrate – this taxonomy makes it clear that the universal enjoyment of human rights is heavily circumscribed. It suggests rights realisation correlates strongly with privileged categories of citizenship.

Remarking that rights realisation is linked to citizenship of just a few states draws into question what the instruments of international human rights law describe as 'beyond question' – the universality of human rights (Vienna Declaration, para. 1). While accepting the reality of widespread rights violations, supporters of the international human rights system argue it is designed to ensure that *one day* all human beings will enjoy all human rights. In the words of a former UN Special Rapporteur on Non-Citizens, '[t]he architecture of international human rights law is built on the premise that all persons, by virtue of their essential humanity, should enjoy all human rights' (Weissbrodt [2003] in Larking 2016, 201). In fact, however, the architecture of international human rights law is built on the premise of sovereignty, which accords states freedom from external interference and equal standing and authority within a global society of states (Larking 2014, 144).[1] As such, the international human rights regime assumes that individuals enjoy human rights – if they do so at all – primarily by virtue of their membership of some rights-recognising state. This suggests there are structural impediments to universalising human rights that are downplayed by many international law scholars and human rights practitioners.

By comparison, international relations scholars tend to emphasise the centrality of sovereignty as a structuring principle of international law.[2] Some also take the claimed universality of human rights seriously and suggest its theoretical import is to fundamentally qualify sovereignty. In the late 1970s, Hedley Bull (1977, 146) suggested that '[c]arried to its logical extreme, the doctrine of human rights and duties under international law is subversive of the whole principle that mankind should be organised as a society of states' (as cited in Noll 2000, 82–3). In a similar vein, in the 1990s many cosmopolitan political theorists described the world as moving towards an era in which the universal realisation of rights might become possible in the form of 'post-national' or 'de-territorialised' rights (see Stasiulis 1997, 198 citing Jacobsen 1996; Sassen 1996; Soysal 1994). Although not presaging the demise of the sovereign state, they took the European Union as an exemplar and suggested that citizenship was no longer a privileged category or precondition for rights recognition. They pointed to 'new forms of post-

---

[1]   I have previously developed versions of this argument in Larking 2004; 2014, ch. 8; and 2016. See also Larking 2012, 72–3.

[2]   While noting Falk's assessment that the concept of sovereignty is – as Mayall couches it – 'in such deep trouble that its use should be left to politicians but discarded in serious academic analysis', Mayall points out that '[t]he formal order of international society continues to be provided, in the main, by the collectivity of sovereign states' (1999, 474). Characterisations of sovereignty as the foundational structuring principle of international law is consistent with widespread scepticism about the degree to which it reliably constrains state behaviour – see Jack Goldsmith's account of this prevailing scepticism (2000, 959–61).

national membership and rights, protected by international human rights provisions...and increasingly accepted and indeed organised by nation states' (Stasiulis 1997).

Yet in a world in which strident nationalism is resurgent, political parties that vilify migrants are gaining ground,[3] and states that once viewed themselves as 'settler societies' no longer see the incorporation of migrants as fundamental to nation building (see Dauvergne 2016), it is becoming clearer that individuals without access to a privileged category of citizenship are individuals without human rights.

After detailing how international law ties human rights to membership in rights-recognising states, I discuss the normative heft of sovereignty, locating it in the principle of political self-determination. I argue that recognising a qualified right to international freedom of movement and placing corresponding limits on how states police their borders would do more for political self-determination than continued deference to the principle of sovereignty in the instruments of human rights and in international frameworks governing migration. Re-casting human rights along these lines may be achieved by the advocacy of citizens within rights-recognising states, combined with international pressure from coalitions of states whose residents are most disadvantaged by the current global institutional order. In order to promote mobilisations in this direction, clarity is necessary about the role currently played by human rights instruments in upholding an outdated conception of sovereignty.

How International Human Rights Recognise and Uphold the Principle of Sovereignty

The international human rights regime is based on multilateral declarations and treaties between states that have bound themselves to recognise the rights contained therein. There is nothing unusual about states as sovereign entities entering into multilateral arrangements that constrain their future behaviour. In the case of human rights instruments, however, sovereignty is preserved as a structuring principle, with only minimal constraints imposed and the freedom of states in relation to border controls protected. The regime's foundational instruments specify that rights should be exercised in a

---

[3]   The election of Donald Trump in the United States and Britain's decision to leave the EU are two of the more notable examples reflecting a resurgence in xenophobic nationalism. Regarding the growing popularity of anti-immigrant parties in Europe, see Chakelian 2017 and Adler 2016. While Adler accepts there has been a rise of nationalism and anti-immigrant sentiment in Europe, she denies this is evidence of a recent lurch to the far-right.

manner consistent with the UN's 'purposes and principles' (Universal Declaration of Human Rights, Art. 29(3)) which include the sovereign equality of all Member States (Charter of the UN, Art. 2(1)). With the *Universal Declaration of Human Rights* (UDHR), the *International Covenant on Civil and Political Rights* (ICCPR) and the *International Covenant on Economic, Social and Cultural Rights* (ICESCR) constitute an international bill of rights, specifying all the key human rights. Although primarily dedicated to individual rights, article 1 of both Covenants affirms that 'all peoples have the right to self-determination', allowing them to 'freely determine their political status', 'freely pursue their economic, social and cultural development', and 'freely dispose of their natural wealth and resources'. I discuss the relationship between peoples, self-determination, and sovereignty in the next section.

As well as upholding sovereignty and self-determination, the international bill of rights imposes obligations on states to protect without discrimination the rights of all individuals subject to their jurisdiction or on their territory (ICCPR, Art. 2(1)). Discrimination on the basis of national or social origin is illegitimate (ICCPR, Art. 2(1) and ICESCR, Art. 2(2)).[4] This would seem to imply that people living in a state that fails to protect their rights are free to migrate to another rights-recognising state, but in fact no human rights instrument accords a right to international freedom of movement. States are entitled to control their borders (Noll 2000, 13) and the sovereign right of states to refuse territorial access or deny naturalisation to non-citizen residents is not questioned by international human rights bodies (Guiraudon and Lahav 2000, 168). States determine the conditions for lawful residence and treat individuals who do not comply with these conditions as unlawfully present. Despite explicitly opposing discrimination, if a person is unlawfully present, international human rights instruments allow that their rights can be qualified. Most significantly, they can be detained and deported. This means they are unlikely to make themselves known to authorities in order to claim other rights to which they may theoretically be entitled, or to protest rights violations (Larking 2014, 132).

The sovereign control that states exercise over matters related to membership has been treated by the European Court of Human Rights as qualifying the rights even of native born or long-standing non-citizen residents. This is telling because the Court is widely celebrated as uncoupling human rights recognition from national status and curtailing the sovereign

---

[4]   With these qualifications: developing countries may determine to what extent they guarantee economic rights to non-nationals (ICESCR, Art. 2(3)), and non-citizens do not have rights of political participation (ICCPR, Art. 25). Note as well that the International Convention on the Elimination of all Forms of Racial Discrimination does 'not apply to distinctions, exclusion, restrictions or preferences…between citizens and non-citizens' (Art.1(2)).

autonomy of EU Member States. Yet in a number of cases, the Court has found that the deportation of non-citizen residents who have committed crimes does not breach their human rights. In hundreds of other cases it has refused even to consider the question, ruling challenges to deportation orders inadmissible (see Dembour 2003).[5]

The right to seek asylum in article 14(1) of the UDHR has not prevented states from constructing elaborate border control regimes to prevent asylum seekers accessing their territory. These regimes have been treated as 'within the letter, if not the spirit' of international law (Goodwin-Gill and McAdam 2007, 360) and the UN *Convention Relating to the Status of Refugees* ('Refugees Convention') itself recognises that an asylum seeker's presence in a Convention state may be unlawful (Art. 31(2)). While parties to the Refugees Convention should consider protection claims of asylum seekers who arrive on their territory, and afford protection to those who have a well-founded fear of persecution in their home state,[6] in practice this protection is afforded to a tiny percentage of refugees globally.[7] It offers little comfort, moreover, to those people impelled to migrate because of poverty or starvation, war or civil conflict, or environmental disaster. In the remainder of this chapter, I use the expression 'forced migrants' to refer to both Convention refugees and people who migrate for any of the reasons just listed.[8]

The Normative Defence of Sovereignty

Given it is states that are parties to international human rights treaties, it is not surprising that these treaties should preserve state sovereignty. But that they do so is not regarded merely as marking the limits of the possible in international relations. Rather, it is defended on the basis that sovereignty is a

---

[5]   See Guiraudon and Lahav (2000, 169) for an account of the few cases in which the Court ruled *against* the legality of deportation on the basis deportation would breach the right to family life or to protection against inhuman or degrading treatment.

[6]   To qualify for protection under the Refugees Convention as amended by its 1967 Protocol, the reasons for persecution must relate to a person's race, religion, nationality, membership of a particular social group or political opinion (Art. 1).

[7]   Border controls prevent most refugees from leaving the region in which their home state is located and thus from accessing protection under the Convention. Official resettlement programs for refugees are also very limited. In 2015, the UN High Commissioner for Refugees estimated there were 21.3 million refugees and another 44 million forcibly displaced people worldwide. In the same year, 107,100 refugees were resettled (UNHCR 2015).

[8]   As indicated above (fn 6), the Refugees Convention defines the term 'refugee' restrictively, requiring a person to be outside his or her country of nationality and unable to return to it 'owing to a well-founded fear of being persecuted for reasons of race, religion [etc.]' (Art. 1(2)).

good in itself, and desirable from the perspective of human rights on the basis that it supports political self-determination. As we saw earlier, this concept is equated in the international bill of rights with the freedom of peoples to 'determine their political status', 'pursue their economic, social and cultural development' (ICCPR and ICESCR, Art. 1(1)), and 'dispose of their natural wealth and resources' (ICCPR and ICESCR, Art. 1(2)). The claim that sovereignty supports political self-determination is true only in a very limited sense. The boundaries of all current states are based on histories of violence and dispossession, and most are host to a number of different national, cultural and ethnic groups – some of which view themselves as politically autonomous or as deserving of political autonomy.

In international law, however, the self-determination principle has been treated primarily as applying to existing states and to the overseas colonies of the European imperial powers (Mayall 1999, 481). Appeals to self-determination have not proved effective as a more general route to sovereign autonomy – international recognition of sovereignty tends to follow in the aftermath of successful secessionist struggles rather than to support them. And while the UN Declaration on the Rights of Indigenous Peoples includes a right to self-determination, this is heavily qualified. Rather than being correlated with the exercise of sovereign powers, the Declaration specifies that the rights it contains cannot be used to undermine the 'territorial integrity or political unity' of the state in which indigenous peoples reside (Art. 46; see also Larking 2014, 145).

Despite the fact that the principle of sovereignty provides only heavily qualified support for political self-determination, it retains powerful normative appeal as a mechanism to ensure some degree of respect for political autonomy, self-government, and the collective right of members of states to freedom from overbearing control by imperial or alien powers. Consistently with this, sovereignty should act as a barrier to global tyranny, preventing the concentration of power in any one state or group of states.

Recognising a Qualified Human Right to International Freedom of Movement

We have seen that an aspect of sovereignty is a state's right to control the composition of its population and those who cross its borders. I want to suggest here that how this right is currently exercised does not advance the principle of political self-determination that provides normative justification for sovereignty. It is, moreover, fundamentally at odds with the aspirational claims of human rights, including the suggestion that 'recognition of the inherent dignity and the equal and inalienable rights of all members of the human family is the foundation of freedom, justice and peace in the world' (UDHR, preamble).

As things currently stand, the burden of hosting and caring for forced migrants is very unevenly shared. The vast majority are contained in their own countries or regions. The capacity of these countries and regions to 'freely pursue their economic, social and cultural development' and 'freely dispose of their natural wealth and resources' (ICCPR and ICESCR, Art. 1) – and thus to be politically self-determining – is limited by the fact that they shoulder most of the costs of accommodating the world's forced migrants.[9] This inequity is both produced and compounded by other forms of inequality within global institutions and regimes. Wealthy and powerful states strongly influence how international trade, finance and other governance regimes function, with the result that they benefit disproportionately from these regimes.[10] Ensuring that these states support a larger share of the financial and social burden of resettling or otherwise assisting forced migrants would provide an incentive to make the international rules of engagement fairer. This would reduce the number of people forced to migrate in the first place. It would also promote the causes of political self-determination and genuinely universal human rights.

One major barrier to achieving more equitable burden-sharing in relation to forced migration – and thus to incentivising the creation of fairer global trade and finance regimes – is the perception within wealthy, rights-recognising states that according even a qualified right to international freedom of movement will undermine social conditions for current citizens. Very large, unregulated influxes of people entering a country in a short space of time do place pressure on social infrastructure, but research suggests that the long-term economic benefits of immigration either outweigh the costs or are cost neutral, and moreover, that immigration may be necessary to fuel the economies of post-industrial states with ageing populations.[11] Globally and within many countries, wealth and income inequalities have reached historically unprecedented levels (see Alston 2015, paras 8–9, 10, 35 and 37). These inequalities impede economic growth and pose greater dangers for social cohesion than the challenges posed by even large-scale migration.

Members of wealthy, rights-recognising states must confront what are genuine threats to their lifestyle, rights and culture. These threats do not stem directly from forced migration, but from global inequalities combined with the

---

[9] See Hansen 2017, 12–3. The discussion primarily concerns refugees but also refers more generally to displaced populations.

[10] See Joseph 2007; George 2004, 53ff. and 57ff.; and Pahuja 2014.

[11] See OECD 2014 and Koser 2007, ch.7, 'The economic impact of immigration'.

corrosive effects on the rule of law within states from designating forced migrants as unlawfully present and denying them equal recognition and protection under the law. The proposition endorsed by the US Supreme Court that 'Congress may make rules as to aliens that would be unacceptable if applied to citizens'[12] is at odds with the idea that even democratically elected parliaments are bound by rule of law principles. It contradicts the 'revolutionary principle of equality' that Hannah Arendt argues must support and legitimate government in all rights-recognising states.[13] Governance in accordance with the rule of law requires that laws are capable of impartial application and do not single out particular groups, including non-citizens, for punitive measures. Building border fences, denying entry, and creating zones of exclusion does not dissolve this problem because border regimes must be administered within the framework of the law, regardless of whether the law is state-based or regional. If democratic states disavow their commitment to a foundational law of equality, they accept the idea that some people have an innate or inherent right to govern. Historically, this idea justified the rule of the monarchy, but it can also be used to justify the rule of larger collectives, as in Hitler's claim that 'right is what is good for the German people' (see Larking 2004, 16; 2014, 45). Who counts as a member of 'the people' is endlessly contestable and revisable. Recognising the threat posed to their own rights by the refusal to accord rights to unwelcome outsiders, privileged individuals who are members of rights-recognising states and who inhabit Castles's top tiers of the citizenship hierarchy must mobilise in support of fairer global rules of institutional engagement, combined with a right to international freedom of movement for all forced migrants.[14]

These mobilisations could be supported by the advocacy of states in the global south whose members are currently disadvantaged by global trade and finance regimes, and by the failure in international human rights instruments and migration frameworks to accord even a qualified right to international freedom of movement. Coalition building among these states and their members, and between them and concerned citizens of wealthy rights-recognising states, would recognise their shared interests. It would promote the ideals of political self-determination and of human rights shared and enjoyed by 'all members of the human family'.

---

[12] *Demore v Kim* 538 U.S. 510 (2003) 11, in Wilsher 2012; and see Larking 2016, 197.

[13] This principle must be protected by 'the complete impartiality of the law' (see Arendt 1968, 11 and 91, and my discussion in Larking 2014, 29–35 and 165–7).

[14] Previously I have argued in support of a right to international freedom of movement only for victims of genocide, but supplemented by obligations on wealthy rights-recognising states to share the burden of resettling or otherwise supporting all forced migrants (Larking 2012; 2014). In *Refugees and the Myth of Human Rights* I suggested obligations in relation to forced migrants who are not victims of genocide could be spelled out in a multilateral resettlement treaty (2014, 164–5).

References

Adler, Katya. 2016. "Is Europe lurching to the far right?" *BBC News,* 28 April 2016. http://www.bbc.com/news/world-europe-36150807

Alston, Philip. 2015. *Report of the Special Rapporteur on Extreme Poverty and Human Rights, Philip Alston, on Extreme Inequality and Human Rights,* 27 May, 29th sess. HRC, UN Doc A/HRC/29/31.

Arendt, Hannah. 1968 [1951]. *The Origins of Totalitarianism.* USA: Harcourt Inc.

Bauman, Zygmunt. 1998. *Globalization: the Human Consequences.* Cambridge: Polity.

Bull, Hedley. 1977. *The Anarchical Society*. London: Macmillan.

Castles, Stephen. 2005. "Nation and Empire: Hierarchies of Citizenship in the New Global Order." *International Politics* 42, no. 2: 203–224.

Chakelian, Anoosh. 2017. "Rise of the Nationalists: A Guide to Europe's Far-Right Parties." *The New Statesman,* 8 March 2017. http://www.newstatesman.com/world/europe/2017/03/rise-nationalists-guide-europe-s-far-right-parties

Dauvergne, Catherine. 2016. *The New Politics of Immigration and the End of Settler Societies*. USA: Cambridge University Press.

Dembour, Marie-Benedicte. 2003. "Human Rights Law and National Sovereignty in Collusion: The Plight of Quasi-Nationals at Strasbourg." *Netherlands Quarterly of Human Rights* 21, no. 1: 63–98.

George, Susan. 2004. *Another World Is Possible If....* New York, USA: Verso.

Goldsmith, Jack. 2000. "Sovereignty, International Relations Theory, and International Law – Review of Sovereignty: Organized Hypocrisy, by Stephen D. Krasner." *Stanford Law Review* 52, no. 4 (April): 959–986.

Goodwin-Gill, Guy S. and Jane McAdam. 2007. *The Refugee in International Law.* USA: Oxford University Press.

Guiraudon, Virginie and Gallya Lahav. 2000. "A Reappraisal of the State Sovereignty Debate: The Case of Migration Control." *Comparative Political Studies* 33, no. 2: 163–195.

Hansen, Randall. 2017. *Constrained by Its Roots: How the Origins of the Global Asylum System Limit Contemporary Protection*. Washington, DC: Migration Policy Institute.

Jacobson, David. 1994. *Rights Across Borders: Immigration and the Decline of Citizenship*. Baltimore and London: The Johns Hopkins University Press.

Joseph, Sarah. 2007. "Human Rights and the World Trade Organization: Not Just A Case of Regime Envy." Research Paper, University of Leicester, 31 October.

Koser, Khalid. 2007. *International Migration: A Very Short Introduction.* UK: Oxford University Press.

Larking, Emma. 2004. "Human Rights and the Principle of Sovereignty: A Dangerous Conflict at the Heart of the Nation State?" *Australian Journal of Human Rights* 10, no. 1: 15–32.

Larking, Emma. 2012. "Human Rights, the Right to Have Rights, and Life Beyond the Pale of the Law." *Australian Journal of Human Rights* 18, no. 1: 57–88.

Larking, Emma. 2014. *Refugees and the Myth of Human Rights: Life Outside the Pale of the Law*. Farnham, UK: Ashgate.

Larking, Emma. 2016. "Irregular Immigrants in Australia and the United States – Rights, Realities, and Political Mobilization." *Journal of Human Rights* 15, no. 2: 189–207.

Mayall, James. 1999. "Sovereignty, Nationalism, and Self-Determination." *Political Studies* XLVII: 474–502.

Noll, Gregor. 2000. *Negotiating Asylum: The EU Aquis, Extraterritorial Protection and the Common Market of Deflection.* The Hague/Boston/London: Martinus Nijhoff Publishers.

Organisation for Economic Cooperation and Development (OECD). 2014. *Is Migration Good for the Economy?* OECD Migration Policy Debates, May.

Pahuja, Sundhya. 2014. "Global Poverty and the Politics of Good Intentions." In *Law in Transition*, edited by Ruth Bechanan and Peer Zumbansen. Oxford and Portland, Oregon: Hart Publishing.

Sassen, Saskia. 1996. "Beyond Sovereignty: Immigration Policy Making Today." *Social Justice*, no. 23: 9-20.

Soysal, Yasemin Nuhoglu. 1994. *Limits of Citizenship. Migrants and Postnational Membership in Europe*. Chicago: The University of Chicago Press.

Stasiulis, Daiva. 1997. "International Migration, Rights, and the Decline of 'Actual Existing Liberal Democracy.'" *Journal of Ethnic and Migration Studies*, no. 23: 197-214.

UN General Assembly. 1945. *Charter of the United Nations,* 24 October, 1 UNTS XVI. http://www.refworld.org/docid/3ae6b3930.html

UN General Assembly. 1948. *Universal Declaration of Human Rights,* 10 December, 217 A (III). http://www.refworld.org/docid/3ae6b3712c.html

UN General Assembly. 1965. *International Convention on the Elimination of all Forms of Racial Discrimination*, 21 December, A/RES/2106.

UN General Assembly. 1966. *International Covenant on Civil and Political Rights*, 16 December, A/RES/2200A, UN Doc. A/6316.

UN General Assembly. 1966. *International Covenant on Economic, Social and Cultural Rights*, 16 December, A/RES/2200A, UN Doc. A/6316.

UN General Assembly. 1966. *Protocol relating to the Status of Refugees,* 16 December, A/RES/2198. http://www.refworld.org/docid/3b00f1cc50.html

UN General Assembly. 1993. *Vienna Declaration and Programme of Action,* 12 July, A/CONF.157/23. http://www.refworld.org/docid/3ae6b39ec.html

UN High Commissioner for Refugees (UNHCR). 2015. "Global Trends 2015: Figures at a Glance." *Statistical Yearbook 2015*. http://www.unhcr.org/en-au/figures-at-a-glance.html

Wilsher, Daniel. 2012. *Immigration Detention: Law, History, Politics* (USA: Cambridge University Press).

Weissbrodt, David. 2003. *The Rights of Non-Citizens: Final Report of the Special Rapporteur, David Weissbrodt*, 26 May, 55th sess. Sub-Commission on the Promotion and Protection of Human Rights, UN Doc E/CN.4/Sub.2/2003/23.

4

From Narratives to Perceptions in the Securitisation of the Migratory Crisis in Europe

SUSANA FERREIRA

The management of migration in the Mediterranean is one of the main challenges that the European Union (EU) currently faces. The intense migratory flows registered since the end of 2013 that peaked in 2015, with over 1.8 million border crossing detections around the EU (Frontex 2017, 19), have put to test the mechanisms of the Union's immigration, border and asylum policies and its capacity to deal with a humanitarian crisis.

The current migratory crisis has revealed the EU's weaknesses regarding the management of migratory flows and the deficiencies of its legal framework on migration, borders and asylum. Furthermore, the EU's actions have been criticised by many (namely civil society organisations and academics) for its focus on security measures, specifically in terms of border management, claiming that the securitisation of migrations is not the answer to the crisis.

The adoption of a set of emergency actions, extraordinary measures that go beyond ordinary politics, and the emphasis on a dialectic between migration and security on political narratives, aims to legitimise the securitisation practices adopted during the current migratory crisis. Hence, in this chapter I focus on the practices and narratives of the EU's political leaders to address the securitisation of migrations during the migratory crisis. I argue that a securitisation of migrations in the EU is taking place during this period (from 2013 to date), through the implementation of emergency actions by the EU and the adoption of securitarian narratives by European political leaders to support these actions.

For a better assessment of the securitisation process, this chapter is organized as follows: firstly, I introduce the academic debate on the securitisation of migrations in the EU, followed by an analysis of the EU's main strategic documents to assess how migrations are presented as a security threat to the EU; afterwards, I address the emergency actions adopted during the current migratory crisis, as well as the discourses of political leaders on migration, and the impact they had on public perceptions and opinions; and, lastly, I present some overall conclusions.

The Securitisation of Migrations

Any matter dealt with at a higher level, often the state, is considered as politicisation. When that subject is regarded as urgent it can lead to securitisation. Securitisation, more than an extreme version of politicisation, goes beyond it, since a special treatment is given to the subject. Thus, there is securitisation only when there is a legitimate existential threat that legitimises the breaking of rules to perform emergency actions (Buzan, Wæver and De Wilde 1998, 24–25).

For the Copenhagen School, the speech that presents an object as an existential threat does not create securitisation on its own; it is rather a securitising move. Acceptance by the audience is necessary so that the issue in question is dealt with as a securitised object (Buzan, Wæver and De Wilde 1998). Thus, the securitising process is only complete when there is an acceptance by the audience. Nevertheless, Balzacq (2011, 22) goes beyond the focus on the speech acts of the Copenhagen School, instead emphasising the role of practices; the security acts. In this sense, an approach that combines both practices (acts) and narratives (speech acts) is a more comprehensive one to analyse the process of securitisation of migrations in the EU.

Over the last two decades, the academic debate on the securitisation of immigration has been a very rich one. This link between international migrations and security has a constructivist matrix at its basis, arising from the creation of a nexus of threats, where different actors share their fears in the creation of a 'dangerous society' (Bigo 2002).

When analysing the migration-security link, we are not only focusing on state security, but on the security of society as a whole and even the security of the various groups that compose it. Immigration can be perceived as a threat to a state's sovereignty, but also as a threat to the freedom of society. In the first case, we are dealing with the immigration problem as political security, whereas in the second, we are under societal security.

Within the framework of societal security, immigration threatens societal identity. Thus, the securitisation of immigration takes place through the securitisation of identity, i.e., 'the European supranational identity is defended against a cultural (or demographic) invasion of other identities' (Brancante and Reis 2009, 82).

Jef Huysmans argues that the securitisation of immigration in Europe is intertwined with the regional integration process (Brancante and Reis 2009, 83). On the one side, this securitisation of immigration is triggered by welfare chauvinism, which, according to the author, is 'a strategy of introducing cultural identity criteria in an area in which belonging is determined on the basis of social policy criteria, such as health, age, disability and employment' (Huysmans 2000, 768). It translates into an economic fear that immigrants might overload the welfare system and jeopardise the internal market. On the other side, immigration may also be perceived as a menace to cultural homogeneity. Within the logic of societal security of the Copenhagen School, Huysmans (2000) suggests that an identity is created in opposition to the identities that surround it, which may lead to the creation of a supranational European identity.

Critics of the societal security concept, Bigo (2002) and Adamson (2006) claim that there is a securitisation of migration to fight transnational crime, such as terrorism and organised crime, within the realm of national security. Bigo (2002, 63) claims that this security prism to analyse migrations 'is the result of the creation of a continuum of threats and general unease in which many different actors exchange their fears and beliefs in the process of making a risk and dangerous society'. In this sense, Bigo's sociological approach focuses on the role of security agencies, which he calls professional 'managers of unease', in the securitisation of migration, by their own practices. These professionals not only have to face the threat, but they have the power to determine what is or what is not a threat (Bigo 2002, 74).

Nevertheless, the rise of terrorism in the security agenda led to the increasing relation between terrorism and migration and the adoption of a human rights-centred perspective, focusing on the human security of individuals. In this sense, authors such as Bhabha (2005) claim that anti-immigrant policies do not work in practice and they should rather be framed within existing human rights law. Thus, states should rethink their policies and protect their borders while safeguarding immigrants' human rights.

Irregular migrations are often conceived as an element of insecurity, as the illicit entrance of migrants might present a direct or immediate challenge to state security (Requena 2015, 61). Nevertheless, the requirements for legal entrance are defined by national immigration policies. Therefore, the political power is the one entitled to declare the entrance of others as regular or irregular. Thus, in a situation of irregularity the immigrant becomes the enemy of the politician (Bigo 2002, 6), and is therefore considered a threat. Moreover, irregular migrations bring along a series of threats to immigrants' human security.

Migrations as a Security Threat to the EU

The definition of security priorities is essential for policy design. Accordingly, an analysis of the EU's main strategic documents allows us to understand the connection between security and migrations in the EU's lexicon, which later translates into its policy making.

In this sense, since the beginning of the twenty-first century, the EU has adopted different security strategies in order to adapt to the new realities, taking into account the threats arising at that moment in time. The 2003 *European Security Strategy* identifies five key threats to European security: terrorism, proliferation of weapons of mass destruction, regional conflicts, state failure and organised crime (European Council 2003). Under the threat of organised crime, it briefly addresses irregular migrations, along with drugs and arms trafficking, as part of the external dimension of organised crime. Furthermore, it focuses on the Mediterranean region as a neighbouring unstable area, which requires the Union's continued engagement. In this sense, the document reflects post-9/11 thinking, focusing on the threat of terrorism and transnational organised crime. Yet, it already reflects the Union's concern over irregular migrations and stability in the Mediterranean area.

Given the changes the EU suffered in the first decade of the twenty-first century, such as the 2004 enlargement and the beginning of the economic crisis in 2007, as well as the international system, and within the framework of the Stockholm programme, the European Council adopted in 2010 an *Internal Security Strategy* for the EU, which aimed to address the new challenges. The strategy defines a 'new' set of common threats to internal security, which are: terrorism, organised crime, cyber-crime, cross-border crime, violence itself, and natural and man-made disasters. Some of these threats had already been outlined by the 2003 European Security Strategy – terrorism and organised crime – yet, new ones emerge as part of the new international order (Council of the European Union 2010).

Finally, in 2015, the Union adopted the *European Agenda on Security*, at a time that the EU faced a migratory crisis. This new agenda aims to be a 'shared agenda' between the Union and its Member States in the creation of an area of internal security. The EU outlines three common threats to its internal security: terrorism, organised crime, and cybercrime. Furthermore, the document stresses the need to effectively implement border management to prevent cross-border crime and terrorism (European Commission 2015c, 6), highlighting the link between border management, migrations and security.

These three documents – the *European Security Strategy*, the *Internal Security Strategy* and the *European Agenda on Security* – define the EU's key priorities in terms of internal security, always taking into account the specific moment in which they are inserted. Still, the connection between security and migrations is clear, depicting irregular migrations as a threat to security and emphasising the role of border management in the management of migrations.

In this sense, the EU mainly focuses on irregular migrations as a threat to its internal security, despite the fact that it only represents a small part of the total migrations to the European territory. Furthermore, the repeated use of the word 'illegal' in the EU's jargon to refer to these flows emphasises this representation of a threat.

Furthermore, the current migratory crisis reiterated the connection with terrorism, previously established with 9/11. Fears that jihadist terrorists could enter the EU's territory using migratory routes were confirmed after the Paris attacks on November 2015, since '[t]wo of the terrorists involved had previously irregularly entered via Leros and had been registered by the Greek authorities, presenting fraudulent Syrian documents in order to speed up their registration process' (Frontex 2016, 12).

To sum up, within the EU, migrations are mainly conceived as a threat to societal and internal security, particularly irregular migrations. Thus, this approach translates into the policy design in the field of migrations.

On the Adoption of Emergency Actions to Face the Migratory Crisis

The endorsement of a set of emergency actions is a fundamental axis in the securitisation process (Buzan, Wæver and De Wilde 1998, 24–25), as previously highlighted. Therefore, it is of great importance to analyse the urgent measures adopted to deal with the migratory crisis, in order to assess the securitisation of migrations.

The sinking of a vessel carrying over 500 refugees in Lampedusa (Italy) in

October 2013 led to the implementation of a Task Force for the Mediterranean, which proposed guidelines and measures to better address migratory flows in this area and prevent deaths at sea (Council of the European Union 2013). The Task Force identified five main areas of action that should be assessed in the following months: strengthening cooperation with third countries; regional protection, resettlement and reinforced legal avenues to Europe; fight against trafficking, smuggling and organised crime; reinforcing border surveillance in order to provide an up-to-date maritime situational picture and the protection and saving of lives of migrants in the Mediterranean; assistance and solidarity with Member States dealing with high migratory pressure. However, despite the Commission's commitment to implement the actions proposed, the ones taken were not enough to prevent the worsening of the crisis and the increasing loss of lives at sea.

The increasing migratory pressure in the Mediterranean since the end of 2013 became again an increasingly pressing issue on the European agenda in April 2015, when a boat sank near the shores of Lampedusa killing near 300 people (Kington, 2013). This humanitarian tragedy left the EU in a crisis mode (Ferreira 2016, 5). The following day, on 20 April, the European Commission presented a ten-point action plan on migration, which defined immediate actions to be taken in response to the humanitarian crisis in the Mediterranean (European Commission 2015e). Among the measures established, the most controversial one was the proposal of a military action to tackle smuggling in the Mediterranean. Finally, in May 2015 the European Commission presented its European Agenda on Migration (European Commission 2015f), setting concrete and immediate actions to tackle the crisis and looking forward in terms of a strategy to better manage migrations.

The European Agenda on Migration aims to give a comprehensive framework to the management of migrations in the EU, combining both internal (immigration, asylum and borders) and external policies (Common Security and Defence Policy), and taking into account the shared responsibility between EU Member States and also countries of transit and origin.

The plan put forward a set of specific measures at two different levels: the first level focuses on the urgent actions needed to respond to the human tragedy lived in the Mediterranean; and the second level identifies the four main pillars to better manage migrations (European Commission 2015f, 3–6). Among the urgent actions, a very controversial issue has been the adoption of a relocation and resettlement scheme (European Commission 2015f, 4), since home affairs and interior ministers could not reach an agreement on the quota of refugees to be relocated and resettled across the EU, given the divergences and controversies between frontline Member States and central and northern Member States. Member States finally reached a consensus in September 2015 to relocate a total of 160,000 people (see Council Decisions of 14 September and 22 September 2015). However, the relocation process has been very slow and thus has fallen very far behind the numbers agreed. According to the European Commission's ninth progress report on the EU's emergency relocation and resettlement schemes, on 8 February 2017 a total of 11,966 refugees had been relocated (8,766 from Greece and 3,200 from Italy) and 13,968 people in need of international protection had been resettled in the EU's Member States. According to the same report, 'Sweden, the United Kingdom, Finland and Netherlands as well as associated countries Switzerland, Liechtenstein and Iceland have already fulfilled their pledges' (European Commission 2017a).

Furthermore, the plan proposes, among other urgent measures: a funding package for Frontex's missions Triton and Poseidon; the implementation of a Common Security and Defence Policy (CSDP) mission on smuggling migrants; a pilot multi-purpose centre established in Niger by the end of 2015; and a 'hotspot' approach to work on the ground with frontline Member States to identify and register incoming migrants (European Commission 2015f, 3–6). However, so far the EU has not been able to deliver the necessary results. In this sense, according to a report of the European Council of Refugees and Exiles, the 'hotspots have certainly not helped in relieving the pressure from Italy and Greece as was their stated objective: instead, they have led to an increase in the number of asylum applicants waiting in Italy and Greece, consolidating the challenges and shortcomings already inherent in the Dublin system' (European Council for Refugees and Exile 2016, 7). Regarding the adoption of the CSDP operation – EUNAVFOR MED Operation Sophia, although this operation has helped to reduce the migratory flow by nine percent (compared to the previous years) in the Central Mediterranean route, it has led to a change in routes and a high increase in the Eastern Mediterranean route (Council of the European Union 2016).

Nevertheless, given the migratory pressure that Greece was being subjected to by the beginning of 2016 due to the closing of borders along the Balkan route, the EU-Turkey Agreement was signed in March 2016. This agreement takes a step further in the externalisation of the EU's borders, making Turkey partly responsible for the management of the EU's eastern border, while creating a new buffer State. The agreement aims to address the overflowing arrival of migrants from Turkey to Greece through the return of any new irregular migrant that arrives in Greece to Turkey. Nevertheless, it raises several questions regarding its legality, as it violates EU law on issues such as detention and the right to appeal (Collett 2016), and even its operationalisation. On the one hand, this agreement denies potential refugees the possibility to request international protection in the EU. On the other hand the mass returns of refugees and migrants to Turkey, despite the establishment of a resettlement scheme, violates international and European law protecting refugees and asylum seekers, namely the principle of non-refoulement. Moreover, it is still questionable if Turkey may be considered a 'safe third country' for refugees or whether Turkey can ensure access to effective asylum procedures for those in need of international protection (Brooks 2016; de Marcilly 2016). Furthermore, this agreement also shows the EU's connivance with totalitarian regimes in order to achieve its goals.

Discourses on Migration

Discourses on immigration create different perceptions within the general public, often supported by the media coverage of these issues. Sometimes the person who presents the discourse is more important than the speech itself. As Balzacq (2005, 172) put it, the discursive techniques used by agents allow '(...) the securitising actor to induce or increase the [public] mind's adherence to the thesis presented to its assent'. Various studies have focused on the different construction of discourses on immigration issues in Europe (see Buonfino 2004; Triandafyllidou 2000). Therefore, I do not aim to do a thorough analysis of European leaders' political discourses on immigration and security, rather to deconstruct the main ideas portrayed by these speeches in this specific moment in time.

Research has shown that there are two main opposite axes on discourses on migrations (Gropas 2015; Triandafyllidou 2012, 389). On the one hand, there is a humanitarian and solidarity approach. In these discourses, the emphasis is placed on equal treatment for immigrants and their contribution to host societies. On the other hand, there are the discriminatory discourses, which emphasise a nationalistic rationale, often linking migrations with criminality, terrorism or prostitution (Triandafyllidou 2012, 389).

Negative political discourses on immigration often resort to different linguistic expressions to describe this phenomenon, particularly with regard to irregular migrations. In this sense, political leaders frequently use metaphors related to natural catastrophes to describe the arrival of large number of migrants. Take for example Italy's former Prime Minister Berlusconi's speech resorting to the wording 'human tsunami' to refer to the growing number of migrants arriving in Italy in 2011 (Corriere Della Sera 2011). Thus, expressions connected to natural disasters serve as a securitarian element in the politicians' speech, as they imply that those migrants pose a threat to internal security. The media also uses those metaphors for greater impact among its audience. That is the case with some of the headlines of the Washington Times – 'Stop the immigration *flood'* (Thomas 2015) ; BBC News – 'Migrants *flood* trains in desperate bid to leave Italy' (Bell 2015) ; or Mail Online – 'Forget the Greek crisis or Britain's referendum, this *tidal wave* of migrants could be the biggest threat to Europe since the war, writes Michael Burleigh' (Burleigh 2015).

From British Prime Minister David Cameron's use of the expression 'swarm' to address the 'Calais crisis' (Elgot 2015), to former French President Nicolás Sarkozy's metaphor of a 'leak in the kitchen' to ridicule the Commission's proposal to relocate refugees – later used by the Spanish Interior Minister Férnandez Díaz (Sánchez 2015) – a number of similar terms were used to depict the refugees reaching European shores during the current migratory crisis. These negative statements by political leaders potentiate racist and xenophobic feelings among local populations, which have been criticised by civil society organisations, such as Amnesty International, and even by the United Nations (United Nations Human Rights, Office of the High Commissioner (UNHCR) 2015).

Furthermore, since 9/11 there has been a growing association between migration and terrorism. The speeches portraying immigrants as terrorists have gained momentum during the current migratory crisis, given the presence of the Islamic State in Syria. In this sense, political leaders have expressed their 'fear' that jihadi terrorists might be among those seeking international protection in Europe. An example of this is the concern expressed by the Spanish Interior Minister that a group of jihadi terrorists might enter Spain along with the refugees relocated to the country (EFE 2014). In the end, these negative discourses and statements portray migrations as a threat to European Member States, generating fear and rejection among host societies.

Nevertheless, a humanitarian and solidarity approach is also present in many other speeches, particularly the ones from the leaders of the EU's institutions. European leaders, such as the President of the European Commission, Jean-Claude Juncker, or the High Representative of the European Union for Foreign Affairs and Security Policy, Federica Mogherini, have called for collective action, solidarity and courage to face the migratory crisis. Jean-Claude Juncker issued a statement which openly showed his concern about the '(...) resentment, the rejection, the fear directed against these people by some parts of the population' (Juncker 2015).

In this line, the Italian Prime Minister Matteo Renzi took a stronger stance threatening to 'hurt' Europe if it remained paralysed in the face of the migratory crisis (Agence France-Presse 2015). French Interior Minister Bernard Cazeneuve criticised the French far-right *Front National* party's proposal to reinstate border checks, calling it a 'stupid' idea (Boudet 2015).

Other political leaders have called for action and solidarity from the EU and its Member States, while sometimes being reluctant to adopt some of the measures on the table. That was the case of the Spanish Prime Minister Mariano Rajoy, who, after the 19 April 2015 tragedy in the Mediterranean claimed that, 'Words are now worthless, we need to act' (Eldiario.es 2015), and later rejecting the scheme proposed for the relocation of refugees.

Another relevant leader worth mentioning is Pope Francis, whose messages reach beyond the Catholic world. When visiting Lampedusa in 2013, remembering the many hundreds of migrants who had died in their attempt to reach European shores, the Pope talked about the 'globalisation of indifference' regarding our current world, calling for international solidarity towards these tragedies (Staff Reporter 2015).

The securitising actor, in this case European leaders, is the one who speaks security. If it is true that the wording used in the speeches may speak for itself and have a great impact in public opinion, the figure of the leader himself or herself is a crucial element in the acceptance of the audience. In this sense, if it is a well-respected leader speaking security it will have a greater acceptance among a wider public.

Public Perceptions and Opinions

Narratives and practices on immigration and security shape citizens' perspectives about immigration. In the EU, public opinion about immigration and racist attitudes has suffered slight changes over the last decades, as well as the perception of threats to internal security.

An analysis of the Eurobarometer surveys on racism and xenophobia and on internal security from the eighties until now allows us to conclude that despite the different critical moments regarding migrations, there has been no significant impact in terms of the public opinion's perceptions. However, in 2015 there was a high increase from the 2011 survey, from 13% to 19%, on the Europeans' perception of migrations as a security challenge (European Commission 2015d, 6–9). In general, European citizens consider the EU as a critical element in the development of policies and strategies to face the different threats to European security. Moreover, Europeans believe that internal security is linked to external events, thus supporting a common answer to these threats. European citizens in general advocate common immigration and asylum policies, while requesting stricter controls of the external borders (European Commission 2015d).

Furthermore, we should also mention the increasing importance that far-right/

right-wing populist parties have in European policies, based on an ethnocentric ideology and often opposing pro-immigration policies. These parties focus on the national identity axis, where the 'other' is not part of the society, thus leading to racist and extremist discourses. The break of the migratory crisis and the terrorist attacks that have spread around Europe over in recent years (Paris, Brussels, or more recently, London) have paved the way for a growing Euroscepticism and an increasing support for these populist parties. They have established and reinforced their presence in Austria, Denmark, Finland, France, Germany, Greece, Hungary, Italy, the Netherlands and Sweden, where they have acquired significant political visibility and power (Gutteridge 2015). It is interesting to observe that the far-right has had a pronounced impact in Central European Member States, which are most of the refugees' host countries.

These results are in line with the slight growth registered in the perception of irregular migrations as a security threat to the EU and its Member States, and demonstrate the acceptance of the anti-immigrant, racist and nationalist discourses of these parties' leaders. In this sense, it would be interesting to analyse discourses of a group of far-right parties around the EU and its impact on the different societies.

Final Remarks

The current migratory crisis has highlighted the handicaps of the EU's common immigration, border and asylum policies, as well as the growing securitisation of these policies. The call for Member States' solidarity to face this crisis has collided with Member States' own political interests, creating internal frictions and dissidences. Most of the measures adopted to face this humanitarian crisis were based on low common denominators, and the EU seems to be falling short in accomplishing them. In March 2017, the European Commission called for renewed efforts from Member States to implement the relocation and resettlement schemes, where progress was slow in its first moment and now seems to be promising, with a total of 13,546 relocations and 14,422 resettlements (European Commission 2017b).

Taking into account the practices and narratives analysed, I conclude that there has been a securitisation of migrations in the EU with the current migratory crisis, through the adoption of exceptional measures that go beyond the sphere of normal politics and the adoption of what might be considered some legally questionable measures (such as the EU-Turkey Agreement). Furthermore, the growing support to far-right parties all around the EU, as well as EU citizens' growing perceptions of migration as a threat to security, legitimises this securitisation of migrations. This should be contrasted with figures regarding migratory flows. In 2015, migrants in the EU represented 6.7% of the total population (around 3.4 million migrants) and in that same year illegal entrances peaked at 5.2%, a representative figure if we consider that there was an increase of 100% in detections of illegal border crossings, compared to the previous year (Eurostat 2016; Frontex 2016 and 2017). In this sense, this feeling of insecurity is the result of a perception of a threat posed by the growing number of irregular migrants entering the EU during this period.

Nevertheless, the adoption of these measures so far has not helped to solve the crisis, rather to circumvent it or even to displace it to other regions, given the EU's incapability to find a common ground to deal with this humanitarian crisis. Therefore, to sustain the Area of Freedom Security and Justice (AFSJ), the EU needs to move beyond a securitarian approach and adopt a coherent and comprehensive strategy regarding migration management, which ensures the security and stability of external borders while preserving the freedom of movement.

References

Adamson, Fiona B. 2006. "Crossing Borders: International Migration and National Security." *International Security* 31: 165–99.

Agence France-Presse. 2015. "We Will Hurt EU If Migrant Crisis Is Not Fixed, Says Italian PM Matteo Renzi." *The Guardian*, 15 June 2015. http://www. theguardian.com/world/2015/jun/15/we-will-hurt-eu-if-migrant-crisis-is-not-fixed-says-italian-pm-matteo-renzi.

Balzacq, Thierry. 2005. "The Three Faces of Securitisation: Political Agency, Audience and Context." *European Journal of International Relations* 11, no. 2: 171–201. doi:10.1177/1354066105052960.

Balzacq, Thierry, ed. 2011. *Securitisation Theory: How Security Problems Emerge and Dissolve*. Oxon, New York: Routledge.

Bell, Bethany. 2015. "Migrants flood trains in desperate bid to leave Italy." *BBC News*, 20 June 2015. http://www.bbc.com/news/world-europe-33204681.

Bhabha, Jacqueline. 2005. "Trafficking, Smuggling, and Human Rights." *Migration Policy Institute*. https://www.migrationpolicy.org/article/trafficking-smuggling-and-human-rights.

Bigo, Didier. 2002. "Security and Immigration: Toward a Critique of the Governmentality of Unease." *Alternatives* 27: 63–92.

Boudet, Alexandre. 2015. "French Interior Minister Calls Border Controls 'Stupid.'" HuffPost, 15 September 2015. http://www.huffingtonpost.com/2015/09/15/border-controls-france_n_8139762.html.

Brancante, Pedro Henrique and Rossana Rocha Reis. 2009. "A 'Securitização Da Imigração': Mapa Do Debate." *Lua Nova* 77. http://www.scielo.br/pdf/ln/n77/a03n77.pdf.

Brooks, Julia. 2016. " EU-Turkey Agreement Undermines Refugee Protection in Law and in Practice". *Atha*, 31 May 2016. http://atha.se/blog/eu-turkey-agreement-undermines-refugee-protection-law-and-practice.

Buonfino, Alessandra. 2004. "Politics, Discourse and Immigration as a Security Concern in the EU: A Tale of Two Nations, Italy and Britain." ECPR Joint Sessions of Workshops. Uppsala: ECPR.

Burleigh, Michael. 2015. "Forget the Greek Crisis or Britain's Referendum, This Tidal Wave of Migrants Could Be The Biggest Threat To Europe Since The War, Writes Michael Burleigh." *Mail Online*, 26 June 2015. http://www.dailymail.co.uk/news/article-3141005/Tidal-wave-migrants-biggest-threat-Europe-war.html.

Buzan, Barry, Ole Wæver and Jaap De Wilde. 1998. *Security: A New Framework for Analysis*. London: Lynne Rienner Publishers.

Collett, Elizabeth. 2016. "The Paradox of the EU-Turkey Refugee Deal." *Migration Policy Institute*. http://www.migrationpolicy.org/news/paradox-eu-turkey-refugee-deal.

Corriere Della Sera. 2011. «Berlusconi: 100 Rimpatri Al Giorno. Apello a Tunisi: 'È Uno Tsunami Umano.'» *Corriere Della Sera*.

Council of the European Union. 2010. "Draft Internal Security Strategy for the European Union: 'Towards a European Security Model.'" 5842/2/10, 23 February 2010.

Council of the European Union. 2013. "Press Release, 3260th Council Meeting Justice and Home Affairs." 14149/13, Luxembourg, 7 and 8 October.

Council of the European Union. 2016. "EUNAVFOR MED - Operation SOPHIA. Six Monthly Report: 22 June to 31 December 2015." Brussels, https://wikileaks.org/eu-military-refugees.

de Marcilly, Charles. 2016. "The EU-Turkey Agreement and its implications." *Robert Schuman Foundation*, 13 June 2016. http://www.robert-schuman.eu/en/european-issues/0396-the-eu-turkey-agreement-and-its-implicationsan-unavoidable-but-conditional-agreement.

EFE. 2014. «Férnandez Díaz: 'Entre las avalanchas de inmigrantes se cuelan terroristas yihadistas.» *ABC.es*, 6 November 2014.

Eldiario.es. 2015. «Rajoy Se Indigna Con Las Muertes En El Mediterráneo Pero Se Opuso a Una Operación Europea de Rescate.» *Eldiario.es*, 19 April 2015. http://www.eldiario.es/desalambre/Rajoy-indigna-Mediterraneo-operacion-europea_0_379012338.html.

Elgot, Jessica. 2015. "Calais Crisis: Cameron Condemned For 'Dehumanising' description of Migrants." *The Guardian*, 30 July 2015. https://www.theguardian.com/uk-news/2015/jul/30/david-cameron-migrant-swarm-language-condemned.

EUR-Lex. 2017. "Justice, Freedom and Security." *EUR-Lex*. http://eur-lex.europa.eu/summary/chapter/justice_freedom_security.html?root_default=SUM_1_CODED%3D23,SUM_2_CODED%3D2307&locale=en.

European Commission. 2017a. "Commission calls for renewed efforts in implementing solidarity measures under the European Agenda on Migration." Press release, 2 March. http://europa.eu/rapid/press-release_IP-17-348_en.htm.

European Commission. 2017b. "Relocation and Resettlement: Member States need to build on encouraging results." Press release, 8 February 2017. http://europa.eu/rapid/press-release_IP-17-218_en.htm.

European Commission. 2015a. "Communication from the Commission to the European Parliament, the Council, the European Economic and Social Committee and the Committee of the Regions: A European Agenda on Migration." 13 May 2015 COM (2015) 240 final.

European Commission. 2015b. "Europeans' Attitudes towards Security." In *Special Eurobarometer*, vol. 432. Brussels: European Commission.

European Commission. 2015c. "Global Approach to Migration and Mobility." http://ec.europa.eu/dgs/home-affairs/what-we-do/policies/international-affairs/ global-approach-to-migration/index_en.htm.

European Commission. 2015d. "International Cooperation and Development." Building Partnerships for Change in Developing Countries.

European Commission. 2015e. "Joint Foreign and Home Affairs Council: Ten Point Action Plan on Migration." Press Release, no. 20. April.

European Commission. 2015f. "Communication from the Commission to the European Parliament, the Council, the European Economic and Social Committee and the Committee of the Regions: A European Agenda on Migration." COM (2015) 240 final.

European Council. 2003. European Security Strategy. *A Secure Europe in a Better World*.

European Council for Refugees and Exile. 2016. *The implementation of the hotspots in Italy and Greece*. A Study. European Council for Refugees and Exile. http://www.ecre.org/wp-content/uploads/2016/12/HOTSPOTS-Report-5.12.2016..pdf.

Eurostat. 2016. "Migration and migrant population statistics." *Eurostat, Statistics Explained*. http://ec.europa.eu/eurostat/statistics-explained/index. php/Migration_and_migrant_population_statistics#Migrant_population.

Ferreira, Susana. 2016. "Migratory Crisis in the Mediterranean: Managing Irregular Flows." *Stability: International Journal of Security & Development* 5, no. 1, 1–6. http://dx.doi.org/10.5334/sta.441.

Frontex. 2017. *Risk Analysis for 2017*. Warsaw: Frontex. http://frontex. europa.eu/assets/Publications/Risk_Analysis/Annual_Risk_Analysis_2017. pdf.

Frontex. 2016. *General Report 2015*. Warsaw: Frontx. http://frontex.europa. eu/assets/About_Frontex/Governance_documents/Annual_report/2015/ General_Report_2015.pdf.

Gropas, Ruby. 2015. "Discourses at the Frontline: Greek Approaches to Migration." *CritCom, A Forum for Research & Commentary on Europe*. http://

councilforeuropeanstudies.org/critcom/discourses-at-the-frontline-greek-approaches-to-migration/.

Gutteridge, Nick. 2015. "MAPPED: Shocking March of the Far-Right across Europe as Migration Fears Reach Fever Pitch." *Express*, 26 December 2015. http://www.express.co.uk/news/world/629022/EU-migration-crisis-far-right-parties-Europe-Germany-Sweden-France.

Huysmans, Jef. 2000. "The European Union and the Securitisation of Migration." *JCMS: Journal of Common Market Studies* 38: 751–77.

International Justice Resource Center. 2017. "Asylum & the Rights of Refugees." www.ijrcenter.org/refugee-law/.

Juncker, Jean-Claude. 2015. "A Call for Collective Courage." European Commission Statement.

Kington, Tom. 2013. "Lampedusa shipwreck: Italy to hold state funeral for drowned migrants". *The Guardian*, 9 October 2013. https://www.theguardian.com/world/2013/oct/09/lampedusa-shipwreck-italy-state-funeral-migrants.

Requena, Miguel. 2015. "International Migrations, Security and Identity." In *Globalization and International Security: An Overview*, edited by Teresa Rodrigues, Rafael García Pérez, and Susana Ferreira, 51–76. New York: Nova Science Publishers.

Sánchez, Gabriela. 2015. "Las Barbaridades de Los Políticos Sobre Refugiados Que Llegan a Europa: 'Gotera', 'Plaga', 'Amenaza.'" Eldiario.es, 17 August 2015. http://www.eldiario.es/desalambre/barbaridades-politicos-refugiados-Europa-amenaza_0_421008475.html.

Staff Reporter. 2015. "Pope Francis Warns against 'globalisation of Indifference' in Lenten Message." *Catholic Herald*, 27 January 2015. http://www.catholicherald.co.uk/news/2015/01/27/pope-francis-warns-against-globalisation-of-indifference-in-lenten-message/.

Thomas, Cal. 2015. "Stop the immigration flood." *The Washington Times*, 25 February 2015. http://www.washingtontimes.com/news/2015/feb/25/cal-thomas-stop-immigration-flood/.

Triandafyllidou, Anna. 2000. "The Political Discourse on Immigration in

Southern Europe: A Critical Analysis." *Journal of Community & Applied Social Psychology* 10: 373–89.

Triandafyllidou, Anna. 2012. "Migration Policy in Southern Europe: Challenges, Constraints and Prospects." *ELIAMEP*: 54–63.

United Nations Human Rights, Office of the High Commissioner (UNHR). 2015. "UN Human Rights Chief urges U.K. to tackle tabloid hate speech, after migrants called 'cockroaches'." *United Nations Human Rights, Office of the High Commissioner*, 24 April 2015. http://www.ohchr.org/EN/NewsEvents/Pages/DisplayNews.aspx?NewsID=15885.

5

Europe's Barbwire Fences: Reflections on Reporting the Refugee Crisis in Greece

MARIANNA KARAKOULAKI

Since the summer of 2015, the Greek islands of the Aegean Sea, that are only a few miles from the coasts of Turkey, and the small village of Idomeni, which is next to Greece's northern border with Macedonia, have become directly associated to the so-called refugee crisis. Thousands of refugees mainly from war-torn areas in the wider Middle East were arriving daily in the country's islands in their attempt to reach safety, and once they left the islands they moved towards Greece's northern borders. The images that were broadcasted from these areas immediately became associated with human loss, sorrow and trauma but also hope, perseverance and global acts of solidarity. At the same time, since 2015 we also observed the rise of barbwire fences as Member States of the European Union (EU) and their neighbours relentlessly tried to keep those arriving away from their territory.

In 2015, I was working as a freelance journalist, reporting on the refugee crisis from Greece's northern border in Idomeni. This chapter is my attempt to reflect on my understanding of borders. For this reason, I examine the way the refugee crisis unfolded in Greece from 2015 until the end of 2017 through my ethnographic observations as a journalist on the ground. However, this chapter is not about the crisis in Greece; it is a series of observations of the violent nature of borders and their impact on those on the move. In order to do that, I recount the story of the refugee crisis in five acts: five stories of individuals I met throughout these years that showcase the violent nature of the border. I do not intend to examine all aspects of the crisis – something like this would be impossible. But I do intend to look at the way borders create violence and the consequences of this for the people on the move. Due to the fact that I focus on people's movements in Greece since 2015, I refer to those on the move as refugees defying the legal limitations of the term because the majority of them but not all came from war-torn areas.[1] At the end of the chapter, I explore the notion of a no borders politics as a method of fighting the violence created by borders.

Violent Borders and Traumatic Experiences: A Story in Five Acts

Act I: Violent Lands

In the morning of 8 May 2015 a local volunteer and activist who was helping refugees at the Greek-Macedonian border[2] was asking for supplies and help in a Facebook post. According to that post, hundreds of Syrian refugees were found locked inside a freight train wagon and they were taken to the police station of Idomeni. At that period, I was working as a field producer on a different story about a gang that was kidnapping refugees in Macedonia[3], so that story's reporter, Ramita Navai, and I thought this incident may be connected to our research. It turned out that it was not related, but that incident exposed a different side of the migration route and the methods used to move people throughout borders. Those who were at the police station had paid thousands of Euros to smugglers in order to take them directly to Germany by train. However, when the train entered Macedonia it was checked by the police who in turn sent it back to Greece without alerting the Greek authorities of those locked inside. Hours later, the Greek authorities found the train abandoned near the border. One of those who were at the police station exclaimed during a short interview,

> I was close to losing my family and my life. When the train stopped, a police officer opened the door. He saw us but he didn't say anything. He then closed the door and told the driver

---

[1]   The term 'refugee' is defined in the 1951 Refugee Convention and the 1967 Protocol among other legal texts and mainly refers to those fleeing conflict or adverse political situations thus the term has legal limitations. For more on this issue see this book's introduction as well as the first chapter, and for an interesting thesis on people on the move see Thomas Nail's *The Figure of the Migrant* (2015).

[2]   By referring to the Greek-Macedonian border, I mean the so-called buffer zone next to the village of Idomeni, and between the railway that crossed Greece and Macedonia and the Axios (Vardar) River.

[3]   'Macedonia: Refugees Kidnap Gangs' was broadcast by the British broadcaster Channel 4 News and exposed an organised gang network of Afghans who were operating in Greece and mainly Macedonia and were kidnapping refugees who were trying to cross the Western Balkan Route (Navai 2015). The film is available here: https://www.youtube.com/watch?v=A5fDgJP2G30.

> to return to Greece. When the train arrived in Greece, we were
> abandoned inside the wagon (Field Notes, 8 May 2015).

That time must have been the fifth time I was at the Greek-Macedonian border since the first time I went to the area on January 2015. Incidents of violence were evident as the refugees who were stuck between the borders always recounted various stories with violent incidents; from beatings and muggings by the Macedonian authorities to being shot (Field Notes, January 2015; April 2015; May 2015). Yet that was the first time that an incident that involved hundreds of people had happened; at least, as far as I was aware at that particular moment.

Every time I visited the Greek-Macedonian border, I was trying to figure out the dynamics of what was happening and where it might all lead. I think the train incident can put the people's movement dynamics at that time into perspective. First of all, the borders were closed; this means refugees had no option other than moving throughout borders in an irregular manner – without any form of legal papers that would have given them the right to cross borders. For this reason, the only way one could cross was by paying someone else to help them cross without getting caught by the authorities; thus people's movements were controlled by smuggling networks who had the know-how of moving irregularly. For example, the incident with the train was one of the methods; someone – possibly a smuggler – had paid train officials in order to hide people inside wagons (for more on how that was done, see Navai 2015). Each one of those in the wagons had paid approximately 1200 Euros in order to go from Greece to Germany, considering there were almost 200 people, the smuggling network that was responsible for this made 240,000 Euros per trip; thus, closed borders was a profitable business for criminal networks (Field Notes, January 2015; April 2015; May 2015). It is important to note here that this concerns the crossing of the Greek-Macedonian border by hiding in a train as prices differed depending on the type of crossing. It is also important to add that crossing the sea border was a different side of the same journey that included different prices and other methods.

Apart from the way smuggling networks were taking advantage of closed borders, the number of people who arrived was rising; local activists said that one day 100 people would arrive and the next up to 500. Moving inside Greece was restricted, as those without papers or a residency permit could not take public transportation, which led to people paying extra money to taxi drivers who took the risk, or even walking for hours to the borders.[4] Physical

---

[4]   The route towards the Greek mainland shifted several times from 2015 until 2016. During May 2015, the most common route someone took once they arrived in Athens

violence was evident as people were beaten by the authorities or by criminal gangs. Yet, hundreds of people were daily defying both restrictions and violence, and kept on arriving in Greece with the tolerance of the authorities, as their movement was no longer a secret for anyone in the areas near Greece's borders.

A large number of researchers support the idea that movement is a political act and those at the centre of it are political actors as they defy politically imposed restrictions in their struggle to move throughout borders (see for example Agier 2016; King 2016; Hess 2017; Jones 2016). Indeed, what was happening at the beginning in 2015 was an act of political resistance as thousands of people resisted state imposed laws and restrictions and marched towards their ultimate goal: a safe area where they could build their lives from the beginning. When one person was down, the rest would help them, when their attempt was unsuccessful, they would keep on trying until they succeeded. In fact, this form of perseverance was successful in the end.

Act II: Violent Seas

The autumn of 2015 was entirely different from the beginning of that year. In July 2015, the authorities of Macedonia passed a law that allowed refugees who entered the country to freely move in it for three days (Associated Press 2015). That meant that those who were entering Macedonia through the Greek-Macedonian border were legally allowed to be in the country for three days. In my understanding that was the beginning of the open borders period[5] in the Balkan Route (Associated Press 2015). One of the immediate impacts of this policy was the gradual disappearance of smuggling networks through-out the route. At that time, I had met several refugees who were on their way to Northern European countries; contrary to those who crossed borders before summer, they managed to reach their final destinations relatively faster

---

from the Greek islands was as follows: from Athens people took the train to Thessaloniki (identification was not necessary); once in Thessaloniki, there were two main options: either take the bus to the small town of Polycastro which is near the border, and then either take a taxi or walk to the village of Idomenito, or walk from Thessaloniki to Idomeni directly, which is approximately 79 kilometres (Field Notes, April 2015; May 2015).

[5]   By referring to the open borders period, I refer to the term that was used mainly by the media in order to describe the movement of people from Greece towards Northern Europe with the tolerance of the authorities who, from the summer of 2015 until the closure of the so-called Balkan Route, managed movements in order to be done in an orderly manner. In reality, the borders were never officially open and this movement never took place in official border crossings. For example, the refugee crossing at the Greek-Macedonian border was on the area that the railroad crossed from Greece to Macedonia.

and most of them without paying excessive amounts to smuggling networks.

In September 2015, thousands of refugees, mainly from Syria, Afghanistan and Iraq were arriving on the Greek islands on a daily basis (United Nations High Commissioner for Refugees 2016). Although the free passage through the Balkan Route had eliminated gang violence throughout the border, the situation at sea was different. The rising number of people who crossed meant a rising demand for smugglers who operated on the Turkish side of the Aegean. The higher demand meant different prices and services. As a result, those who did not have enough money to guarantee their safe passage put their lives at risk by wearing cheap fake life vests and using unsafe rubber boats (Hubbard 2015; BBC News 2016).

At that moment, I had not been to the Greek islands as I was focused on reporting from the northern part of the border. However, I had gained multiple contacts with refugees, reporters, government officials and activists in order to be as well-informed as possible for someone not on the ground.

On 2 September, I received a message on Facebook from Zahra, a 19-year-old refugee girl that I met at the bus station in Thessaloniki. 'Hi, I need your help', she said. Zahra had already arrived in Sweden so at the beginning I was confused about why she may need my help. Zahra had settled in Sweden, however, members of her extended family had fled from Syria a few weeks before she contacted me. When she sent me that message, her sister-in-law was in a sinking rubber boat in the middle of the Aegean Sea. None of the passengers could get hold of the Greek authorities and time was running out. They could, however, contact their families and friends and as such that message reached me. Due to the urgency of the situation help had to be sent immediately. Zahra wrote:

> Call the police. Please we need help. I am waiting. There are children and they are afraid. The boat is destroyed. Please hurry, they are drowning. They are wearing life vests but they are not so strong. They can't hold them for long time.

I called one of my contacts in the Greek military who in turn informed the Greek Coast Guard. I had already sent him their location, as Zahra had sent me a Google Maps screenshot that had the coordinates on it. Their rescue was not an easy task, as they had to be located in the middle of the night. That night, the authorities rescued more than one boat. Since that day, I have had several discussions with my contact from the military regarding that incident. As he mentioned one time, he felt responsible for those people's rescue despite not being directly involved. I felt the same. That sense of responsibility for someone else's life would have been even stronger for Zahra as it involved a person she knew well, but also, an experience she herself went through – the precariousness of crossing the sea in a rubber boat.

Act III: Violent Camps

The previous incident took place during the same period that the German Chancellor Angela Merkel announced the opening of the borders for refugees who were fleeing conflict (Hall and Lichfield 2015; De La Baume 2017; Dockery 2017). Largely because of Angela Merkel's statement, the number of those who decided to cross the borders reached new levels. In 2015 more than one million people reached Europe through the Mediterranean Sea including the Aegean Sea; of those an estimated number of 800,000 people arrived through Greece (Clayton and Holland 2015). The open border policy that created the Balkan Route provided a safe and fast way for people to reach their final destinations as the route was no longer controlled by smugglers.

A couple of months later, however, borders started shutting down unexpectedly as European countries were not able to cope with the rising numbers of arrivals (Karakoulaki 2015; Siegfried 2015). The final straw came in March 2016 with the introduction of the EU-Turkey statement that was drafted in such a way as to intentionally reduce refugee arrivals (AFP 2016). The EU-Turkey Statement, which is more commonly known as the EU-Turkey Deal, is an agreement between Turkey and the EU regarding Syrian refugees. In short, for each Syrian refugee who returns from Greece or Italy to Turkey, one Syrian refugee from Turkey is accepted to the EU.[6]

It is important to note that as people were arriving in thousands at the buffer zone of the Greek-Macedonian border, and their crossing was officiated by the Greek and Macedonian authorities, there was a need to set up several facilities including medical centres or waiting areas. That need created what became known as the camp of Idomeni – from now on Idomeni – which took its name from the nearby village. Because Greece did not at that moment officially recognise Idomeni as an official camp, it did not built any facilities for the people who were there. For that reason, humanitarian organisations, and mainly the Médicins Sans Frontières [Doctors without Borders] (MSF), started building emergency infrastructure. By the beginning of January 2016, the camp had expanded throughout the fields near the buffer zone (Field Notes, August 2015–May 2016).

---

[6]   For a detailed discussion on the EU-Turkey Statement see Jenny Poon, Benjamin Hulme and Dora Kostakopoulou's chapters in this book.

Between the end of February and the beginning of May 2016, I was going to the Greek-Macedonian border at least three times a week, if not on a daily basis. Following the new developments, thousands of people were stranded in Idomeni and around March 2016 thousands of people were in limbo (Karakoulaki 2016b; 2016c; 2016d). Information by official authorities was limited, if not non-existent, and day after day it became clear that there was no plan by either the Greek government or the European Union. The situation at the time created a cloud of uncertainty and this, along with the harsh winter conditions, seemed to take its toll on people. Protests, either large or small, that resulted in violence were almost daily – fake rumours about the opening of the borders even had severe results (Tosidis 2016). Becoming a refugee already has psychological implications, thus the ongoing uncertainty of that time seemed to take its toll on those stranded (Papadopoulos 2007; Field Notes, 18 March 2016; Karakoulaki 2016c). I still vividly remember when I first met Ibrahim, a former interpreter for the US forces in Iraq, who broke down in tears as we were talking:

> I feel very stressed about everything. I am 26 and I haven't lived anything. When I was in Iraq, I was studying and working at the same time. Then I went to Turkey, and I was working for nothing. When I finally left Turkey and crossed the sea, I thought I made it. I thought I would go to Germany and I would bring my wife. Then I came here... I came to nothing. I don't know what I will do (Karakoulaki 2016c).

This was not the first time that someone broke down in tears in the middle of a discussion and it turned out it would not be the last. The common factor among all times was the fact that it occurred when there was some sort of disruption of refugees' movement throughout borders.

According to Renos Papadopoulos (2007), the closest theory that a psychologist can use in order to describe what is happening to refugees during their flight is trauma theory. However, refugee trauma and psychological trauma are different notions. Refugee trauma is a more general term that refers to various phenomena that are connected to a specific reality – the refugee reality and everything associated to it. On the other hand, psychological trauma does not necessarily have to do with external causes (Papadopoulos 2007, 303). Yet, not every person exposed to similar experiences has the same reaction (Papadopoulos 2007).

For some, the loss of home can lead to the loss of belonging and an environment where everything is new can cause frustration (Alcock 2003). Refugee trauma can have great effects on people's lives. Some of those who have fled from conflict suffer or have suffered physical trauma but for Kalsched (1996), physical trauma 'doesn't split the psyche. An inner psychological agency ...does the splitting'. While refugees were on their journey they did not allow themselves to be influenced by what they had experienced in their countries; their only goal was to reach their final destination (Field Notes, March–April 2016). Those who experience trauma block their memories in order to cope with their daily lives, yet, when this mechanism is disrupted their trauma resurfaces (Alcock 2003). For those in Idomeni, when their destination and consequently their goal was disrupted, the memories of their experiences resurfaced (Field Notes, March–April 2016).

Act IV: Violent States

As days were passing by and people had no information on their status or situation, tension was imminent. On 10 April 2016, refugees had organised a protest. By 9 am, hundreds that became thousands gathered in the middle of Idomeni. The protests were calm and all of us who were reporting on it thought it was going to die out as it happened almost every day. After a couple of hours of peaceful protests, a refugee delegation asked to speak with the Macedonian authorities who were gathered on the other side of the border. The Greek police negotiated with the Macedonians who in turn agreed to speak to refugees. Several police officers, journalists and the five delegates went to the side of the Macedonian border. After the negotiations had no actual result, the delegation left and went to inform the thousands who were protesting behind. In the beginning, I thought that the protest was over but those who were protesting had had enough. Approximately ten minutes later, thousands started marching towards the Macedonian-built fence and the first teargas from the Macedonian side fell on the ground. The Macedonian authorities had thrown teargas inside Greek territory before due to protests by refugees, but what was to follow was unexpected.

Teargas, rubber bullets, stun-grenades and water cannons with water that seemed to have chemicals were employed non-stop and with unprecedented force. At one point, my colleague and I left in order to file our report, and when we returned the clashes continued. For approximately eight hours, the Macedonian police and military were responding to the clashes with an extraordinary display of force towards men, women and children while refugees were responding by throwing rocks. As one of the protesters said: *'This is like Palestine, Gaza.'* (Field Notes, 10 April 2016). It is interesting to note that while these events were happening, the Greek authorities did not respond despite the fact that the Macedonian authorities were clearly violating Greece's sovereignty by firing teargas and other riot control agents inside Greek territory that included the village of Idomeni.

The lengths that states go to in order to protect their borders in peaceful times became even more evident to me that day. By using a variety of riot control measures, the Macedonian authorities made it clear that their border was not going to open and anyone who tried to trespass was going to face the consequences.

Act V: Violent Isolation

A month and a half after the events of 10 April 2016, the makeshift camp at the Greek – Macedonian border was evicted by the Greek authorities and a new phase of the refugee crisis in Greece started. Before the closure, the Greek government hurriedly prepared refugee camps isolated from urban settings and in many cases in areas that were not suitable due to hazardous conditions.[7] On 11 November 2016, my colleague and I were working on a story about the conditions of refugee camps during winter; at that time a popular narrative was the winterisation of refugee camps and the unpreparedness of the Greek government. Little did we know that a conversation that we would have that day would leave us in a state of shock; not because of the contents of the discussion – these were not dramatic, shocking or traumatic – but because of the way these stories were told and the feelings they conveyed.

We arrived at the camp of Nea Kavala in Northern Greece early in the morning, and after passing the police check we started working. That camp was one of the good ones in Greece as instead of tents it had ISO boxes that had been converted into houses. A few hours after doing a series of interviews and photographs, we decided to leave as we had all the material we needed. As we were walking out, I noticed a handmade shoe cabinet outside a house. I stood for a second and mentioned it to my colleague who went close to see it. This is when Idris came. Idris is a Kurdish Syrian who had been in Greece for a little less than a year at that time. He was with his whole family. He invited us for coffee and we sat next to a fire outside. Nawras, a young Syrian English Literature student whom we met earlier, came to help us with the translation as Idris and his family did not speak any English. After asking the same questions I did with others, I thought of asking something different, something that has now become a standard question: 'How would you describe your situation in one word?'

---

[7] This observation is based on various visits to several refugee camps in Northern Greece, Athens and several Greek islands between 2016 and 2017.

There was silence for a while. And then Idris said: 'I left war from Syria and I expected to see a better life. After I came here, *I saw another war; a psychological war*.' (Field Notes, 11 November 2016)

I then turned to Nawras and asked him the same question; his reply was equally emotionally charged: 'I feel *lost*. This is the first time I have been confused to such a degree. I cannot even think of what I am supposed to do in the future. Nothing. I am *literally confused*.' (Field Notes, 11 November 2016)

Although the discussion with Idris and Nawras took place at the end of 2016, the conditions in Greece have not improved. The situation is even more critical in the islands of the Aegean where there is a geographical restriction; that means that refugees who arrived in Greece after the EU-Turkey Statement are not allowed to go to the Greek mainland before a decision regarding their asylum application is made. A recent report published by Médecins Sans Frontières [Doctors without Borders] (MSF) characterised the refugees' situation in Greece as a mental health emergency to such a degree that their mental health services were overwhelmed (MSF 2017).

Cathy Zimmerman, Ligia Kiss and Mazeda Hossain (2011) recognise five phases of the migratory process that are related to health considerations: pre-departure phase, travel phase, destination phase, interception phase and return phase. Although all phases are relevant to refugees in Greece, it is particularly important to note the impacts of the interception phase, which relates to refugees in detention or in refugee camps.

Immigration detention centres or refugee camps often have deleterious effects on mental or physical health and are commonly sites of human rights abuses. There are clear associations between the length of detention and the severity of mental disorders, especially for individuals with prior exposure to traumatic events, which is common among forced migrants (Zimmerman et al., 2011).

As mentioned, Greece initially set up refugee camps, both on the islands and on the mainland, in isolated areas with limited capacities and few, if any, provisions. More than a year later, problems in the camps remain. However, none of Greece's or the EU's actions regarding the refugee crisis are surprising. The deteriorating conditions of the camps can work as deterrence to refugees who plan to cross international borders in order to reach European countries. For this reason, both Greece and the EU are blatantly ignoring delays in setting up suitable refugee camps in the mainland and camps in deteriorating, inhuman and degrading conditions on the islands, as well as human rights abuses by the authorities (Council of Europe 2017; Banning-Lover 2017; Howden and Fotiadis 2017).

Final Reflections: Toward a No Borders Approach

While commenting on the militarisation of borders and the construction of the wall between the United States and Mexico, Noam Chomsky emphasised the violent nature of borders: 'The US-Mexican border, like most borders, was established by violence – and its architecture is the architecture of violence' (Chomsky 2013).

In this chapter, I looked at five examples of what I perceive as border violence. While reporting these events, I eventually came to a twofold conclusion: first, that borders are inherently violent – something that Reece Jones examines in depth in his book *Violent Borders: Refugees and the Right to Move* (2016); and second, that the forms of violence created by borders can be fought through a no borders politics approach – the theory of which is analytically examined by Natasha King in her book *No Borders: The Politics of Immigration Control and Resistance* (2016). Indeed, after observing the constant changing nature of the refugee crisis, I came closer to believing that Europe's reaction to the refugee crisis creates violence. In order to fight this violence a different approach to borders is needed. This different approach to borders can start with an open borders policy that will eventually lead to a no borders politics.

An open border policy does not necessarily mean the end of casualties. For instance in 2015, 300 people lost their lives at sea in September and October of that year when there was a sort of an open borders policy (MSF 2015). Thus, open borders cannot be successful without the provision of safe passage. In the event described in Act II for example, the borders were open, however, the sinking of the boat was not preventable as those on it did not have a safe option of crossing the sea border between Greece and Turkey; although there were no victims that day, the experience left its mark on everyone involved. Taking into consideration that people will continue to cross borders, for various reasons, the concept of safe passage includes the provision of safe and legal ways for people to seek asylum. One of these ways was the implementation of the EU's emergency relocation scheme which promised to safely relocate 65,000 refugees from Greece and Italy to other European countries (European Commission n.d; International Organization on Migration n.d.). The EU's relocation scheme offers safe access to asylum to thousands of refugees in Greece and Italy but it is far from perfect as, at the time of this writing, it is scheduled to discontinue without meeting its promised limit (Amnesty International 2017). Relocation was eventually a failed policy. The way it was implemented did not take into consideration people's needs and family ties as they were selected by European states and they did not have the chance to choose their destination. This, in turn, meant that some ended up in countries where they had no connections.

At the same time, the EU did not take into consideration the continuation of refugee arrivals in Greece and the shifting of the routes. Once the EU-Turkey Statement was implemented, numbers were limited remarkably but arrivals did not stop. Considering that the Statement does not allow the transfer of people from the Greek islands where refugees arrive at the mainland to await processing of their asylum application, the Greek islands overflowed, as there is very limited capacity. For example, as of November 2017, the Greek islands hosted 14,586 refugees while their capacity is currently under 8,000 (UNHCR 2017; Roberts 2017). The camps in turn are in dire conditions and those living there suffer from various abuses including refugee trauma (Human Rights Watch 2017a and 2017b). Thus, one can say that the way the EU has responded to the crisis has resulted in the continuation of violence as described in this chapter.

The failure of states and the European Union to protect refugees amounts to their failure to discontinue the violence created by borders. This is where a no borders politics comes as an answer. A no borders politics can eventually eliminate the violence created by border regimes. However, in order to achieve this goal we need to take into consideration that a no borders politics involves the refusal of both the border and the state (King 2016, 126–132). The theory of no borders politics recognises that there are several tensions involved, as those at the centre of this politics – those on the move – seek political recognition. How can one refuse the existence of the state but at the same time seek political participation and recognition? As King concludes, we can overcome these tensions through collaboration of various actors involved in the dismissal of the border.

> Negotiating borders even as we aim towards their negation is always an ongoing process of overcoming – of being attentive to the presence of borders while also trying to render them redundant. A no borders politics is not just a naïve demand to bring down all borders. It's a constant, *deeply realistic* practice that undermines their logic and makes other worlds in their gaps (King 2016, 152–153).

Constantly working on issues around the refugee crisis in Europe has left me with a feeling of unease. The stories I have heard, especially the ones I never told in public, have taken their toll on me multiple times. At the same time, this period made me reflect and, to a degree, change my perceptions of the border and the state. One chapter is not enough to fully explain or even understand the concepts of violent borders and the theory of a no borders politics. However, I hope it can be a starting point of the discussion on how these two notions interconnect and how we can take them one step further in order to find new ways of approaching the notion of borders.

References

AFP. 2016. "Greece marks first day without migrant arrivals after EU-Turkey deal." *Ekathimerini,* 24 March 2016. http://www.ekathimerini.com/207308/article/ekathimerini/news/greece-marks-first-day-without-migrant-arrivals-after-eu-turkey-deal.

Agier, Michel. 2016. *Borderlands*. Translated by David Fernbach. Cambridge: Polity Press.

Alcock, Miranda. 2003. "Refugee Trauma – the Assault on Meaning." *Psychodynamic Practice* 9, no 3: 291–306.

Associated Press. 2015. "Macedonia Allows Migrants to Legitimately Transit Country." *Voice of America*, 18 June 2017. https://www.voanews.com/a/macedonia-migrants-asylum-law/2828577.html.

Banning-Lover, Rachel. 2017. "Greek refugee camps remain dangerous and inadequate, say aid workers." *The Guardian*, 10 February 2017. https://www.theguardian.com/global-development-professionals-network/2017/feb/10/greek-refugee-camps-dangerous-inadequate-aid-workers.

BBC News. 2016. "Migrant crisis: Turkey police seize fake life jackets." 6 January 2016. http://www.bbc.co.uk/news/world-europe-35241813.

Chomsky, Noam. 2013. "Hidden Power and Built Form: The Politics Behind the Architecture." Interview by Graham Cairns. *Architecture_MPS*. https://chomsky.info/20131001/.

Clayton, Jonathan and Hereward Holland. 2015. "Over one million sea arrivals reach Europe in 2015." *UNHCR*, 30 December 2015. http://www.unhcr.org/afr/news/latest/2015/12/5683d0b56/million-sea-arrivals-reach-europe-2015.html.

Costa Riba, Monica. 2017. "Why The End of the Refugee Relocation Scheme Should Not Mean the End to Relocation." *Amnesty International*, 26 September 2017. https://www.amnesty.org/en/latest/news/2017/09/why-the-end-of-the-refugee-relocation-scheme-should-not-mean-the-end-to-relocation/.

Council of Europe. 2017. "Report to the Greek Government on the visits to Greece carried out by the European Committee for the Prevention of Torture and Inhuman or Degrading Treatment or Punishment." 26 September 2017. http://www.politico.eu/wp-content/uploads/2017/09/CPT-report.pdf.

European Commission. n.d. "European Solidarity: A Refugee Relocation System." https://ec.europa.eu/home-affairs/sites/homeaffairs/files/what-we-do/policies/european-agenda-migration/background-information/docs/2_eu_solidarity_a_refugee_relocation_system_en.pdf.

De La Baume, Maïa. 2017. «Angela Merkel Defends Open Border Migration Policy.» *POLITICO*, 27 August 2017. https://www.politico.eu/article/angela-merkel-defends-open-border-migration-refugee-policy-germany/.

Dockery, Wesley. 2017. "Two years since Germany opened its borders to refugees: A chronology." *Deutsche Welle*, 04 September 2017. http://www.dw.com/en/two-years-since-germany-opened-its-borders-to-refugees-a-chronology/a-40327634.

Hall, Allan and John Lichfield. 2015. "Germany Opens Its Gates: Berlin Says All Syrian Asylum-Seekers Are Welcome To Remain, As Britain Is Urged to Make a 'Similar Statement'." *The Independent*. 24 August 2015. http://www.independent.co.uk/news/world/europe/germany-opens-its-gates-berlin-says-all-syrian-asylum-seekers-are-welcome-to-remain-as-britain-is-10470062.html.

Hess, Sabine. 2017. "Border Crossing as Act of Resistance: The Autonomy of Migration as Theoretical Intervention into Border Studies." In *Resistance: Subjects, Representations, Contexts,* edited by Martin Butler, Paul Mecheril and Lea Brenningmeyer. Bielefeld: Transcript.

Howden, Daniel, and Apostolos Fotiadis. 2017. "The Refugee Archipelago: The Inside Story of What Went Wrong in Greece." *Refugees Deeply*, 6 March 2017. https://www.newsdeeply.com/refugees/articles/2017/03/06/the-refugee-archipelago-the-inside-story-of-what-went-wrong-in-greece.

Hubbard, Ben. 2015. "Money Flows With Refugees, and Life Jackets Fill the Shops." *The New York Times*, 26 September 2015. https://www.nytimes.com/2015/09/27/world/middleeast/money-flows-with-refugees-and-life-jackets-fill-the-shops.html.

Human Rights Watch (HRW). 2017a. "Greece: Asylum Seekers in Abysmal Conditions on Islands." 23 October 2017. https://www.hrw.org/news/2017/10/23/greece-asylum-seekers-abysmal-conditions-islands.

Human Rights Watch (HRW). 2017b. "Greece: Dire Risks for Women Asylum Seekers." 15 December 2017. https://www.hrw.org/news/2017/12/15/greece-dire-risks-women-asylum-seekers.

International Organisation for Migration (IOM). n.d. «EU Relocation Programme.» https://greece.iom.int/en/eu-relocation-programme.

Jones, Reece. 2016. *Violent Borders: Refugees and the Right to Move*. London: Verso Books.

Kalsched, Donald. 1996. *The Inner World of Trauma*. Sussex: Routledge.

Karakoulaki, Marianna. 2015. "Stranded in the Balkans." *IRIN*, 20 November 2015. https://www.irinnews.org/analysis/2015/11/20/stranded-balkans.

Karakoulaki, Marianna. 2016a. "Chaos and Desperation at the Greek-Macedonian Border." *Deutsche Welle*, 29 February 2016. http://www.dw.com/en/chaos-and-desperation-at-the-greek-macedonian-border/a-19083418.

Karakoulaki, Marianna. 2016b. "No Hope, Limited Options for Refugees in Idomeni." *Deutsche Welle*, 11 March 2016. http://www.dw.com/en/no-hope-limited-options-for-refugees-in-idomeni/a-19111009.

Karakoulaki, Marianna. 2016c. "Idomeni's Refugees Suffer Mental Anguish." *Deutsche Welle*, 02 April 2016. http://www.dw.com/en/idomenis-refugees-suffer-mental-anguish/a-19157879.

Karakoulaki, Marianna. 2016d. "Macedonia Police Deploy Tear Gas on Refugees at Idomeni." *Deutsche Welle*, 10 April 2016. http://www.dw.com/en/macedonia-police-deploy-tear-gas-on-refugees-at-idomeni/a-19177170.

King, Natasha. 2016. *No Borders: The Politics of Immigration Control and Resistance*. London: Zed Books.

Médecins Sans Frontières (MSF). 2015. "People Need Safe and Legal Ways to Seek Asylum and Migrate." 10 November 2015. https://msf.exposure.co/provide-safepassage.

Médecins Sans Frontières (MSF). 2017. "Greece: EU border policies fuel mental health crisis for asylum seekers." 10 October 2017. http://www.msf.org/en/article/greece-eu-border-policies-fuel-mental-health-crisis-asylum-seekers.

Nail, Thomas. 2015. *The Figure of the Migrant*. Stanford: Stanford University Press.

Navai, Ramita. 2015. "Macedonia: Tracking Down the Refugee Kidnap Gangs." *Channel 4 News*, 5 June 2015. https://www.youtube.com/watch?v=A5fDgJP2G30.

Papadopoulos, Renos. 2007. "Refugees, Trauma and Adversity-Activated Development." *European Journal of Psychotherapy and Counselling* 9, no. 3: 301–312.

Roberts, Rachel. 2017. "Refugees Face Deadly Winter on Greek Islands As Charities Call on Government to Prevent Deaths." *The Independent*, 1 December 2017. http://www.independent.co.uk/news/world/europe/greece-refugees-winter-deaths-charities-call-on-government-help-a8087996.html.

Siegfried, Kristy. 2015. "Balkan Countries Impose 'National Segregation' at Borders." *IRIN*, 19 November 2015. http://www.irinnews.org/news/2015/11/19.

Tosidis, Dimitris. 2016. "From Idomeni on the road to nowhere." *Deutsche Welle*, 15 March 2016. http://www.dw.com/en/from-idomeni-on-the-road-to-nowhere/g-19117947.

United Nations High Commissioner for Refugees (UNHCR). 2010. "Convention and Protocol Relating to the Status of Refugees." http://www.unhcr.org/3b66c2aa10.

United Nations High Commissioner for Refugees (UNHCR). 2016. "Refugees and Migrants Sea Arrivals in Europe." *The UN Refugee Agency*. https://data2.unhcr.org/ar/documents/download/49921.

United Nations High Commissioner for Refugees (UNHCR). 2017. "Fact Sheet: Greece/ 1–30 November 2017." *The UN Refugee Agency*. https://data2.unhcr.org/en/documents/download/61158.

Yeung, Peter. 2016. "Idomeni: Macedonian Police Fire Tear Gas and Rubber Bullets at Refugees Trying to Break through Greek Border." 10 April 2017. http://www.independent.co.uk/news/world/europe/idomeni-macedonia-police-tear-gas-refugee-border-greece-a6977141.html.

Zimmerman, Cathy, Ligia Kiss and Mazeda Hossain. 2011. "Migration and Health: A Framework for 21st Century Policy-Making." PLoS Med 8 no. 5. https://doi.org/10.1371/journal.pmed.1001034.

Field Notes

NB: The Field Notes are categorised in months unless there is reference to a specific event in the text.

Field Notes, January 2015.
Field Notes, April 2015.
Field Notes, May 2015.
Field Notes, 8 May 2015.
Field Notes, August 2015.
Field Notes, September 2015.
Field Notes, October 2015.
Field Notes, November 2015.
Field Notes, December 2015.
Field Notes, February 2016.
Field Notes, March 2016.
Field Notes, 18 March 2016.
Field Notes, April 2016.
Field Notes, 10 April 2016.
Field Notes, May 2016.
Field Notes, 11 November 2016.

6

Empathy and Othering: Framing Syria's Refugee Crisis in the British Press

NICOLA LANGDON

'Choices about words do matter'
United Nations High Commissioner for Refugees (2016)

Since 2011, an increasingly protracted civil war has ravaged Syria, resulting in a large-scale refugee crisis. Under threat from the Assad regime, Islamic State militants and coalition airstrikes, thousands of refugees and migrants prefer to risk the tumultuous seas of the Mediterranean in order to seek refuge on Europe's borders, generating the largest mass movement of people in recent history (European Commission 2015, 1). In 2015, the number of 'sea arrivals' to Europe totalled 1,004,356, almost five times the figure for 2014 (International Organisation for Migration (IOM) 2016). For many of those travelling by boat to seek sanctuary in the European Union (EU), the journey is a perilous one. The boats used are often small, overcrowded or unsea-worthy, and many have perished in the Mediterranean Sea. The IOM estimates the number of fatalities in the Mediterranean at 3,771 in 2015 (IOM 2016).

Desperate images of overcrowded boats and a mountain of discarded lifejackets on the Greek island of Lesbos have appeared in the media over the preceding months (see BBC 2015c; CNN 2016). However, none pricks the consciousness like the image of a small boy face-down in the lap of the waves. On 2 September 2015, Turkish photojournalist Nilüfer Demir immortalised the tragedy of the refugee crisis by tweeting a photo of Aylan Kurdi, a Syrian toddler who drowned crossing the Mediterranean to Turkey alongside the hashtag #KiyiyaVuranInsanlik (English translation 'humanity washed ashore' (Demir 2015). British print media remediated this harrowing image and presented it to us as the epitome of human vulnerability and Western shame (see Burrows 2015; Dubuis 2015; Hartley-Brewer 2015; Rayner and Dominiczak 2015; Smith and Goddard 2015). A cosmopolitan outlook was created as we imagined Aylan Kurdi, in his shorts and t-shirt, as our son and brother. The converse framing saw the Western media talking of the dangers of the refugee crisis. Calais was a 'war zone' or 'gauntlet', and 'swarms' of people were trying to 'storm' the UK (Bland 2015; Fricker 2015; Ingham 2015; Saunders 2015; Whitehead 2015), or risk their children's lives in precarious border crossings, or to unknown traffickers.

This chapter considers the ways in which we imagine such large-scale movements of people by considering the British press reporting of the crisis. In doing so, the chapter highlights ways in which the Syrian refugee crisis is constructed and presented, contributing to our understanding of this humanitarian emergency. The first is a 'threat' framing of the crisis which considers those in flight as threatening to the UK through criminality, immorality, fraud and divergent identities. The vulnerability of those in flight is perpetuated through dehumanisation, indifference and 'othering' as we elevate the perception of threats to the UK above the individual suffering of those who are displaced. The second framing draws the crisis near to us in proximity, perception and empathy, instilling a cosmopolitan conception of this as the moral responsibility of humanity. This chapter discusses the discursive construction of the crisis within the British media, considering how such understandings may shape our perceptions, affecting our compassion for those suffering from forms of violence and insecurity, and our support for policy-making that seeks to manage such crises. Scott Blinder has examined such latent perceptions of immigrants in British public opinion, and while not establishing causality, highlights the capacity of media coverage to indirectly influence attitudes on immigration (Blinder 2015, 96). Similarly, a study by Duffy and Frere-Smith for the Social Research Institute Ipsos MORI highlights that 'cause and effect' runs in all directions between the public, politicians and the media on the issue of immigration. The study finds that there is sufficient evidence 'to suggest that the media have an independent effect on views of immigration and therefore that the accuracy and balance of their coverage needs careful scrutiny' (Duffy and Frere-Smith 2014).

Media Framing: Power and Perception

The media are the primary channel through which domestic and foreign politics are disseminated to the public (McCombs and Shaw 1972). The press therefore plays an extremely significant role in shaping our understandings of issues such as migration (Allen 2016; Blinder and Allen 2015) and may do this through the notion of media framing. A frame is a 'central organizing idea' (Gamson and Modigliani 1987, 143), or way of viewing the world that may lead to the promotion of particular understandings (Lawlor 2015, 329). This is achieved through the use of select information, language constructions and linguistic tools. Within the field of political communication, interest lies in how frames may shape political understandings and influence policy decision-making. The media form a significant site within which 'various social groups, institutions, and ideologies struggle over the definition and construction of social reality' (Gurevitch and Levy 1985, 19), and as such frames are not value-neutral. Media texts utilise language and image to present information and events through particular frameworks. As such, they play a constitutive role (Lamont 2015, 92) and also perpetuate latent power;

> We walk around with media-generated images of the world, using them to construct meaning about political and social issues. The lens through which we receive these images is not neutral but evinces the power and point of view of the political and economic elites who operate and focus it. And the special genius of this system is to make the whole process seem so normal and natural that the very art of social construction is invisible (Gamson et al. 1992, 374).

Frames often operate through the use of cultural resonance or magnitude (Entman 2004, 6). Cultural resonance involves discursive constructs that appear culturally familiar to the audience, or which 'strike a responsive chord' (Snow and Benford 1988, 207). This may be through the use of language that is 'noticeable, understandable, memorable, and emotionally charged' (Entman 2004, 6). Magnitude, refers to the weight or strength of the frame, and may involve the repetition of words or themes to stimulate effect or metaphor, exemplars, catchphrases, depictions and visual images (Gamson and Modigliani 1989, 3–4). A frame is successful to the extent that it is unconsciously accepted by its recipient audience. The ramification of this is that we are insentiently influenced by what we see and hear through the media, and thus the promotion of certain understandings and policy reactions appear naturalised.

Forced Migration and Discursive Representation

The extant migration literature base has focussed upon empirical exp-eriences, the normative and legal basis for migration and the role of institutions like the United Nations High Commission for Refugees (UNHCR) (Loescher 2001), or political and security implications (Loescher et al. 2008). However, a developing field addresses the discursive construction of forced displacement. Much of this literature has considered migrants and refugees entering Australia, which has pursued a notoriously strict border policy towards non-nationals entering the country in recent years through the 'Pacific Solution' (2001–2007)[1]. Such stringent policies have stimulated research into the attitudinal factors surrounding migration. There have been a variety of studies focussing upon the perceptions of those entering Australia (Lueck et al. 2015; McKay et al. 2011). Others discuss how these perceptions are generally negative and involve marginalisation through specific identity constructions such as 'illegal immigrant' or 'boat people' (O'Doherty and Lecouteur 2007), or dehumanisation through the establishment of a culture of fear around refugee-hood and displacement (Bleiker et al. 2013; Esses et al. 2013).

British media narratives on migration have addressed similar topics, such as the construction of asylum seekers as a 'threat' and legitimisation of subsequent restrictive policies towards immigration (Innes 2010) and the difference in attitudes between British public and experts working closely on asylum issues (Pearce and Stockdale 2009). Lawlor (2015) looks specifically at the media framing of immigration in Canadian and British newsprint. Balch and Balabanova (2016) have considered the communitarian and cosmopolitan framing of immigration within the British media with regard to the free movement of Romanians and Bulgarians from 2006–2013. Their study highlights the prevalence of communitarian framings of immigration within the British press, to the almost exclusion of cosmopolitan ideals.

Studies are emerging that examine the forced migration towards Europe that has been occurring since 2014; considering Mediterranean border policies (Lendaro 2016), discursive representations within Germany (Holmes and Castañeda 2016), or of Syrian refugees within social media (Rettberg and Gajjala 2016). Stuart Allan has looked specifically at the stereotypes surrounding the Syrian refugee crisis, focussing upon the visual images of the Syrian child, Aylan Kurdi, who drowned in an attempt to cross from Turkey to Greece in September 2015 (Allan 2016). Furthermore, a key development has been a contemporary report prepared for the UNHCR, and also in conjunction with Cardiff University, which examines the press coverage of the EU refugee and migrant crisis through a content analysis of the newsprint in five European Countries, including the UK (Berry et al. 2015). This significant study arose from the evident mixed reportage of the migration, leading the

---

[1]   The 'Pacific Solution' refers to the Howard Government's 2001 policy to intercept asylum seekers on 'unauthorised' or 'irregular maritime arrival' (IMA) vessels in Australian waters and transfer them to processing centres on the Pacific islands of Nauru or Manus. The policy was contentious and received a great deal of criticism due to the conditions and length of stay within the offshore processing centres (Phillips 2012).

UNHCR to commission a report examining the drivers of such coverage. The findings of the study suggested there were significant differences between the five countries' coverage of the crisis, from the sources used and language employed, to the problematising of the crisis, as well as the dominant themes presented. The report suggests that out of the five countries under analysis (Spain, Italy, Germany, UK, Sweden), UK coverage had the most negative and polarised coverage of the crisis, often presenting the issue as a social or cultural threat. This chapter develops upon these existing works, considering the discursive framing of the Syrian refugee crisis within the British press and the consequences of such ways of viewing the world.

'Threat Framing' and 'Othering' within British Newsprint

The presence of negative framings were clearly evident within the British press in 2015 during the height of refugee migration towards the EU. The dominant negative construction involved the attachment of some kind of 'threat' to those displaced. This threat framing was constructed from a variety of negative portrayals, racial stereotypes (Allan 2016), fallacious attachments to acts of criminality or terrorism, and a questioning of refugees' authenticity. These negativities were projected through the use of selective terminology and misleading information, the use of metaphorical statements and the evocation of past experiences of mass migration, such as during the Rwandan Genocide and World War II. The creation and projection of a threat frame played to domestic audiences already experiencing social anxiety due to financial austerity, the wars in Iraq and Afghanistan, terror incidents in the UK and Europe and increasing Islamophobia and racial tensions. Such anxieties led to an ingroup-outgroup mentality (Holmes and Castañeda 2016, 13) as well as increased support for right-wing political parties in the UK and Europe, such as the UK Independence Party (UKIP) who utilised the immigration debate to further their cause (Berry 2015, 1).

During the EU Referendum campaign, immigration formed the central foundation of the 'Leave campaign', supported by UKIP. A consequence was the stoking of social fears through the promulgation of an 'immigration as threat' framing, which was repeated through the press. This was particularly stark within traditionally right partisan press, but also evident throughout more liberal media in perhaps less pejorative ways (see Balch and Balabanova 2017). At the height of the campaign, UKIP produced a billboard poster showing a throng of 'migrants' making the journey to the Croatia-Slovenia border. The people in the poster appear to be Arab and predominantly male, and it carries the tagline 'Breaking Point'. The poster was internationally criticised within the media (Bilefsy 2016; Hopkins 2016; Safdar 2016; Stewart and Mason 2016), however despite condemnation the poster and the ensuing discussion reinforced already evident social constructions. Firstly, that this was a 'crisis' – a situation at 'breaking point'. Secondly, that those making the journey towards the refugee camp are young males – usually outside of the social constructs of victimhood (Bleiker et al. 2013, 408). Such imagery immediately leads to questions of authenticity. If this was a genuine humanitarian situation, where are the women, children and elderly – those assumed 'most vulnerable' in society? Instead, the poster shows primarily males under 65, providing the implication that they are seeking socio-economic opportunities rather than fleeing persecution and violence, and establishing those in flight as 'cowardly' (Rettberg and Gajjala 2016, 180). Thirdly, the photo is hauntingly reminiscent of Nazi propaganda of Jewish refugees during World War II. These links were highlighted on *Twitter* and within some of the British press where UKIP leader Nigel Farage was widely berated for his insensitive 'gutter politics' (Stewart and Mason 2016).

The British press referred frequently to the refugee movement as a 'crisis'. By describing the situation in this way, the event is instantly magnified as something critical and uncontrolled. Such speech acts take the issue out of the normal political process, placing it on the security agenda as something threatening; portraying 'enemies at the gate' (Esses et al. 2013, 519). Similarly, the situation was often referred to using metaphorical language or statements. These frequently were of an ecological nature, such as descri-bing a 'flood', 'deluge', 'tide' or 'swamp' (Holmes and Castañeda 2016, 18; Parker 2015, 7), or using descriptors such as 'swarm'. In the following statement, published in *The Independent*, Fergusson describes the situation as a 'storm', highlighting the scale of its 'force', and suggests a lack of situational control. 'This is not a passing storm. We are in the grip of forces that have already accelerated beyond our control' (Fergusson 2015).

The ecological nature of the language used suggests a natural power that is overwhelming or uncontrollable. Such terms reduce the event to an anonymous mass movement without consideration of the individual human element contained within. Terms such as 'swarm' suggest an individual element as part of a large collectivity, but degrades that individual element to the level of an insect or pest. We rarely use the word 'swarm' outside of descriptors about insects. Prime Minister David Cameron was criticised for his description of a 'swarm of people' entering the UK. While he defended this as an attempt to convey the scale of the situation, such terms reduce the displaced to numbers rather than people, which leads to a 'denial of humanity' (Esses et al. 2013, 519) and promotes the idea of people as dirty or diseased – associations we commonly make with pests. Nigel Farage and *The Independent* utilised theological metaphors to illustrate the scale of the refugee movement, suggesting this was something of magnitude and out of human control.

[E]xodus of biblical proportions (Farage, in *Mail Online* 2015).

The figures already sound biblical (Fergusson 2015).

Both uses of metaphorical language dehumanise the vulnerable people affected. It is such dehumanisation that distances us from those experiencing such displacement, and leads us to consider them apart from ourselves. Instead of part of global humanity, they are the distant 'other', the 'huddled masses' (The Daily Telegraph 2015) or 'irregular' (Fergusson 2015). Furthermore, terms such as 'swarm' that conjure imagery of refugees as insects are disturbingly redolent of the hate language utilised to incite militias during the Rwandan genocide (1994) in their denunciation of the Tutsi as cockroaches (Melvern 2000, 227), or the Nazi regime descriptions of Jews as parasites (Kenez 2013, 91). The statements below are illustrative of this dehumanisation. The first is made by Katie Hopkins, a former columnist for *The Sun* who is recognised for rather vitriolic opinion pieces. In it, she makes explicit, distasteful references to cockroaches and the Ethiopian famine during the early 1980s. The second statement from an article published by *The Express* uses the water metaphor of a 'torrent'. This statement also describes those in flight as 'migrant stowaways'. This has the consequence of implying that these are economic migrants and that they are partaking in illegal activity – 'stowing away to get into Europe'.

> Make no mistake, these migrants are like cockroaches. They might look a bit "Bob Geldof's Ethiopia circa 1984", but they are built to survive a nuclear bomb (Hopkins 2015).

> MIGRANTS SWARM TO BRITAIN: Torrent of stowaway migrants on a typical day in borderless UK [emphasis in original] (Chapman 2015).

The identity constructions of the refugees within the media also shape our perception of the forced migration. The UK media overwhelmingly referred to this as a 'migrant' crisis rather than utilising any other term for those displaced. The use of the term 'migrant' does not acknowledge the reasons for flight in the first instance. Rather, it suggests a level of agency in the decision-making process that for many is illusory. While there is always a choice to be made on an individual level to take particular action, the use of the term 'migrant' trivialises the complexities of this decision. It also associates those taking flight in the most precarious and dangerous of situations with economic migrants, emigrating for socioeconomic opportunities. The extracts below suggest an animal or gang-like group of 'migrants' and asks us to question how many people can realistically be resettled in the UK and Europe. The last extract suggests 'migrants' are 'invading' the UK. Such rhetoric appeals to nationalistic sentiments and notions of strengthening sovereignty and border controls.

> MIGRANTS: HOW MANY MORE CAN WE TAKE? [emphasis in original] (Doughty et al. 2015).

> [R]oaming packs of migrants (Gutteridge 2015).

> New migrant 'invasion' of Britain bigger than the Vikings, Romans and Norman Conquest (Barnett 2016).

The normative categorisations of displacement are not made cogent within the press reports of the issue. The interchangeable use of the terms migrant/ asylum-seeker/refugee is damaging, leading to the undermining of public support for refugees and the denial of legal protection at the most vulnerable times (UNHCR 2016). While it is evident that some of those making the hazardous crossing to Europe are doing so for socioeconomic reasons, it is unwise to refer to this as a 'migrant' crisis when so many of those people are forcibly displaced by conflict and persecution. Moreover, the reasons for flight are at best trivialised, and at worst denied through a confusion between the push of conflict and insecurity and the draw of improved socioeconomic circumstances.

This delegitimisation is further compounded by overt claims to the sincerity and lawfulness of those in flight. The British press frequently made claims to the authenticity of those crossing to Europe, suggesting these were economic migrants, or suggesting they were fraudulent claims for asylum in order to 'get into the country', or that they should not be allowed into the UK as it was not the entry EU Member State under the Dublin Regulation[2].

> [The BBC] carried an interview with a *remarkably healthy looking* Syrian refugee *claiming not to have eaten* for 16 days and who said he was going to be a European table tennis champion [emphasis added] (Clark 2015).

> [W]e have been too quick to listen to the sob stories of terrorists disguised as asylum seekers and too quick to ask whether there might be a good reason that their home countries were out to arrest them (Clark 2015).

---

[2]   Under the Dublin Regulation, asylum claims should be made within the first state entered (Lendaro 2016, 151).

Frequently the press made references to 'migrants' receiving welfare in the UK being privileged above UK nationals (Berry et al. 2015, 253). Such reports, more prevalent within the British tabloid press demarcate those entering the UK as receiving preferential treatment, exacerbating social tensions and overall perceptions of refugees and migrants as untrustworthy (Parker 2015, 8), unlawful (Lueck et al. 2015, 619), 'cheating the British system' (Esses et al. 2013, 523) or causing injustices to British citizens and values.

As well as questions over the genuineness of those seeking asylum, the British press often made explicit links between those in flight and criminality, trafficking gangs or terrorists. Such accusations, often spurious, serve to cognitively link those vulnerable and in need of assistance with criminality (Lendaro 2016, 153; Lueck et al. 2015, 617; Parker 2015, 6), reinforcing the negative threat framing through which the forced migration is constructed.

> What we can't do is allow people to break into our country (Cameron, in Chapman 2015).

> Armed gangs smuggling migrants to UK for £2,000 (Sheldrick 2015).

> Britain at risk of Mediterranean migrant crisis after second boat reaches UK in two weeks (Barnett and Sykes 2016).

In the statements above, *The Express Online* perpetuate the construction of refugees and migrants as criminals. They reproduce a comment from Cameron suggesting that people are 'breaking in' to the UK. The second extract illustrates the trafficking of refugees and migrants, suggesting gangs are violent and hold links to the UK. That the passport of a Syrian refugee was found near the body of one of the suicide bombers responsible for the Paris terror attacks in November 2015 solidified claims that terrorists were entering Europe under the pretence of refugee-hood (Lendaro 2016, 150). Links to people smugglers (often the only way for many to commence the arduous journey over land or sea)(UNHCR 2017, 1), constructs the desire for safety and asylum as a shady or 'deviant' activity (McKay et al. 2011, 117, 124) pursued by those without a genuine need for assistance; human desperation is not sufficient cause.

These discursive devices combine to construct those journeying to the EU in search of sanctuary in a negative and threatening way, where those experiencing insecurity are constructed as perpetuating insecurity (Innes 2010, 462). In framing refugees in this way, we protract the geographical and cultural distance between the observer 'us' and the suffering 'them'. The British press were complicit in promoting an ingroup-outgroup perception of the refugee emergency. This was a terrible situation, but these people were constructed as culturally dissimilar, economic migrants, criminals, fraudsters, terrorists or immoral.

'Cosmopolitan Framing' and the Death of Aylan Kurdi

In contrast to the negative 'threat' frame construction of those experiencing displacement, the British press also promoted a 'cosmopolitan' frame which emphasised a shared understanding of morality and the universality of humanity. Rather than perceiving those displaced as threatening, this frame identified with their vulnerabilities and may also provoke calls for some form of official assistance or aid in the drive to alleviate the suffering of others. In recognising the universality of human experience, it draws the event closer in our consciousness so that we are viewing from a position of morality, empathy and solidarity rather than distance and apathy. Those experiencing displacement are constructed as part of global humanity by reporting that highlights personal experience, tragedy or 'human-interest'. This point is illustrated in the statement below by Zena Agha in *The Independent*, who describes the fate of her cousin who died crossing the Mediterranean.

> Just because he was a migrant doesn't mean his life was worthless – geography was the only difference between us and him (Agha 2015).

Agha also highlights the fickleness of the media, whereby certain human interest stories become the hooks upon which an article is hung, while many more people suffer without voice or media attention. Her point was valid and came two days before the death of three-year old Aylan Kurdi, who has been credited with a change in UK public interest and attitudes towards the emergency (BBC 2015b; Gunter 2015; Kingsley and Timur 2015). However, a cosmopolitan framing was evident prior to this tragedy and is illustrated by the first two extracts below which emphasise the UK's moral position in the world and the universality of humanity. The third statement illustrates the converse, suggesting that the UK cannot help all of the people all of the time and thus we should expect individual tragedies like Agha's cousin and Aylan.

> Europe has to help – just as we did in generations past. We cannot carry like this. It's immoral, it's cowardly and it's not the British way (Wintour 2015).

> Those of us lucky enough to live in stability must understand that the problems of those less fortunate are, in a sense both practical and moral, our problems, too (The Times 2015).

> [C]ommon sense says that Britain cannot save the world (The Express Online 2015).

The cosmopolitan framing of this movement of people towards the EU apexes with the death of Aylan Kurdi, alongside his mother Rehana and brother Galip as they crossed from Turkey to Greece. The image of Aylan lying face down on the sandy shoreline was picked up globally by the media and the British press were no exception. With Aylan's death was felt a shift in the media framing of the refugee movement (BBC 2015b; Gunter 2015; Kingsley and Timur 2015). Rather than a threat, the image of Aylan was one of innocence and tragedy. The little boy was portrayed as a victim of a tragic situation rather than a criminal. Aylan was not a terrorist. This image of death and innocence was a profound and shocking one, resonating with audiences, encouraging us to view Aylan as our child or little brother (Nicole Itano, in Gunter 2015; Bouckaert, in Laurent 2015). This was, in part, easy to do. Aylan looked like any toddler in shorts and t-shirt, his clothing no doubt aided this imagining for those in the West. While many images of death and violence shown in the media are grisly and bloody, this photo was shocking for its calmness – 'he could have been sleeping except for the context' (Itano, in Gunter 2015). What goes comparatively unnoticed is that Aylan's mother and brother both perished alongside him. It is, however, the visual power of Aylan that is symbolic and resonates in our consciousness. The visual element of the frame provides evidence of his suffering and experience that is more emotionally affecting than any statistic (Bleiker et al. 2013, 399, 408). We are led to question with outrage how this little boy came to end up face down in the sand. What would drive this terrible situation? And what can be done about it?

Despite this sorrowing event, some of the British tabloid press still questioned the authenticity of the family's refugee status, with *The Express Online* suggesting the family had been safe in Turkey and were 'not in deadly peril' (Lee 2015). This illustrates how some elements of the British press continued to construct this event through a 'threat frame', seeking to disparage the validity of the Kurdi family's vulnerability and experience, thereby suggesting less legitimate reasons for their displacement and encouraging us to doubt and distrust. This may of course reflect the partisanship of *The Daily Express*, a traditionally right-wing paper showing support to UKIP (Mason 2015) who utilised the immigration debate to underpin their campaign for the UK to rescind its EU membership in the 2016 referendum.

The consequence of this potent symbolism was to bolster a cosmopolitan framing of the refugee movement, encouraging us to look beyond the negative imagery of 'swarms' of 'migrants' and recognise a responsibility to humanity. We are reminded that these people are human too. That in order for families to be making this perilous crossing of the Mediterranean, the situation at home must be more insecure, and that for Aylan and his family this was a journey of necessity not choice. This cosmopolitan framing encourages us to consider the refugee movement in a more proximate way, encouraging empathy and assistance rather than fear and 'othering'.

These two ways of perceiving the refugee crisis were conflictual and prod- uced a competing narrative. This contestation was more evident after the death of the toddler Aylan Kurdi which seemed to alter, albeit temporarily, the discursive vista towards a more cosmopolitan moral frame. While these diverse ways of constructing reality may provide an equilibrium of sorts – what Entman has termed 'frame parity' (2010, 418), the reality is more like a swinging pendulum, where one frame tends to dominate with some cont- estation from a counterframe. Furthermore, such frame contestation may in part reflect the partisan nature of British newsprint. It is regarded that the British press have traditionally held political leanings and we could therefore anticipate that those standpoints may in part be reflected in the media framing of a highly politicised issue such as immigration.

Conclusion

Why is it that some refugees are considered legitimate, innocent and worthy of assistance and others are criminals, illegitimate and not worthy of ass- istance? How the media frames such events has the ability to shape our understandings and perceptions. By framing the refugee movement as a threat, we cognitively distance it and shift the social responsibility for assistance away from ourselves. The threat frame allows us to perceive this as the suffering of a distant 'other'. The proximity of the event is distanced geographically and cognitively, and any cultural resonance is minimised. We are permitted to voyeur from afar or turn away from the suffering 'other'. Subsequently, empathy is diminished alongside compassion and forms of moral responsibility, permitting us to legitimise certain policy responses. The projection of a threat resonates to cognitive schema already primed by financial, social and racial tensions, the visibility of atrocities committed by terrorists such as ISIS, and stoked in some cases by nationalist politics. Cultural stereotyping creates social and racial boundaries, whereby refugees belong to the same geographical region or religion as those we see as committing heinous terror attacks like in Paris (2015) or Brussels (2016). We form false collectivities and perpetuate the persecution of those suffering through simplistic stereotypes and indifference, which leads to 'revictimisation' (Bleiker et al. 2013, 411). We fail to recognise that many of those seeking asylum in Europe are fleeing civil war, external intervention and the terror of ISIS as well.

A cosmopolitan framing helps us to perceive this as an issue for global humanity that we are all responsible for, and compels us to assist in the mitigation of suffering. The image of Aylan Kurdi cognitively resonates as we think of him as our own child or brother. The symbolism of his image forces us to reconsider this morally as a humanitarian issue requiring social responsibility and assistance. In encouraging us to view through a cosmopolitan frame, the media may go some way to alleviate the hostility around issues such as immigration, strengthening human bonds and moral responses, and mitigating against a dereliction of the suffering of 'others' or the perpetuation of difference and indifference that contributes to a 'threat' construction and fear response. However, the longevity of such a framing is in question, and we must wonder how many Aylan's are required for such ways of perceiving the world to resound – 'It shouldn't take a viral image to make us care about other people' (Agha 2015). At the time of writing the British media have a new symbol in Omran Daqneesh, a five-year-old rescued from the carnage of an airstrike in Syria. He sits shocked and bloodied in the back of an ambulance as the world press captured his photograph and the headlines resound once again with 'global outrage' (Coghlan and Philp 2016).

References

Agha, Zena. 2015. "All my cousin wanted to do was flee the horrors of Syria, but he ended up drowning in the sea; Just because he was a migrant doesn't mean his life was worthless – geography was the only difference between us and him." *The Independent,* 21 April 2015. http://www.independent.co.uk/voices/comment/all-my-cousin-wanted-to-do-was-flee-the-horrors-of-syria-but-he-ended-up-drowning-in-the-sea-10192831.html.

Allan, Stuart. 2016. "Shattering Stereotypes: Crisis reporting and the Alan Kurdi images" Invited paper at *Communication and Conflict: Iraq and Syria Conference*, SOAS University of London, 7 May.

Allen, William, L. 2016. "A Decade of Immigration in the British Press." Migration Observatory Report, COMPAS, University of Oxford. www.migrationobservatory.ox.ac.uk.

Balch, Alex and Ekaterina Balabanova. 2016. "Ethics, Politics and Migration: Public Debates on the Free Movement of Romanians and Bulgarians in the

UK, 2006–2013." *Politics* 36, no. 1:19–35.

Balch, Alex and Ekaterina Balabanova. 2017. "A Deadly Cocktail? The Fusion of Europe and Immigration in the UK Press." *Critical Discourse Studies*: 1–20. doi:10.1080/17405904.2017.1284687.

Barnett, Helen. 2016. "New migrant 'invasion' of Britain bigger than the Vikings, Romans and Norman Conquest." *Express,* 30 May 2016. http://www.express.co.uk/news/uk/601177/European-net-migration-Britain-largest-history.

Barnett, Helen and Selina Sykes. 2016. "Britain at risk of Mediterranean migrant crisis after second boat reaches UK in two weeks" *The Express*, 30 May 2016.

BBC. 2015a. "David Cameron criticised over migrant 'swarm' language." 30 July 2015. http://www.bbc.co.uk/news/uk-politics-33716501.

BBC. 2015b. "Alan Kurdi: Has one picture shifted our view of refugees?" 3 September 2015. http://www.bbc.co.uk/news/blogs-trending-34142804.

BBC. 2015c. "10 Moving Photos of Europe's Migrant Crisis." 4 September 2015. http://www.bbc.co.uk/news/magazine-34137358.

Berry, Mike, Inaki Garcia-Blanco and Kerry Moore. 2015. "Press Coverage of the Refugee and Migrant Crisis in the EU: A Content Analysis of Five European Countries." *Report prepared for the UNHCR.* http://www.unhcr.org/uk/protection/operations/56bb369c9/press-coverage-refugee-migrant-crisis-eu-content-analysis-five-european.html.

Bilefsky, Dan. 2016. "As Migrants Face Abuse, Fear That 'Brexit' Has Given License to Xenophobia." *The New York Times*, 27 June 2016. https://www.nytimes.com/2016/06/28/world/europe/as-migrants-face-abuse-fear-that-brexit-has-given-license-to-xenophobia.html?_r=0.

Bland, Archie. 2015. "Speaking of migrants as a 'swarm' is on the same spectrum as suggesting we send in the army. It dehumanises, and presents an animalistic threat." *The Guardian*, 30 July 2015.

Bleiker, Roland, David Campbell, Emma Hutchison and Xzarina Nicholson. 2013. "The Visual Dehumanisation of Refugees." *Australian Journal of Political Science* 48, no.4: 398–416.

Blinder, Scott. 2013. "Imagined Immigration: The Impact of Different Meanings of 'Immigrants' in Public Opinion and Policy Debates in Britain." *Political Studies* 63, no. 1: 80–100.

Blinder, Scott and William L. Allen. 2015. "Constructing Immigrants: Portrayals of Migrant Groups in British National Newspapers, 2010–2012." *International Migration Review* 50, no. 1: 3–40.

Burrows, Thomas. 2015. "Bob Geldof Says He'll Take In Four Migrant Families as He Lambasts Politicians' Response to Crisis As a 'Sickening Disgrace'." *MailOnline*, 4 September 2015. http://www.dailymail.co.uk/news/article-3222233/Bob-Geldof-says-ll-four-migrant-families-lambasts-politicians-response-crisis-sickening-disgrace.html.

Chapman, John. 2015. "MIGRANTS SWARM TO BRITAIN: Torrent of stowaway migrants on a typical day in borderless UK." *The Express*, 29 August 2015, 4–5.

Clark, Ross. 2015. "Left wing media wallow in migrant crisis sob stories says Ross Clark." Express, 26 August 2015. http://www.express.co.uk/comment/expresscomment/600688/Ross-Clark-left-wing-migrant-crisis.

CNN. 2016. "Europe's Migration Crisis in 35 Photos." 31 May 2016. http://edition.cnn.com/2015/09/03/world/gallery/europes-refugee-crisis/.

Coghlan, Tom and Catherine Philp. 2016. "Boy Victim becomes a symbol of Assad's war." *The Times*, 19 August 2016.

Demir, Nilüfer. 2015. 'http://www.dha.com.tr/suriyeli-kacak-gocmenleri-tasiyan-bot-batti-7-olu_1016088.html … #KıyıyaVuranİnsanlık', *Twitter*, 2 September 2015. https://twitter.com/refuliinn/status/639158640641986560. Accessed 25 March 2017.

Doughty, Steve, Ian Drury and John Stevens. 2015. "MIGRANTS: HOW MANY MORE CAN WE TAKE?" *The Daily Mail*, 28 August 2015.

Dubuis, Anna. 2015. "Harrowing Moment Grieving Migrant Mum Breaks Down After Seeing Dead Bodies of Her Two Young Sons in Morgue." *Mirror.co.uk*, 2 September 2015. http://www.mirror.co.uk/news/world-news/harrowing-moment-grieving-migrant-mum-6370424.

Entman, Robert M. 2004. *Projections of Power: Framing News, Public Opinion, and US Foreign Policy.* Chicago: The University of Chicago Press.

Entman, Robert M. 2010. "Cascading Activation: Contesting the White House's Frame After 9/11." *Political Communication* 20, no. 4: 415–432.

Esses, Victoria, M., Stelian Medianu and Andrea S. Lawson. 2013. "Uncertainty, Threat, and the Role of the Media in Promoting the Dehumanization of Immigrants and Refugees." *Journal of Social Issues* 69, no. 3: 518–536.

European Commission. 2015. "Syria Crisis: ECHO Factsheet." *European Commission.* https://ec.europa.eu/echo/files/aid/countries/factsheets/syria_en.pdf.

Fergusson, James. 2015. "The Refugee Crisis Is No Passing Storm." *The Independent*, 23 August 2015.

Fricker, Martin. 2015. "They've Got Knives So Sharp You Could Shave with Them': Mirror Man Runs Gauntlet In Calais With Trucker." *mirror.co.uk*, 25 June 2015. http://www.mirror.co.uk/news/uk-news/theyve-knives-sharp-you-could-5949207.

Gamson, William A. and Andre Modigliani. 1987. "The Changing Culture of Affirmative Action." In *Research in Political Sociology* edited by Braungart, R. G. and Margaret M. Braungart. JAI Press: Greenwich.

Gamson, William A. and Andre Modigliani. 1989. "Media Discourse and Public Opinion on Nuclear Power: A Constructionist Approach." *American Journal of Sociology* 95, no. 1: 1–37.

Gamson, William A., David Croteau, William Hoynes and Theodore Sasson. 1992. "Media Images and the Social Construction of Reality." *Annual Review of Sociology* 18: 373–393.

Gunter, Joel. 2015. "Alan Kurdi: Why One Picture Cut Through." *BBC*, 4 September 2015. http://www.bbc.co.uk/news/world-europe-34150419.

Gurevitch, Michael and Mark R. Levy. 1985. "Preface." *Mass Communication Review Yearbook 5*. California: Sage.

Gutteridge, Nick. 2015. "Euro 2016 Sparks New Migrant Threat: Calais Jungle to Exploit Weakened Security during Cup." *Express,* 20 April 2015. http://www.express.co.uk/news/uk/662696/Euro-2016-new-Calais-refugee-threat-migrants-exploit-weakened-security-sneak-UK.

Hartley-Brewer, Julia. 2015. "If You Really Want to Save Syrian Children, Save Syria." *Telegraph.co.uk*, 3 September 2015. http://www.telegraph.co.uk/news/worldnews/middleeast/syria/11841292/If-you-want-to-save-Syrian-children-save-Syria.html.

Holmes, Seth M. and Heide Castañeda. "Representing the 'European Refugee Crisis' in Germany and the Beyond: Deservingness and Difference, Life And Death." *American Ethnologist* 43, no. 1: 12–24.

Hopkins, Katie. 2015. "*Rescue Boats? I'd Use Gunships to Stop Migrants*." *The Sun,* 17 April 2015. https://www.thesun.co.uk/news/1541491/rescue-boats-id-use-gunships-to-stop-migrants/.

Hopkins, Steven. 2016. "Nigel Farage's Brexit Poster Is Being Likened to 'Nazi Propaganda', Compared to Auschwitz Documentary Scene." *The Huffington Post*, 16 June 2016. http://www.huffingtonpost.co.uk/entry/nigel-farages-eu-has-failed-us-all-poster-slammed-as-disgusting-by-nicola-sturgeon_uk_576288c0e4b08b9e3abdc483.

Ingham, John. 2015. "WE CAN'T STOP MIGRANT CHAOS; Calais Still In Crisis As French Say It's Not Their Problem Calais Turned Into A 'War Zone'" *The Express*, 25 June 2015.

Innes, Alexandria, J. 2010. "When the Threatened Become the Threat: The Construction of Asylum Seekers in British Media Narratives." *International Relations* 24, no. 4: 456–477.

International Organization for Migration (IOM). 2016. "IOM Counts 3,771 Migrant Fatalities in Mediterranean in 2015." *International Organization for Migration*, 1 May 2016. http://www.iom.int/news/iom-counts-3771-migrant-fatalities-mediterranean-2015.

Kingsley, Patrick and Safak Timur. 2015. "Stories of 2015: How Alan Kurdi's Death Changed the World." *The Guardian*, 31 December 2015. https://www.theguardian.com/world/2015/dec/31/alan-kurdi-death-canada-refugee-policy-syria-boy-beach-turkey-photo.

Kenez, Peter. 2013. *The Coming of the Holocaust: From Antisemitism to Genocide*. Cambridge: Cambridge University Press.

Lamont, Christopher. 2015. *Research Methods in International Relations*, London: Sage Publications.

Laurent, Olivier. 2015. "What the Image of Aylan Kurdi Says About the Power of Photography." *TIME*, 4 September 2015. http://time.com/4022765/aylan-kurdi-photo/.

Lawlor, Andrea. 2015. "Framing Immigration in the Canadian and British News Media." *Canadian Journal of Political Science* 48, no. 2: 329–355.

Lee, Adrian. 2015. "Migrant Crisis: The Truth About The Boy On The Beach Aylan Kurdi." Express, 15 September 2015. http://www.express.co.uk/comment/expresscomment/604590/Migrant-crisis-the-truth-about-the-boy-the-beach-Aylan-Kurdi.

Lendaro, Annalisa. 2016. «A 'European Migrant Crisis'? Some Thoughts on Mediterranean Borders." *Studies in Ethnicity and Nationalism* 16, no. 1: 148–157.

Loescher, Gil. 2001. *The UNHCR and World Politics: A Perilous Path*, Oxford: Oxford University Press.

Loescher, Gil, James Milner, Edward Newman and Gary Troeller. 2008. *Protracted Refugee Situations: Political, Human Rights and Security Implications*, Tokyo: United National University Press.

Lueck, Kerstin, Clemence Due and Martha Augoustinos. 2015. "Neoliberalism And Nationalism: Representations Of Asylum Seekers In The Australian Mainstream News Media." *Discourse and Society* 26, no. 5: 608–629.

Mail Online. 2015. *"Eurosceptics 'In Chaos' As THIRD Campaign to Leave EU Is Launched By Ukip with Warning Over 'Biblical Wave of Migration from Syria."* 1 September 2015. http://www.dailymail.co.uk/news/article-3217622/Nigel-Farage-says-immigration-number-one-concern-voters-predicts-huge-impact-EU-referendum.html.

Mason, Rowena. 2015. "Daily Express owner Richard Desmond hands UKIP £1m'" *The Guardian*, 16 April 2015. https://www.theguardian.com/politics/2015/apr/16/daily-express-owner-richard-desmond-ukip-donation.

McCombs, Maxwell E. and Donald L. Shaw. 1972. "The Agenda-Setting Function of Mass Media." *The Public Opinion Quarterly* 36, no. 2: 176–187.

McKay, Fiona H., Samantha L. Thomas and Susan Kneebone. 2011. "It Would be Okay If They Came through the Proper Channels': Community Perceptions and Attitudes toward Asylum Seekers in Australia." *Journal of Refugee Studies* 25, no. 1: 113–133.

Melvern, Linda R. 2000. *A People Betrayed: The Role of the West in Rwanda's Genocide*. London: Zed Books.

O'Doherty, Kieran and Amanda Lecouteur. 2007. "'Asylum seekers", "boat people" and "illegal immigrants": Social categorisation in the media." *Australian Journal of Psychology* 59, no. 1: 1–12.

Parker, Samuel. 2015. "'Unwanted invaders': The representation of refugees and asylum seekers in the UK and the Australian print media." *eSharp* 23. http://www.gla.ac.uk/media/media_404384_en.pdf.

Pearce, Julia M. and Janet E. Stockdale. 2009. "UK Responses to the Asylum Issue: A Comparison of Lay and Expert Views." *Journal of Community & Applied Social Psychology* 19, no. 2: 142–155.

Phillips, Janet. 2012. "The 'Pacific Solution' Revisited: A Statistical Guide to the Asylum Seeker Caseloads on Nauru and Manus Island." Report of Social Policy Section, *Parliament of Australia*, 4 September 2012. http://www.aph.gov.au.

Rayner, Gordon and Peter Dominiczak. 2015. "Plight of Migrant Children Stirs Europe's Conscience." *The Daily Telegraph*, 3 September 2015.

Rettberg, Jill W. and Radhika Gajjala. 2016. "Terrorists or Cowards: Negative Portrayals of Male Syrian Refugees in Social Media." *Feminist Media Studies* 16, no. 1: 178–181.

Safdar, Anealla. 2016. 'Brexit: "UKIP's 'Unethical' Anti-Immigration Poster', *Al Jazeera*, 28 June 2016. http://www.aljazeera.com/indepth/features/2016/06/brexit-anti-immigration-ukip-poster-raises-questions-160621112722799.html.

Saunders, Craig. 2015. "IT'S A WAR ZONE; ...so send in Brit Troops." *Daily Star*, 30 July 2015: 4–5.

Sheldrick, Giles. 2015. "Armed Gangs Smuggling Migrants to UK For £2,500." *The Express*, 22 August 2015. http://www.express.co.uk/news/uk/600018/Armed-gangs-smuggling-migrants-UK-2-000.

Smith, Hannah, L. and Jacqui Goddard. 2015. "Everyone Was Screaming... My Two Boys Slipped From My Hands'; Images of His Dead Son Stopped Us In Our Tracks." *The Times*, 4 September 2015: 8–9.

Snow, David A. and Robert D. Benford. 1988. "Ideology, Frame Resonance, and Participant Mobilization." *From Structure to Action: Comparing Social Movement* Research across Cultures, edited by Bert Klandermans, Hanspeter Kriesi and Sidney Tarrow. Greenwich: Jai Press.

Stewart, Heather and Rowena Mason. 2016. "Nigel Farage's Anti-Migrant Poster Reported to Police." *The Guardian*, 16 June 2016. http://www.theguardian.com/politics/2016/jun/16/nigel-farage-defends-ukip-breaking-point-poster-queue-of-migrants.

The Express Online. 2015. "Swarms of Migrants Are the Norm in the UK in 2015." *The Express Online*, 28 August 2015. http://www.express.co.uk/comment/expresscomment/601512/Swarms-migrants-are-the-norm-the-UK-2015.

The Daily Telegraph. 2015. "Europe Can't Ignore These Huddled Masses." *The Daily Telegraph,* 29 August 2015.

The Times. 2015. "Doing More: The Lack of a Simple Answer to the European Migrant Crisis Is No Excuse for Stasis. Britain Can and Should Help Syrian Refugees, Both Here and in the Middle East." *The Times*, 4 September 2015.

United Nations High Commissioner for Refugees (UNHCR). 2016. "UNHCR Viewpoint: 'Refugee' or 'migrant' - Which is right?" 11 July 2015. http://www.unhcr.org/uk/news/latest/2016/7/55df0e556/unhcr-viewpoint-refugee-migrant-right.html.

United Nations High Commissioner for Refugees (UNHCR). 2017. "Desperate Journeys: Refugees and Migrants Entering and Crossing Europe via the Mediterranean and Western Balkans Routes." February 2017. http://www. unhcr.org/uk/news/updates/2017/2/58b449f54/desperate-journeys-refugees-migrants-entering-crossing-europe-via-mediterranean.html.

UN News Centre. 2016. "As Mediterranean Death Toll Soars, Ban Urges Collective Response to Large Refugee and Migrant Movements." 31 May 2016. http://www.un.org/apps/news/story.asp?NewsID=54092#. V6SvETXnjE9.

Whitehead, Tom. 2015. "Calais Closed Down As Migrants Swarm." *The Daily Telegraph*, 24 June 2015.

Wintour, Patrick. 2015. "Yvette Cooper: UK Should Take In 10,000 Middle East Refugees; Labour Leadership Contender Says It Is Immoral And Cowardly For Britain To Turn Its Back On Those Fleeing War And Turmoil." *The Guardian*, 1 September 2015.

Part Two

Drivers and Responses

7

Conflict and Migration in the Middle East: Syrian Refugees in Jordan and Lebanon

KAMEL DORAÏ

Since the outbreak of the Syrian conflict in 2011, nearly five million refugees settled in neighbouring countries. This massive refugee movement follows others, such as the forced exile of Palestinians after the creation of the State of Israel in 1948, Lebanese from 1975 to 1990 or Iraqis since the early 1980s (Chatty 2010). Refugee movements are one of the major consequences of the political crises in the Middle East in recent decades. As a result, the region is hosting one of the largest refugee populations in the world, while most of the host countries (except Turkey and Israel with time and geographical restrictions) are not signatories of the Geneva Convention of 1951. In consequence there is no specific asylum legislation in these host countries (Kagan 2011). The region is also characterised by strong and ancient human mobility as a result of regional economic disparities and transnational social ties (Marfleet 2007). Today's forced migration movements appear to be linked with previous cross border migration at a regional level. Current geographical distribution of Syrian refugees is partially shaped by pre-existing ties and regional labour migration. This chapter will focus first on the socio-political consequences of the mass arrival of Syrian refugees in Lebanon and Jordan. It will focus more specifically on the gradual changes of migration policies in both countries and their consequences on migration patterns. Special attention will be placed on Palestinian refugees from Syria, who face double displacement. It will then analyse the forms of settlement of Syrian refugees in both countries, with a focus on Jordan. The Syrian crisis has led to a shift in the Jordanian settlement policy. Until 2012, when Zaatari camp opened in Northern Jordan, the reluctance of the authorities of the host countries to open new camps was based on the fear of permanent settlement of refugees on their territory, as is the case for Palestinians.

Conflict, Migration and the Syrian Crisis in the Middle East

The current Syrian forced migration movement has produced deep changes in the Middle East migration system. Before 2011, Syria was hosting large numbers of refugees, comprised mainly of Palestinians and Iraqis but also Sudanese and Somalis (Doraï 2011). Meanwhile hundreds of thousands of Syrian labour migrants were working in Lebanon and in the Gulf countries (Shah 2004). Since the outbreak of the conflict in 2011, Syria is one of the main countries of origin of refugees in the world, with more than five million Syrians fleeing their home, mostly to neighbouring countries. According to the United Nations High Commissioner for Refugees (UNHCR), Turkey, Lebanon, Jordan and Iraq are currently hosting the vast majority of the Syrian refugees.

A Massive Refugee Movement Concentrated in Neighbouring Countries

Country	Registered refugees
Turkey	2,733,655
Lebanon	1,033,513
Jordan	656,400
Iraq	225,455
Egypt	117,350

Syrian refugees registered at the UNHCR, Oct. 2016 (UNHCR n.d.b)

The high concentration of Syrian refugees in the Middle East can be partly explained by the historical and previous migratory links existing between the countries in the region. Bilateral agreements existed to facilitate the circulation and employment – with restrictions – of people. Regional mobility pre-existed the independence of states in the region. When national borders were created at the beginning of the twentieth century, this circular migration transformed into transnational networks. The settlement of Syrian refugees is also the result of an open door policy during the first two years of the conflict. The Middle East is not an exception as most of the refugees in the world find asylum in neighbouring countries (UNHCR 2016, 15). The settlement of these refugees is also linked to the development of increasingly restrictive migration policies by most of the European countries, with the exception of Germany and Sweden. These two countries have received 64% of the total asylum applications in Europe (UNHCR n.d.a).

The recent agreement between Turkey and the European Union aims to stabilise Syrian refugees outside EU territory (Krumm 2015). European Union countries try to limit new entries, while the causes of departures are not addressed effectively both for those who continue to leave Syria or their country of first asylum (Jordan, Lebanon, Iraq). Some new agreements are being implemented in neighbouring countries. For example, since April 2016, Jordan has adopted a new regulation to give Syrian workers access to the labour market, but it still concerns a limited number of refugees (according to the Jordan Ministry of Labour, 37,000 Syrian workers had obtained a work permit by the end of 2016). The permanence of conflict is always a determining factor that leads to more departures. Meanwhile, the condition of exile in neighbouring countries leads to increasing impoverishment of the poorest refugees who have limited access to the legal labour market and resources. The Syrians are mostly confined to the informal sector and very exposed to competition with other migrant groups, such as Egyptian workers. Their precarious legal status is also a source of instability. The combination of all these factors explains the continuing migration to Europe.

From Cross-Border Circulation to Restrictive Migration Policies

The current Syrian refugee movement cannot be understood without taking into consideration the history of cross-border mobility in the region. Before 2011, migratory circulation was sustained by the existence of well-established transnational networks. Circulation from Syria towards Lebanon or Jordan had different purposes: family visits, marriage or commercial activities. If the presence of Syrians is well documented in Lebanon (Chalcraft 2009; Longuenesse 2015), the current Syrian crisis has shed light on the growing presence of Syrians in Jordan (Al Khouri 2004). Historical links existed between Southern Syria and Northern Jordan – especially tribal and family links – even if it is difficult to evaluate their number before 2011. There was also a group of Syrians who found asylum in Jordan in 1982 after the Hama massacre. Some of them settled permanently in Jordan and opened businesses. They are well integrated in the Jordanian society and participate actively in the private sector.[1]

Migration policies of neighbouring states have dramatically changed since 2011. Syrians were enjoying relative freedom of cross-border mobility towards Lebanon and Jordan. They also had access – with some restrictions in both countries – to the labour market. Both countries had signed agreements with the Syrian government to facilitate the circulation of migrant workers. Due to the mass arrival of Syrians after 2011 and the fear of their permanent

---

[1]   Interviews by Kamel Doraï and Myriam Ababsa in Sahab (Jordan) in 2016 with municipality representatives and Syrian investors.

settlement in the country, Lebanon suspended a bilateral agreement in 2014 – originally implemented in 1994 – on the access of Syrians to the labour market (Longuenesse 2015). At the same time, refugees were still arriving *en masse* in the country, trying to find jobs. If the conflict in Syria has led to the forced migration of hundreds of thousands of refugees, economic migration did not disappear. Nearly 400,000 Syrians were working in Lebanon before 2011 (Chalcraft 2009). Most of them became *de facto* forced migrants, as they could not go back home. A large portion of them registered with the UNHCR (Knudsen 2017). Jordan has also gradually implemented restrictive entry policies for Syrians (Ababsa 2015). The opening of the Zaatari refugee camp in July 2012 can be considered a first turning point to regulate entries of Syrian refugees. Then more restrictions were imposed. Today, even if the border is still officially open, very few Syrian refugees are allowed to enter. The main consequence is that the camp of Rukban on the eastern part of the border transformed from a transit place into a camp. It now hosts more than 85,000 Syrian refugees in a no man's land between the two countries with very limited access to humanitarian assistance (UNHCR 2017).

One important element to take into consideration is that there is no clear distinction between migration policy and asylum policy in Lebanon and Jordan. Like other countries in the region, they are not signatories of the Geneva Convention of 1951 on refugees (Zaiotti 2006). Only Palestinians are recognised as refugees in the state where they have their permanent residency when they are registered with United Nations Relief and Works Agency for Palestine Refugees in the Near East (UNRWA). Thus, both countries have no national asylum system. It is the UNHCR that establishes asylum procedures in cooperation with host governments. Lebanon and Jordan have signed a Memorandum of Understanding with the UNHCR that specifies the mandate of the international organisation (Kagan 2011, 9), from which Palestinians (covered by another international organisation, UNRWA) are excluded.

Palestinians and Iraqis: From Refugees in Syria to Asylum Seekers?

The massive forced migration of Syrians should not conceal the fact that other refugee groups who were residing in Syria have also been forced to escape war and violence. UNRWA estimated the total number of Palestinian refugees displaced inside Syria at just over 250,000 (half of the total number registered in Syria), a large portion originating from Yarmouk camp in Damascus. More than 70,000 of them were forced to seek asylum in neighbouring countries mainly to Lebanon (50,000), Jordan (6,000) and Egypt (9,000) (UNRWA n.d.). Those who are still in Syria, reside in safer places than their habitual place of residency (some camps, like Yarmouk in Damascus or

Handarat close to Aleppo have been subject to heavy destruction and blockade). Eight thousand refugees whose homes were destroyed live in UNRWA facilities, generally in schools. Some Internally Displaced Persons (IDPs) were able to return to their homes, but the number of new refugees that moved *en masse* remains higher.

The current conflict has had dramatic consequences for the Palestinian population in Syria. Palestinians were enjoying access to education and the labour market without particular discrimination in Syria before 2011 (Shiblak 1996). The outbreak of the Syrian conflict in 2011 consigned Palestinians to their stateless status. All this seems to replicate a scenario already seen with Palestinians from Iraq in the aftermath of the fall of Saddam Hussein in 2003 (Doraï and Al Husseini 2013). Palestinian refugees are not covered by the UNHCR mandate, as they already receive assistance from the UNRWA (Feldman 2012). They lack legal protection transforming them *de facto* into illegal migrants subject to potential deportation towards Syria. Palestinian refugees tend to be transformed into asylum seekers by conflicts. Jordan quickly decided to close its doors to this category of refugees, limiting drastically their possibility to escape violence from Syria. As written by Jalal Al Husseini (2015),

> after a relatively tolerant phase during which some 10,000 Palestinian refugees have been able to enter the country, Jordan has tightened its entry policy since late 2012 on behalf of the need to counter the Israeli vision of Jordan as Palestinian homeland of substitution.

Lebanon, until 2013, had adopted a more flexible policy, and hosted more than 75% of the Palestinian refugees from Syria. For the same reasons, Lebanon also decided in 2014 to close its borders for them (Doraï 2015).

The absence of a legal framework concerning Palestinian refugees, who are forced to leave their country of residence as well as the political treatment of the Palestinian refugees by states in the region, raises the problem of secondary migration during conflict. Refugees already residing in Syria (mainly Iraqis and Palestinians) face several limitations to their mobility and protection. Because Middle Eastern countries are not signatories of the 1951 Geneva Convention, they lack protection when they escape a conflict for a second time.

Today, other refugees, such as Iraqis who were in Syria before 2011, can face similar problems. Iraqi refugees who sought refuge in Syria, mostly in the suburbs of Damascus (Doraï 2014), have also been forced to leave their countries of first asylum. The majority returned to Iraq, despite continuing violence. Others were able to continue their journey to Europe, North America or Australia. According to UNHCR, around 20,000 are still in Syria because they cannot leave the country. These populations, already refugees before the Syrian conflict, find themselves therefore forced to new mobility in a context where Syrian neighbouring countries are reluctant to give them asylum. Not being part of the 1951 Geneva Convention, they do not want to be considered resettlement countries. As most of these refugees are unable to move, even temporarily, in the Middle East, a growing number of them are seeking more sustainable solutions outside the region. Jordan and Lebanon consider themselves as only temporary host countries and develop policies that incite refugees to immigrate to third countries to settle permanently and access a new citizenship (Chatelard 2002).

From Exile to Temporary Settlement: Refugees in Camps and Urban Refugees

The Syrian crisis has reopened the debate in the region on the creation of new refugee camps. While Middle Eastern states chose not to open refugee camps during the last Iraqi crisis in 2003[2], Jordan and Turkey took a different decision after 2011 (Achilli et al. 2017). In Lebanon, no official camps have been opened. As a result, a myriad of unofficial refugee camps of small sizes mushroomed, where refugees are especially vulnerable due to lack of coordination of assistance. Most of the current Syrian refugee population settle in urban areas or already existing villages to access resources and develop their own social and economic activities in certain localities, thereby contributing to urban change and development.

The Palestinian Experience and Its Current Consequences

As mentioned earlier in this chapter, host states in the Middle East are reluctant to open new refugee camps. The Iraq wars of 1990–1991 and post-2003 demonstrated for Jordan, Syria and Lebanon that the absence of camps, combined with a relative freedom of entry and residence at the beginning of the crises and a fairly easy access to public services and employment in the informal labour market, have increased the possibility of mobility of refugees and therefore their re-emigration to third countries (Chatelard and Doraï 2009). Additionally, the decision not to open refugee camps is the result of both state policies that try to avoid the creation of camps, and the refugees' very own reasoning. Most of the refugees prefer to

---

[2] Only Palestinians from Iraq were denied entry in neighbouring countries after 2003. Three refugee camps were created at the Iraqi border with Syria to host them before being resettled in third countries.

settle in urban settings or in agricultural areas where they can find employment.

Lebanon, where the Palestinian presence – and therefore the camps – is marked by a history of conflict (Sayigh 1991) and a complex relationship with Palestinian refugees prevails, has so far refused to officially open camps for Syrians on its territory. The fear of creating 'Syrian' spaces in Lebanon, which could lead to the development of political and/or armed movements, remains strong for the Lebanese political leaders. Political parties are also deeply divided on the Syrian conflict. Some pro-regime groups not belonging to the Palestine Liberation Organisation (PLO) or Hamas, such as the Popular Front for the Liberation of Palestine – General Command (PFLP-CG), support the Assad regime while others, through the creation of 'organizational committees'[3], support Syrian opposition groups (Napolitano 2012).

In Jordan, the camp of Azraq, built to accommodate 130,000 people when the number of arrivals of refugees was very high, is now largely empty. The UNHCR has registered almost 55,000 refugees in August 2016, half of Azraq's capacity. Most of the Syrian refugees, when they have the possibility, prefer to settle in urban areas where the opportunities of finding a job are higher and where rebuilding a 'normal' life is easier.

Unlike Lebanon, that hosts more refugees, Jordan opened refugee camps in the north of the country to control the flow of new arrivals. Turkey has also opened camps along its border with Syria. Nevertheless, at a regional scale, still less than 20% of the refugees live in camps. Most of the refugees prefer to settle outside camps to integrate into the local economy and develop links with the host societies, while refugee camps recently created cannot accommodate such a large number of refugees. Jordan opened three main camps. Most of the refugees transited through Zaatari, and to a lesser extent Azraq camps. Transit camps (Ruqban and Hadalat) have been opened on the border between Syria and Jordan parallel to the gradual closure of the border. These transit camps have been created to enable Jordanian authorities to make safety checks before allowing refugees to enter their territory. The waiting time in these camps varies with profiles of the refugees. Those who come from territories controlled by Daesh[4] have to go through a long security

---

[3]   *lijan al-tansiq* in Arabic. On the model created in Syrian cities, these committees contribute to coordinating actions and exchange information with other groups (Napolitano 2012).

[4]   Daesh is the acronym in Arabic for the Islamic State in Iraq and Sham (Bilad al Sham is an Arabic term for Mashrek including Syria, Lebanon, Jordan and Palestine). It is widely used in Arabic countries for Islamic State (IS), the group controlling a portion of the Syrian and Iraqi territories.

procedure, especially young men without family. Until the spring of 2016, most of the refugees spent only a few days in these camps before being accepted or rejected. Since then, and following an attack on Jordanian border guards in June 2013, only a very limited number of refugees were allowed to enter through the camp of Ruqban. Once accepted, they are then directed to one of three settlement camps. If they have a Jordanian *kafil* (sponsor) they can move and settle elsewhere in the country.

The Urban Integration of Syrian Refugees

Despite current conflicts, refugee movements in the region are generally long lasting (the Palestinian refugee problem started in 1948 and the Iraqi one in the early 1980s), and the end of conflict does not always mean return for the entire refugee population. The settlement of these populations generates significant changes of entire neighbourhoods. Thus, refugees should not be considered only as recipients of humanitarian assistance, waiting for an eventual return or resettlement to a 'third country', but also as actors who contribute, through their initiatives and coping strategies, to the development of the cities that host them. In an unstable Middle Eastern political context, the settlement of different refugee populations demonstrates the importance of forced migration in urban development and its articulation with other forms of migration such as internal migration and international labour migration.

In Jordan, the physiognomy of the northern villages and cities has been deeply transformed by the settlement of refugees. The coexistence between Jordanians and Syrians is facilitated by the historical ties that bind the south of Syria and the north of the Kingdom. In some border areas, as in the northwest of Jordan or in the Beqaa valley in Lebanon, the effects of the protracted settlement of a large number of refugees had major effects for the local population. The poorest and the most marginalised populations suffer from the pressure on the rental market. In the northern cities, such as Irbid, Mafraq or Ramtha, rents have increased significantly and are inaccessible to the poorest households. Some services, such as schools or the medical sector, are also affected. For example, according to the United National Development Programme (UNDP),

> with Syrian arrivals, many school classrooms are overcrow-
> ded. Many schools have adopted double schedules, which
> entails shortening classes to 35 minutes from 45, and means
> that teachers are now working overtime that they are not
> compensated for (UNDP 2014).

Syrian Refugee Camps in Jordan

Since mid-2012, three official refugee camps have been opened in Northern Jordan (Zaatari, Azraq and Mrajeeb Al Fhood) that host around 140,000 refugees (22% of the total registered population at the UNHCR). Zaatari camp in Northern Jordan, which has nearly 80,000 inhabitants today, is the best known for the settlement of Syrian refugees, and today is a makeshift city where prefabricated constructions and a few tents are juxtaposed. This area concentrates all the paradoxes of the Syrian presence in Jordan. Humanitarian organisations (such as UNHCR, UNICEF, WFP, Save the Children, MSF, etc.) are omnipresent, symbolising the vulnerability of an exiled population deprived of resources. Unlike Iraqi refugees who arrived in Jordan after the fall of Saddam Hussein's regime, mostly from the urban middle classes, and who had settled in the Jordanian capital, a large proportion of Syrian refugees today are from rural areas and therefore more vulnerable. They have limited access to the labour market, although measures to facilitate obtaining a work permit were made before the summer of 2016.

Today it is quite difficult to characterise the Syrian refugee camps, as their demographic development has been rapid due to the mass arrival of refugees in a short time. Most of the refugees arrived between mid-2012 when 50,000 were registered, and mid-2013 with more than 500,000 registered. The morphology of the camps has changed substantially, from a densely populated area where tents and prefabricated housing were situated closely next to each other to more urban areas where refugees have built small courtyards or small gardens in-between prefabricated housing structures growing vegetables. Initially, the camp of Zaatari was a settlement area for Syrian refugees. Until 2013, they had the possibility to go back and forth without particular control. Exile extending, and the number of refugees increasing significantly, the Jordanian authorities gradually started to control the camp's entrances and exits. Today it is a closed space, and refugees wishing to leave must obtain a temporary permit that allows them to go to a medical appointment in an embassy or see relatives. Similarly, foreigners who wish to enter the camp must obtain prior authorisation from the Jordanian authorities.

The progressive closure of Zaatari refugee camp aims to better control the Syrian refugee population. This process directly impacts the socio-spatial organisation of the camp. Despite the constraints linked to strict regulations imposed by the host state in coordination with the UNHCR, the camp became an area of social and economic life. The refugees are divided by family and sometimes by village of origin. Prefabricated housing and tents have been rearranged to create new forms of housing that allowed the creation of private spaces. Small shops (such as groceries, hair salons, or restaurants) and other small income-generating positions (such as carpenter or electrician) developed in the camp. The refugees have tried, whenever possible, to recreate a normal life in a highly constrained situation. The camp is shaped by international organisations and Non-Governmental Organisation (NGOs) but also by the dynamics generated by the refugees themselves. Despite the strict control of the camp, a city has emerged, completely shaped by its inhabitants. As soon as the camp opened, an informal economy developed throughout the different neighbourhoods of the camp. At the entrance, a shopping street – the Souk Street, referred to as 'Champs Elysées' by the inhabitants of the camp – has emerged. Shops of all kinds mushroomed: mobile phone shops, groceries, bakeries, small restaurants, hair salons, among others. Street vendors stroll around the camp selling all kinds of products. This street has become a central living space symbolising the economic dynamism of the refugees.

Controlling the Border: From Transit Camp to Temporary Settlement Place?

The reality of the camps is itself multiple. In the Middle East, alongside the main official camps run jointly by humanitarian organisations (local and international) and host states, there are also many other forms of encampment. In October 2016, more than 80,000 Syrians were trapped in the Ruqban transit camps east of the Syria-Jordan border, in a no man's land between the two countries. From crossing points to enter Jordan, these spaces have become transit camps where the refugees initially were spending between one to ten days. They are now becoming places of temporary settlement where refugees spend several weeks or months. The tightening of the entry policy in Jordan has turned this entry points into a *de facto* camp at the border. Despite the intervention of the International Committee of the Red Cross, the humanitarian situation is extremely difficult. The question of the camps is intrinsically linked to that of asylum policy and border management. As the conflict continues, the tightening of entry policies in the territories of Syria's neighbouring countries jeopardises the possibility of circulation for refugees with two main consequences. On the one hand, it challenges the role of transnational networks developed by refugees to adapt in their host societies. On the other hand, it contributes to the emergence of new camps at the borders of the host states, where refugees who are trying to leave the violence gather. This situation has created an incentive for refugees to seek asylum outside the Middle East, contributing to the 'European migration crisis'. At a regional level, given the protracted nature of the Syrian refugee crisis, host states face a new dilemma: they have to facilitate their economic and social integration to avoid the development of poverty pockets while preserving the temporary nature of their presence.

Conclusion

The Syrian crisis has deeply transformed the Middle Eastern migration system. Syrians were mostly migrant workers, especially in Lebanon. Since 2011, they constitute one of the most important refugee populations since World War II. The large influx of refugees had one main consequence: the development of restrictive migration policies in the neighbouring countries. The mass arrival of forced migrants concentrated in certain areas (such as border cities and villages, or poor neighbourhoods in the main cities of the host countries) has significant local impact on host societies. The consequences of the influx of refugees in the global South – where most of the world's refugees find asylum – are manifold. The settlement of hundreds of thousands of refugees put pressure on the rental market and can lead to the deterioration of security in some areas. In most cases, the role of the refugee population in these processes has not been evaluated. Middle Eastern countries are not an exception. The arrival of refugees, currently Syrians, often leads to this type of controversy. The development of new refugee camps has given a new dimension to the debate on the forms of settlement for refugees in the Middle East. But this reflection on the role of refugee camps is no longer confined to the Middle East region, and the Syrians have had to go through many camps throughout their quest for asylum. The camps will therefore come in different forms throughout the trajectories of refugees, oscillating between transit camps to settlement places.

References

Ababsa, Myriam. 2015. «De la crise humanitaire à la crise sécuritaire. Les dispositifs de contrôle des réfugiés syriens en Jordanie (2011–2015).» *Revue Européenne des Migrations Internationales* 31, nos. 3 and 4: **73**–101.

Achilli, Luigi, Nasser Yassin and Murat Erdogan. 2017. *Neighbouring Host-Countries' Policies for Syrian Refugees: The Cases of Jordan, Lebanon, and Turkey*, 19 Papers IE Med.

Al Husseini, Jalal. 2015. «D'exode en exode: Le conflit Syrien comme révélateur de la vulnérabilité des réfugiés palestiniens.» *allegralaboratory.net*, http://allegralaboratory.net/dexode-en-exode-le-conflit-syrien-comme-revelateur-de-la-vulnerabilite-des-refugies-palestiniens/.

Chalcraft, John. 2009. *The Invisible Cage, Syrian Migrant Workers in Lebanon*. Stanford, California: Stanford University Press.

Chatelard, Géraldine and Kamel Doraï. 2009. "The Iraqi Presence in Syria and Jordan: Social and Spatial Dynamics, And Management Practices by Host Countries." *Maghreb-Mashreq* 199: 43–60.

Chatelard, Géraldine. 2002. *Incentives to Transit: Policy Responses to Influxes of Iraqi Forced Migrants in Jordan*, EUI Working Papers, Florence: European University Institute RSC n° 2002/50 – Mediterranean Programme Series.

Chatty, Dawn. 2010. *Displacement and Dispossession in the Modern Middle East*. Cambridge: Cambridge University Press.

Doraï, Kamel. 2015. «Les Palestiniens Et Le Conflit Syrien. Parcours De Réfugiés En Quête D'asile Au Sud-Liban.» *Revue Européenne des Migrations Internationales* 31, nos. 3 and 4: 103–120.

Doraï, Kamel and Martine Zeuthen. 2014. "Iraqi Migrants' Impact on a City. The Case of Damascus (2006-2010)". In *Syria from Reform to Revolt, Volume 1. Political Economy and International Relations*, edited by Raymond Hinnebusch and Tina Zintl, 250–265. Syracuse, New York: Syracuse University Press.

Doraï, Kamel and Jalal Al Husseini. 2013. «La Vulnérabilité Des Réfugiés Palestiniens À La Lumière De La Crise Syrienne.» *Confluences Méditerranée* 87 (Automne): 95–108.

Feldman, Ilana. 2012. "The Challenge of Categories: UNRWA and the Definition of a 'Palestine Refugee'" *Journal of Refugee Studies* 25, no. 3: 387–406.

Kagan, Michael. 2011. "We live in a country of UNHCR." The UN Surrogate State and Refugee Policy in the Middle East." UN High Commissioner for Refugees (UNHCR), http://www.refworld.org/docid/4d8876db2.html.

Al Khouri, Riad. 2004. "Arab Migration Patterns: The Mashreq." *Arab Migration in a Globalized World*. Genève: IOM.

Knudsen, Are. 2017. "Syria's Refugees in Lebanon: Brothers, Burden, and Bone of Contention." In *Lebanon Facing The Arab Uprisings,* edited by Rosita Di Peri and Daniel Meier, 135–154. Palgrave Macmillan UK.

Krumm, Thomas. 2015. "The EU-Turkey Refugee Agreement of Autumn 2015 as a Two-Level Game." *Alternatives: Turkish Journal of International Relations* 14, no. 4: 20–36.

Longuenesse, Élisabeth. 2015. «Travailleurs étrangers, réfugiés syriens et marché du travail.» *Confluences Méditerranée* 92: 33–47. DOI: 10.3917/come.092.0033.

Marfleet, Philip. 2007. "Refugees and History. Why We Must Address the Past?" *Refugee Survey Quarterly* 26, no. 3: 136–148.

Napolitano, Valentina. 2012. «La Mobilisation Des Réfugiés Palestiniens Dans Le Sillage De La 'Révolution' Syrienne: S'engager Sous Contrainte.» *Cultures & Conflits* 87: 119–137.

Sayigh, Rosemary. 1991 [1979]. *Palestinians : From Peasants to Revolutionaries*. London: Zed Books.

Shah, Nasra M. 2004. "Arab Migration Patterns in the Gulf." *Arab Migration in a Globalized World*, Genève: IOM.

Shiblak, Abbas. 1996. "Residency Status and Civil Rights of Palestinian Refugees in Arab Countries." *Journal of Palestine Studies* 25, no. 3 (Spring): 36–45.

UNDP. 2014. *Municipal Needs Assessment Report. Mitigating the Impact of the Syrian Refugee Crisis on Jordanian Vulnerable Host Communities*, United Nations Development Programme. http://www.jo.undp.org/content/dam/jordan/docs/Poverty/UNDPreportmunicipality.pdf.

United Nations High Commissioner for Refugees (UNHCR). n.d.a. "Europe: Syrian Asylum Applications From Apr. 2011 to Oct. 2016." http://data.unhcr.org/syrianrefugees/asylum.php.

UNHCR. n.d.b. "Syria Regional Refugee Response." http://data.unhcr.org/syrianrefugees/regional.php.

UNHCR. 2016. "Global Trends: Forced Displacement in 2015." http://www.unhcr.org/statistics/unhcrstats/576408cd7/unhcr-global-trends-2015.html.

UNHCR. 2017. "Jordan UNHCR Operational Update, January 2017." reliefweb, 24 January 2017. http://reliefweb.int/report/jordan/jordan-unhcr-operational-update-january-2017.

United Nations Relief and Works Agency for Palestine Refugees in the Near East (UNRWA). n.d. "Syria Crisis." https://www.unrwa.org/syria-crisis.

Zaiotti, Ruben. 2006. "Dealing with Non-Palestinian Refugees in the Middle East: Policies and Practices in an Uncertain Environment." *International Journal of Refugee Law* 18, no. 2: 333–53.

8

Forced Migration and Security Threats to Syrian Refugee Women

ÖZLEM ÖZDEMIR

There are many reasons why people are forced to migrate, including conflict, natural disasters, famine or unemployment. In Syria's case the main reason for people's forced migration is the country's conflict which, since its beginning in 2011, has forced people to migrate to other countries or be internally displaced. According to the United Nations High Commissioner for Refugees (UNHCR) 6.5 million were displaced within Syria and 4.8 million have fled to neighbouring countries such as Turkey, Lebanon, Jordan and Iraq (United Nations Office for the Coordination of Humanitarian Affairs 2016). Despite the fact that the largest number of Syrian refugees moved to countries in the Middle East such as Iraq (245,022), Egypt (117,658), Lebanon (1,069,111), Jordan (637,859) and Turkey (2,620,553) (UNHCR 2016), thousands of Syrians are on the move to European countries seeking protection, asylum and safety. However, their journey to European countries, either by land or sea, is often not safe. The route through Turkey into Greece is highly risky for refugees. They mostly travel in unseaworthy boats and dinghies across the Mediterranean. These overcrowded boats could sink in a matter of minutes and coast guards for rescue may not arrive in time (International Rescue Committee 2015, 7; Dearden 2016). Similarly, the land routes pose danger (see, for example, Navai 2015).

Not only the migratory routes[1] but also transit camps can be unsafe for

---

[1]   There are six main migratory routes that Syrian refugees are using to enter the European countries. These are the Eastern border routes (crossing the border between Belarus, Moldova, Ukraine, the Russian Federation and its eastern Member States such as Estonia, Finland, Hungary, Latvia, Lithuania, Norway, Poland, Romania and

refugees. A survey carried out by the Refugee Rights Data Project (2016) in nine refugee camps in Greece focused predominately on individuals over the age of 18. Many respondents mentioned they had witnessed others being hurt or killed during their journey to Europe. Rather than finding safety and security in camps in Greece, many refugees continued to face risks to their lives on a daily basis. According to the report, 31.6% of respondents knew of at least one death having taken place inside their camp. Causes for the deaths ranged from violence between residents to chronic disease and lack of adequate medical treatment. Almost half of all respondents (45.3%) replied that they 'don't feel safe at all' or 'don't feel very safe' in camps. On the other hand, countries such as Hungary, Greece, Bulgaria and Macedonia built fences to prevent the refugee flow as refugees are perceived as a threat to national security (Baczynska and Ledwith 2016).

Countries are mostly concerned that armed elements among civilian refugee populations may spread conflict into neighbouring countries (UN Report of the Commission on Human Security 2003). Balkan countries such as Serbia and Macedonia, due to the sudden closure of European borders, had to deal with an unprecedented situation as hundreds of people were blocked inside transit camps – either official or unofficial. Refugees were pushed back by authorities in Bulgaria, Croatia, Hungary, Romania and Spain. There were also allegations of access to asylum procedures being denied and violence (UNHCR 2017). At several borders between Balkan countries refugees were subjected to excessive force and harsh treatment by police (Amnesty International 2015). Some of the European States have taken steps to investigate allegations of human rights abuses at borders (UNHCR 2017).

Violence, however, is gendered during this process. Refugee women's perception and experience of violence, and their vulnerability are crucial for human security. A 'bottom-up' security approach addresses the gender specific insecurity for individuals during displacement (Rosenow-Williams and Behmer 2015). Many women experience numerous traumatic events and are exposed to sexual and gender-based violence[2] at every stage of their refugee

---

Slovakia), the Eastern Mediterranean route (from Turkey, Greece, southern Bulgaria or Cyprus), the Western Balkan route, the Apulia and Calabria route (from Turkey, Greece and Egypt), the Central Mediterranean route (from Northern Africa towards Italy and Malta through the Mediterranean Sea) and the Western Mediterranean route (from North Africa to the Iberian Peninsula, as well as the land route through Ceuta and Melilla), according to the Frontex Migratory Routes Map (https://frontex.europa.eu/along-eu-borders/migratory-map/)

[2]   'Sexual violence, gender-based violence and violence against women are terms that are commonly used interchangeably. They refer to physical, sexual and psychological harm that reinforces female subordination and perpetuates male power and control' (UNHCR 2003, 10).

journey (Pittaway and Bartolomei 2004; Women's Commission for Refugee Women and Children 2006).

This chapter discusses the risks that Syrian refugee women have to deal with during forced migration, and examines what kind of insecurities they face in situations of displacement in the context of human security. International media coverage, NGO and UN reports referencing migrated Syrian refugee women were analysed by using feminist critical discourse analysis to reveal different kinds of threats. Feminist critical discourse analysis (FCDA) investigates how gender ideology is produced in social practices, in social relationships between individuals, and in individuals' social and private identities through written and oral sources (Sunderland 2004; Lazar 2007, 151).

This chapter aims to contribute to feminist studies and international security studies in three ways. Firstly, by investigating the vulnerability of Syrian refugee women during and after forced migration. Secondly, by showing the gendered nature of forced migration. Thirdly, by illustrating the security threats to Syrian refugee women in the context of human security.

Forced Migration and Human Security

Not only traditional state-centric perspectives but also more recent critical approaches to security studies have been applied to address the side effects of forced migration (Betts 2009, 60), and forced migration of refugees and their displacement became an important research area of international security studies (Newman 2003, 4; Gasper and Truong 2010). According to a state-centric traditional security studies approach, national security is considered as the core of international security, and forced migration is seen as a source of insecurity to the state (Betts 2009, 62). Methodologically, traditional security studies literature on forced migration and security examines the empirical relationship between migration and military threats to the state (Betts 2009, 62; Vietti and Scribner 2013).

However, by the 1990s intra-state conflicts were no longer considered as only a threat to security of the state, but to humans (Betts 2009, 62–66). Thus, human security as a concept was included as a policy in the 1990s in The United Nations Human Development Report (UNHDR 1994). The report classifies security in seven categories: economic security; food security; health security; environmental security; personal security; security of the community; and political security. In addition, population growth, economic disparities, migration pressures, environmental degradation, drug trafficking and international terrorism were considered as threats (Booth 2007, 321).

These classifications of security and variations of threats are crucial for people to realise what security means (MacFarlane and Khong 2006, 11).

According to the Report of the United Nations Commission on Human Security in 2003 (UN Report of the Commission on Human Security 2003), the fear and experience of threats changes from person to person. Consequently, human security is related to the protection of individuals' vital freedoms. This human-centred definition is related to security, protection and survival of forced migrants. They must be considered as a vulnerable group that needs protection from threats. Refugees suffer from being displaced and they suffer while being displaced. During their displacement, flight or movement, they experience specific vulnerabilities (Newman 2003, 16) such as rape, persecution, social exclusion or detention (Women's Commission for Refugee Women and Children (WCRWC) 2006). According to Freedman (2016, 3), 'when listening to the stories of forced migrants and studying their experiences, it does seem clear that migration does entail considerable threats to human security [...]'. Poku and Graham (2000, 3–4) also emphasise the link between human security and forced migration in the context of threat. Forced migration is no longer the by-product of war, but a goal in its own right such as ethnic cleansing, genocide, human rights abuses or unemployment (Poku and Graham 2000).

However, in the case of Syria, conflict is the reason for forced migration. Currently, Syrian refugees are considered one of the biggest refugee challenges of European and bordering countries (UNHCR 2016). For some states, they are treated as a threat, for others they are considered people in need of protection. Turkey, Lebanon, Jordan, Iraq and Egypt were the first countries to accept large numbers of Syrian refugees (UNHCR 2016). On the other hand, Greece, Italy, Sweden, Austria, Germany, France and Britain were the European countries that accepted a large number of Syrian refugees (UNHCR 2016). However, Hungary, Macedonia, Serbia, Slovenia and Croatia considered Syrian refugees or asylum-seekers a security threat to their nations (Šabić and Borić 2016). The Hungarian government, for example, declared a nationwide state of emergency in response to the ongoing refugee crisis in Europe, and announced the deployment of additional troops and police officers on its border with Serbia following Slovenia's border crossings closure, blocking the Balkan route that refugees used to reach Western Europe (Strickland 2016). Consequently, the Syrian refugee crisis has become a security issue for states.

Of all refugees, women are likely the most vulnerable group. Physical, environmental, socio-economic and political reasons are the roots of their vulnerability. 'Vulnerability can be seen as a state of high exposure to certain risks and uncertainties, in combination with a reduced ability to protect or defend oneself against those risks and uncertainties and cope with their negative consequences' (UN 2001). Types of vulnerabilities may vary in the case of migration, journey, flight or displacement. Moreover, vulnerability of refugee women increases during this process.

Security Threats to Syrian Refugee Women

Wars and conflicts pose major risks to people's survival, livelihoods and dignity and thus to human security (UN Report of the Commission on Human Security 2003). Therefore, it is not surprising that vulnerability of women increases during forced migration due to a lack of security. They are often targeted with sexual and gender based violence during flight, displacement and migration (WCRWC 2006). Perpetrators, who are mostly unpunished, could be gangs, civilians, bandits, border guards, humanitarian workers and even peacekeepers (Fowler, Dugan and Bolton 2000; Laville 2015). In this sense, it is crucial for international security studies to pay specific attention to the threats experienced by women during forced migration. Feminist intellectuals are concerned that the gendered dimensions of threats have not been analysed adequately (Bunch 2004; Basu 2013; Young and Chan 2015). In this sense, feminist studies emphasise the importance of bottom-up approaches and micro-level perspectives to analyse the threats that are experienced and witnessed by refugee women having different fears and threat perceptions. These approaches and perspectives necessitate giving importance to each refugee woman individually, as a human-centric approach will be more useful to understand their vulnerabilities and also protect them from threats.

According to research conducted by Amnesty International (2016), the 40 refugee women who were interviewed described feeling threatened and unsafe during their journey from Turkey to Greece and then across the Balkans. Many reported that in almost all of the countries they passed through they experienced physical abuse and financial exploitation, they additionally mentioned being groped or pressured to have sex by smugglers, security staff or other refugees.

Furthermore, the UNHCR report (2014) 'Woman Alone: The fight for survival by Syria's refugee women' is the result of field work conducted with 135 female heads of household in order to provide a snapshot of what it means to be a refugee woman in Jordan, Lebanon and Egypt. All women who were interviewed – aged between 17 to 85, with most being between 26 and 59 – said that they have security problems in host countries. After being forced to migrate these women faced sexual and verbal harassment and exploitation due to the fact that they were living without an adult male or husband who would otherwise provide social and physical protection. Several Syrian refugee women also said they experienced harassment or received exploitative offers from persons at local charity associations or landlords that offer services, assistance and free accommodation to Syrian refugees. This insecurity situation, besides bringing feelings of isolation and desperation, often leads to mental health issues such as depression, anxiety and suicidal thoughts (United Nations Population Fund 2014).

A number of women attributed their experiences specifically to the fact that they were living without an adult male, and some said that men made inappropriate proposals for intimate relationships, or asked for their telephone number in an attempt to be 'friends'. Several women in Lebanon had even been approached for temporary marriages, also because marriage is seen as protection from sexual violence (The Freedom Fund 2016).

The vulnerability of Syrian refugee women continues after fleeing from conflict. Elizabeth Tan summarised the situation: 'Women affected by the conflict in Syria continue to be easy targets of sexual violence and harassment in the countries of asylum, in addition to the plight of leaving your own country and being dispossessed of everything' (UNHCR 2014, 50).

Furthermore, refugee women are afraid to speak of their harrowing experiences during their journey as they face the risk of honour killings by their relatives; consequently, perpetrators usually go unpunished (Strickland 2016). At the same time, NGO workers who work with refugee women mentioned that some were even forced to work for smugglers or drug dealers (Strickland 2016).

For female refugees, and especially mothers, needs vary from male refugees. Many Syrian refugee women are forced to take on responsibilities of family members while coping with dwindling resources. For this, they have been forced to turn to prostitution to make money for food, rent or other needs. Some of them engage in 'survival sex' taking lovers in exchange for food, clothing and shelter (The Freedom Fund 2016). They are mostly afraid of sexual harassment from male guards, police or other male refugees (Van Der Zee 2016). For those with children specifically, their primary concern for the protection of their children places a double burden on their shoulders. To stress this situation, Van Der Zee (2016) mentions the experiences and fears of Syrian refugee women in a European transit camp. For example, a Syrian refugee mother of three and pregnant with her fourth child, who had travelled for two weeks crossing the Mediterranean in a rubber boat and walking for kilometres, explains:

There is also the threat of rape and sexual assault by smugglers, security guards, policemen and fellow refugees. Some smugglers try to coerce the women into having sex with them in exchange for a shorter waiting time or a lower price for the crossing.

According to the Women's Refugee Commission, transit camps fail to offer women adequate basic services or protection from violence or exploitation. This is mostly due to the lack of female-specific shelters. In such places, sexual and verbal harassment or assault occur. Therefore, women take their own precautions such as sleeping outside of the tent shared with other male refugees (Van Der Zee 2016).

Shower facilities in transit camps are also of concern. Refugee women reported having to use the same bathroom and shower facilities as men. For example, according to refugee women in a transit camp in Germany, some men would watch women as they went to the bathroom. Some women took measures such as not eating or drinking to avoid having to go to the toilet where they felt unsafe. Seven pregnant women described lack of food and basic healthcare. A dozen of the women interviewed told that they had been touched, stroked or leered at in European transit camps (Amnesty International 2016).

Moreover, the geographical location of a refugee camp increase the risk of sexual violence, especially when the camp is located in a high crime area. The design and social structure in camps are also a problem for refugees. Unrelated families share communal living and sleeping space due to overcrowding. This is a great security problem for women refugees. On the other hand, poor design of services such as poorly lit toilet facilities may also contribute to risk of insecurity. The lack of police protection in some camps is another security problem for refugee women. Police may accept sexual intercourse in exchange for food or services (UNHCR 1995).

In a 2015 study, I explored the various forms of sexual and gender-based violence which take place in refugee camps. Five major British daily newspapers (*Guardian, Independent, Daily Telegraph, Times* and *Sun*) were used for research purposes. According to newspaper coverage, the most common forms of sexual and gender-based violence in Syrian refugee camps are forced marriage, early marriage, dowry and polygamy. In many cases, these different forms of sexual violence are in fact interrelated. For example, parents are afraid of their young daughters being raped or sexually abused at the camps, which brings shame to the family. Therefore, parents force their daughters to marry in favour of dowry or protection. The most frequently mentioned words related to Syrian refugee women discourses at refugee camps are: *afraid, scare, victim/survivor, at risk, in danger, isolation, shame, weak, morality, honour, vulnerable, submission, femininity, passive, defenceless, dependent* and *alone* (Özdemir 2015).

As it is seen from the aforementioned reports, mostly qualitative data-gathering methods were practiced on sexual violence in the context of Syrian refugee women. The use of qualitative rather than quantitative research methods makes it difficult to evaluate the number of Syrian refugee women exposed to violence and risks. Additionally, survivors are usually reluctant to talk about their experiences during migration due to cultural and social pressures, as it is seen as shameful (MacTavish 2016). Syrian refugee women face the risk of honour killings by their relatives and hence prefer to remain silent, which leads to perpetrators going unpunished.

On the other side, refugee-receiving countries have been unprepared for the large number of refugee influx and are failing to protect the refugees during migration adequately. According to research conducted by the Women's Refugee Commission (2016), there is no consideration of gender-based violence along the migration route to ensure safe places. Refugee women are unable to access basic services in transit centres. The lack of clear informat-ion and inability to access interpreters to talk about their vulnerability hinders refugee women from accessing services and leaves them vulnerable to smugglers and other opportunists.

Human security includes not just protecting people but also empowering them. In his article called 'Security and Emancipation', Booth (1991, 319) states that:

> Emancipation is the freeing of people (as individuals and groups) from those physical and human constraints which stop them from carrying out what they would freely choose to do. War and the threat of war is one of those constraints, together with poverty, poor education, political oppression and so on. Security and emancipation are two sides of the same coin. Emancipation, not power or order, produces true security. Emancipation, theoretically, is security. 'Security' means the absence of threats.

Syrian refugee women will be more emancipated if they are far from the threats when they migrate. Their security should be considered at all phases of a refugee cycle. Absence of the threat of pain, fear, hunger and poverty during their migration is an essential element in the struggle for emancipation

(Jones 1999, 126). To prevent Syrian refugee women from sexual and gender-based violence, humanitarian actors should increase knowledge of sexual and gender-based violence programmes. It will also help to develop recommendations for future sexual and gender-based violence programmes (UNHCR 2001).

On the other side, most organisations' leadership dealing with refugees are male dominated. In this situation, female interests are rarely recognized. Organizations should support women as equal decision-makers. Inclusion of refugee women in leadership structures has increased the level of women's involvement in decision-making process. More precisely, in situations where there are refugee women representatives, their appreciation as leaders and their inclusion in leadership structures has led to increased presentation of sexual and gender-based violence issues. They will ensure that gender issues are not left aside (UNHCR 2001). For example, the Women's Learning Partnership (2017) is adapting programmes to realize the Empowering Syrian Refugee Women for a Better Future project with local partner organizations. They provide Syrian refugee women with leadership participation and support a number of young Syrian women to develop their advocacy skills in decision-making processes. Hence, refugee women will have the skills to make their voices heard.

Another project carried by Sawa Association for Development in Lebanon targeted 30 Syrian women aged between 25 and 45 years. The main goal of the project is to empower Syrian refugee women in Lebanese camps by raising their awareness to their civil and social rights, and provide awareness on rights to reduce the vulnerabilities of Syrian women refugees subjected to sexual and gender-based violence, stress and trauma resulting from war. At the economic level, the project aims to ensure women's ability to provide for themselves and their families, and at the legal level, education about the legal aspects of their rights will empower them to stand up against violence. The project will contain workshops that aim to raise women's awareness of their rights, and trainings on empowering women with professional skills to improve their economic situation (Sawa Association for Development 2016).

The United Nations, Governments, NGOs and humanitarian authorities in general should define the kinds of threats Syrian refugee women face during migration. Gender-based analysis, interviews and research programmes should be made to understand the gender-based human security perspective of refugee women. A gender-based human security perspective, during and after forced migration, will empower refugee women. Putting refugee women at the centre of a human security approach will help to decrease their vulnerabilities and number of threats to their individual security (UNHCR 1995 and 2001). Besides, creating awareness via mass media will help to disseminate information on available services, rights of refugees and host country laws. This advocacy work emphasizes how to prevent sexual and gender-based violence incidents at individual, family and community levels, and how to support would-be survivors (UNHCR 2001).

Conclusion

This chapter tried to illustrate the vulnerability of Syrian refugee women and the need of gendering human security during migration. Because of their gender roles, needs and status, refugee women are differently affected and particularly vulnerable. In that, forced migration creates specific threats and insecurities for Syrian refugee women throughout their journeys to their final destinations and while in transit areas. Therefore, gender sensitivity and gender awareness are important issues for the human security of refugee women, enhancing not only the protection of refugees from violence but also their health and livelihoods. A 'gendered human security' concept will not see the refugee women as victims or marginalized groups. Instead, they will be considered as people with different experiences and facing diverse insecurities during migration.

Host governments' collaborations with the UN and NGOs should reveal the kinds of threats that refugee women come across. First of all, priority should be given to the voices of refugee women. Wherever possible female experts from the host community should be engaged to provide sexual and gender-based violence training and service delivery. Funding should be given to experts to institutionalize plans and protocols to address the violence. Females should be actively recruited to international security or security forces to enable women refugees to freely talk about their witnesses.

When refugee women are empowered economically, socially and politically, they will have the ability to play a key role in preventing the spread of violence. On the other side, security forces should improve their monitoring of personnel who may directly or inadvertently contribute to coerced or forced prostitution, sexual exploitation, trafficking and other forms of sexual and gender-based violence (Ward 2002).

Host governments and NGOs, and humanitarian agencies should establish sexual and gender- based violence cases databases. A strong methodology for addressing the needs of women refugees will be available for adoption in future crises (Ward 2002). Of course, it is not easy for authorities and researchers to collect or gather the data on these different types of vulnerabilities and threats that Syrian refugee women face during migration, as they are mostly reluctant to talk about their experiences due to cultural and social pressures such as honour killing or exclusion, which creates an important limitation for research on women and migration. This is a critical difficulty, because qualitative rather than quantitative data-gathering methods are mostly employed.

As emergent and short-term policies, easy access to health services, gender specific security precautions, paying attention to cleaning facilities and hygiene, accommodations for unaccompanied women, and trusted service providers will help to decrease the number of threats. More important than this, international organizations such as the United Nations, NGOs and official authorities should develop a gender-based perspective paying more attention to the specific needs of refugee women. Therefore, besides the official emergent efforts on the ground to elevate the status of refugee women, careful analysis of the practices, experiences and needs of female refugees should be undertaken to determine long-term policies to maintain safer environments for refugee women during and after their journeys.

References

Amnesty International. 2015. "Balkans: Refugees and migrants beaten by police, left in legal limbo and failed by EU." July 2015. https://www.amnesty.org/en/latest/news/2015/07/balkans-refugees-and-migrants-beaten-by-police/.

Amnesty International. 2016. "Female Refugees Face Physical Assault, Exploitation And Sexual Harassment On Their Journey Through Europe." 18 January 2016. https://www.amnesty.org/en/latest/news/2016/01/female-refugees-face-physical-assault-exploitation-and-sexual-harassment-on-their-journey-through-europe/.

Baczynska, Gabriela and Sara Ledwith. 2016. "How Europe Built Fences to Keep People Out." *Reuters*, 04 April 2016. http://www.reuters.com/article/us-europe-migrants-fences-insight-idUSKCN0X10U7.

Basu, Soumita. 2013. "Emancipatory Potential in Feminist Security Studies." *International Studies Perspectives* 14: 455–458.

Betts, Alexander. 2009. *Forced Migration and Global Politics*. West Sussex, UK: John Wiley & Sons, Ltd., Publication.

Bilgin, Pinar. 2008. "Critical Theory, Security Studies: An Introduction." In *Security Studies*, edited by Paul D. Williams, 89–102. New York: Routledge.

Booth, Ken. 1991. "Security and Emancipation." *Review of International Studies* 17: 313–326.

Booth, Ken. 2007. *Theory of World Security*. Cambridge: Cambridge University Press.

Bunch, Charlotte. 2004. "A Feminist Human Rights Lens on Human Security." *Peace Review* 16, no. 1: 29–34.

Buzan, Barry, Ole Wæver and Jaap de Wilde. 1998. *Security: A New Framework for Analysis*. Boulder: Lynne Rienner Publishers.

Collett, Elizabeth. 2016. "The Paradox of the EU-Turkey Refugee Deal." *Migration Policy Institute*. March 2016. http://www.migrationpolicy.org/news/paradox-eu-turkey-refugee-deal.

Dearden, Lizzie. 2016. "Refugees Dying from Hypothermia as Deadly Mediterranean Boat Crossings Continue into Winter." *The Independent*, 9 December 2016. http://www.independent.co.uk/news/world/europe/refugee-crisis-migrants-asylum-seekers-mediterranean-boat-disasters-sinkings-hypothermia-rescues-a7461416.html.

Diskaya Ali. 2013. "Towards a Critical Securitization Theory: The Copenhagen and Aberystwyth Schools of Security Studies." *E-International Relations*. http://www.e-ir.info/2013/02/01/towards-a-critical-securitization-theory-the-copenhagen-and-aberystwyth-schools-of-security-studies/.

Fowler, Carolyn, Julie Dugan and Paul Bolton. 2000. "Assessing the Opportunity for Sexual Violence against Women and Children in Refugee Camps." *The Journal of Humanitarian Assistance*. Feinstein International Centre at Tufts University.

Freedman, Jane. 2016. "Engendering Security at the Borders of Europe: Women Migrants and the Mediterranean Crisis." *Journal of Refugee Studies:* 1–15.

The Freedom Fund. 2016. "Struggling to survive: Slavery and Exploitation of Syrian Refugees in Lebanon." London.

Gasper, Des and Thanh-Dam Truong. 2010. "Development Ethics through the Lens of Caring, Gender and Human Security." In *Capabilities, Power and*

Institutions: Towards a More Critical Development Ethics, edited by Stephen Esquith and Fred Gifford, 58–95. University Park, PA: Penn State University Press.

Graham, David and Nana Poku. 2000. *Migration, Globalisation, and Human Security*. New York: Routledge.

Huysmans, Jef. 2006. *The Politics of Insecurity: Fear, Migration and Asylum in the EU*. London: Routledge.

International Rescue Committee. 2015. *The Refugee Crisis in Europe and the Middle East A Comprehensive Response*. New York: International Rescue Committee.

Jones, Richard Wyn. 1999. *Security, Strategy and Critical Theory*. Boulder CO: Lynne Rienner.

Krause Keith and Williams Michael, eds. 1997. *Critical Security Studies: Concepts and Cases*. London: UCL Press.

Laville, Sandra. 2015. "UN Aid Worker Suspended for Leaking Report on Child Abuse By French Troops." *The Guardian*, 29 April 2015. https://www.theguardian.com/world/2015/apr/29/un-aid-worker-suspended-leaking-report-child-abuse-french-troops-car.

Lazar, Michelle. 2007. *Feminist Critical Discourse Analysis: Gender, Power and Ideology in Discourse*, 2nd Edition, New York: Palgrave Macmillan Press.

MacFarlane, S. Neil, and Yuen Foong Khong. 2006. *Human Security and the UN: A Critical History*. Bloomington: Indiana University Press.

MacTavish, Emma. 2016. *Barriers of Reporting Sexual Violence in Syrian Refugee Camps*. A Thesis Submitted to the Faculty of Social and Applied Sciences in Partial Fulfilment of the Requirements for the Degree of Master of Arts In Human Security and Peacebuilding. British Columbia, Canada: Royal Roads University Victoria.

McDonald, Matt. 2008. 'Constructivism' In *Security Studies*, edited by Paul D. Williams, 59–72. New York: Routledge.

Navai, Ramita. 2015. "Macedonia: Tracking Down The Refugee Kidnap

Gangs"" Channel 4 News, 5 June 5 2015. https://www.youtube.com/watch?v=A5fDgJP2G30.

Newman, Edward, 2003. "International Security, and Human Vulnerability: Introduction and Survey." In *Refugees and Forced Displacement: International Security, Human Vulnerability, and The State*, edited by Edward Newman and Joanne van Selm, 3–31. New York: United Nations University Press.

OCHA (United Nations Office for the Coordination of Humanitarian Affairs). 2016. "About the Crisis." http://www.unocha.org/syrian-arab-republic/syria-country-profile/about-crisis.

Özdemir, Özlem. 2015. "UK National Print Media Coverage of Sexual and Gender-Based Violence (SGBV) against Refugee Women in Syrian Refugee Camps" *Syria Studies* 7(4), 53–77.

Pittaway, Eileen and Linda Bartolomei. 2004. *From Asylum to Protection: Ensuring the Effective Protection of Refugee Women at Risk*. Centre for Refugee Research, University of New South Wales.

Poku, Nana. K. and David Graham, eds. 2000. *Migration, Globalisation and Human Security*. London: Routledge.

Refugee Rights Data Project. 2016. *Life in Limbo: Filling Data Gaps Relating to Refugees and Displaced People in Greece*. Refugee Rights Data Project.

Rosenow-Williams, Kerstin and Katharina Behmer. 2015. "A Gendered Human Security Perspective on Humanitarian Action in IDP and Refugee Protection." *Refugee Survey Quarterly* 34: 1–23.

Šabić, Senada Šelo and Sonja Borić. 2016. *At the Gate of Europe A Report on Refugees on the Western Balkan Route*. Regional Office Zagreb for Croatia and Slovenia: Friedrich Ebert Stiftung.

Sawa Association for Development. 2016. *Resilience and Empowerment of Syrian Women Refugees*. Lebanese: Sawa Association for Development.

Strickland, Patrick. 2016. "Refugee Crisis: Hungary Sends More Troops to Border.' Al Jazeera, 10 March 2016. http://www.aljazeera.com/news/2016/03/refugee-crisis-hungary-sends-troops-border-160309134453267.html.

Sunderland, Jane. 2004. *Gendered Discourses*. New York: Palgrave Macmillan.

United Nations. 2001. *Report on the World Social Situation*. United Nations Press.

UN Report of the Commission on Human Security. 2003. *Human Security Now: Protecting and Empowering People*. New York: UN.

UN Security Council. 2000. Resolution 1325 (2000).

United Nations Population Fund (UNFPA). 2014. *Situation Analysis of Youth in Lebanon affected by the Syrian Crisis*. United Nations Population Fund.

United Nations High Commissioner for Refugees (UNHCR). 1967. *Convention and Protocol Relating to the Statue of Refugees*. United Nations High Commissioner for Refugees.

UNHCR. 1995. *Sexual Violence against Refugees*. Geneva: UNHCR.

UNHCR. 1999. *Protecting Refugees: A field guide for NGOs*. United Nations High Commissioner for Refugees.

UNHCR. 2001. *Prevention and Response to Sexual and Gender-Based Violence in Refugee Situations*. United Nations High Commissioner for Refugees.

UNHCR. 2003. *Sexual and Gender-Based Violence against Refugees, Returnees and Internally Displaced Persons*. United Nations High Commissioner for Refugees.

UNHCR. 2010. *Text of the 1951 Convention Relating to the Status of Refugees*. United Nations High Commissioner for Refugees.

UNHCR. 2014. *Woman Alone: The fight for survival by Syria's refugee women*. United Nations High Commissioner for Refugees.

UNHCR. 2016. *Syria Regional Refugee Response*. United Nations High Commissioner for Refugees.

UNHCR. 2017. "As Europe Refugee And Migrant Arrivals Fall, Reports Of Abuses, Deaths Persist." United Nations High Commissioner for Refugees, 24 August 2017. http://www.unhcr.org/news/press/2017/8/599ec5024/europe-refugee-migrant-arrivals-fall-reports-abuses-deaths-persist.html.

United Nations Human Development Report (UNHDP). 1994. *United Nations Human Development Report*. New York: Oxford University Press.

Van Der Zee, Renate. 2016. "Life As A Female Refugee: You Don't Know Who To Trust." *Al Jazeera*, 15 February 2016. http://www.aljazeera.com/indepth/features/2016/02/life-female-refugee-don-trust-160210092005932.html.

Vietti, Francesca and Todd Scribner. 2013. "Human Insecurity: Understanding International Migration from a Human Security Perspective." *Journal on Migration and Human Security* 1: 17–31.

Ward, Jeanne. 2002. *If Not Now, When? Addressing Gender-based Violence in Refugee, Internally Displaced, and Post-conflict Settings A Global Overview*. The Reproductive Health for Refugees Consortium.

Women's Commission for Refugee Women and Children (WCRWC). 2006. *Displaced Women and Girls at Risk: Risk Factors, Protection Solutions and Resource Tools*. New York: Women's Commission for Refugee Women and Children.

Wæver, Ole. 1995. "Securitization and Desecuritization." In *On Security*, edited by Ronnie D. Lipschutz, 46–86. New York: Columbia University Press.

Women's Learning Partnership. 2017. "Empowering Syrian Refugee Women for a Better Future." 24 August 2017. http://www.learningpartnership.org/empowering-syrian-refugee-women-better-future.

Women's Refugee Commission 2016. *No Safety for Refugee Women on the European Route: Report from the Balkans*. New York: Women's Refugee Commission.

Young, Marta Y. and K. Jacky Chan. 2015. "The Psychological Experience of Refugees: A Gender and Cultural Analysis." In *Psychology of Gender Through the Lens of Culture*, edited by Saba Safdar and Natasza Kosakowska-Berezecka, 17–36. Springer Press, doi: 10.1007/978-3-319-14005-6.

9

Australia's Extraterritorial Asylum Policies and the Making of Transit Sites

SALLY CLARK

Developed nation-states are pursuing aggressive border security policies designed to exclude forced migrants from territories where the rights of asylum are enshrined. In many instances these policies reach beyond the sovereign state into extra-territorial regions, blurring the traditional and functional elements of the national borders they seek to protect. One of the implications of this is that developed states of the Global North now protect themselves from unwanted migration through direct incursions on the sovereignty of less powerful neighbours. These policies are designed to impede access to protection spaces and foster the creation of transit zones where asylum seekers become immobilised. While there is extensive literature that charts this process across the Global North, less attention has been paid to this phenomenon in Southeast Asia, despite the insights such a comparison provides.

This chapter explores the effects of these exclusionary practices on forced migrants and the transit countries that host them. It will begin by providing an overview of the European literature, drawing attention to the significant pattern of state behaviour and its effects on asylum flows across the region. A consideration of how similar processes can be witnessed in the relationship between Australia and Indonesia will then be enunciated. It is argued that Australia's border security policies designed to reduce the number of asylum seekers with whom it must deal have played an instrumental role in reconfiguring the search for asylum in Southeast Asia through policies that shift the burden of protection onto regional neighbours – replicating the discernible European pattern of human rights avoidance. One consequence of this is that in recent years Indonesia has become the prime processing centre for asylum seekers otherwise destined for Australia.

The Refugee Convention and State Responsibility

The 1951 *Convention Relating to the Status of Refugees* is the primary legal instrument relating to the protection of refugees, and provides the most comprehensive codification of the rights of refugees at the international level. The document outlines the responsibility of all signatory states towards asylum seekers and refugees and provides states the framework for the assessment of protection claims. The Convention is one of the most active and drawn upon pieces of international human rights law to date, with aspects such as Article 33 *prohibition of expulsion or return* (refoulement) taking on the status of customary international law (United Nations High Commissioner for Refugees (UNHCR) 2001, 16–18). Yet, despite its successes in developing a near universal architecture of protection, there are deficiencies in the legal framework that have been exploited by powerful states. Of concern here is the narrow interpretation and application of the geographical limitation at the heart of the Convention. In recent years, this geographical limitation has been erroneously interpreted by states to mean that their protection obligations are not activated until an asylum seeker has physically set foot on national soil. While this interpretation has been critiqued in the literature (Taylor 2010; Francis 2009; Hyndman and Mountz 2008; Brouwer and Kumin 2003), state practice continues to operate on this basis.

As a result of this interpretation, powerful states now direct significant resources towards ensuring asylum seekers are not able to physically arrive in their territories. This is achieved through a series of border control policies designed to intercept, interdict and detain potential asylum seekers before the border. Thus, states are able to significantly limit the activation of their Convention obligations through the implementation of 'non-arrival regimes' that aim to directly impede access to asylum (Gibney 2005, 4). These practices, that are largely invisible to the natural citizen, highlight the oft ignored logic of border control in a globalised world – that it rarely takes place at or near the border. As Vaughan-Williams notes, 'states are increasingly ephemeral, electronic, non-visible, and located in zones that defy straightforwardly territorial logic' (Vaughan-Williams in Jerrems 2011, 2)

Non-Arrival Regimes across the Global North

There is a significant body of literature that has explored the creation of non-arrival regimes across Europe. The key themes that emerge from this body of work highlight a substantial pattern of state behaviour that has a significant impact on both neighbouring states and the asylum seekers who become entangled in the exclusionary zones these practices create. The examination of these patterns is important for our understanding, as they foreshadow a similar logic practiced by Australia in regards to the Asia Pacific.

One of the prime ways the European Union (EU) performs its border control is through the paradoxical approach of blurring rather than fortifying its boundaries, creating what many have dubbed the EU's *borderlands* (Del Sarto 2009; Gibney 2005; Papadopoulou 2005; Kirisci 2004; Boubakri 2004). These borderlands function as an effective buffer zone between core and peripheral states, with the new frontier capable of performing traditional border functions, denying access to would be asylum seekers to the EU. Importantly, developed states do not guard their borders against unwanted incursions through strength of arms or military force, but rather through the co-option of economically subordinate states.

Powerful states are able to negotiate cooperation arrangements on border control with neighbouring countries in return for favourable treatment in areas such as trade, security and development (Del Sarto 2009; Balwin-Edwards 2007; Gibney 2005). An asymmetric power dynamic is central to the forging of these types of agreements, as they are achieved by providing much needed economic and political support to peripheral states on the proviso that they adopt the preferred migration policies of their benefactors (Klepp 2010; Balwin-Edwards 2007; Zhyznomirska 2006; Gibney 2005; Papadopoulou 2004; Collinson 1996).

One of the key policy levers Western Europe (and later the EU more broadly) has used to export its migration agenda to the region at large has been the development of policies such as the European Neighbourhood Program (ENP). Through this policy, core EU governments are able to penetrate sovereign states through diplomatic, economic, trade, travel and security alliances, blurring the traditional borders between powerful EU states and their less developed neighbours. This is based on what Del Sarto labels 'positive conditionality', whereby 'cooperative southern states undoubtedly obtain a better deal from Brussels' (Del Sarto 2009, 11).

Beyond the exercise of 'positive conditionality', the EU has developed a raft of policies designed to construct a non-arrival regime that specifically excludes would-be asylum seekers from the common Schengen area. This has been achieved through a variety of complex and interlocking processes that shift the burden for refugee processing and protection onto peripheral states and transit countries. These strategies include the 'Safe Third Country' policy (codified in the Dublin II Regulation), readmission agreements with EU and non-EU states, and the shifting of migration control to the private sector through the introduction of carrier sanctions.

Pre-departure initiatives, such as the requirement that foreign nationals hold a valid entry visa prior to arrival in the common territory, transform the nature of immigration control away from the physical border to a range of new places such as the high seas, consular officers, and foreign airports. These initiatives allow the EU to restrict legitimate travel opportunities to people based on nationality, economic or character grounds, allowing for the 'screening out' of undesirable migrants (read potential asylum seekers) before they are able to arrive at the border (Francis 2009; Weber 2006; Brouweer and Kumin 2003).

Coupled with pre-departure initiatives are carrier sanctions, whereby commercial airlines and other authorised migration carriers face heavy penalties if detected bringing in persons without proper authorisation or documentation (Rodenhauser 2014; Francis 2009; Brouwer and Kumin 2003). By imposing harsh carrier sanctions, states effectively shift the onus of border control away from government regulated borders and government officials to private enterprises and their employees in third countries.[1] Such targeted closure of legal migration channels interrupts linear travel, so that forced migrants have little choice but to travel irregularly, either by land or sea, crossing multiple frontiers in their search for refuge.

The third major strategy in Europe's non-arrival regime is the implementation of the 'safe third country' concept, that allows for the shifting of responsibility for claim processing from one EU state to another if it can be proven that the claimant transited through that state prior to arriving in the destination state. This has led to accusations that developed states are playing a central role in the construction of transit migration through policies that funnel forced migrants into peripheral regions, while simultaneously demanding that these same transit countries do more to stop onward movements to their regions (Lutterbeck 2009; Kirisci 2004; Koser 1997; Lavenex 1998; Collinson 1996). According to Lavenex (1998) the 'safe third country' concept was designed to prevent 'migration shopping' or the simultaneous lodgement of asylum applications across multiple states. Additionally, it was conceived of by the EU as a 'redistributive mechanism' to ensure appropriate burden-sharing for refugee protection across the common Schengen area. Yet in reality, this concept has been used to shift the protection burden away from core states to the periphery of the EU where asylum seekers are now funnelled into by

---

[1]   While many of these pre-emptive measures appear to perform the legitimate function of border control they must be considered problematic when they lack the appropriate safeguards to ensure the rights of people with genuine protection claims are not violated (see for example Francis 2009).

design.

The 'safe third country' concept also includes non-EU member countries considered 'safe' by the EU. To facilitate this, EU states have sought readmission agreements with selected states from Eastern Europe and North Africa to ensure asylum seekers who pass through these regions can be forcibly returned and that the responsibility to process protection claims is that of the first 'safe country' which the forced migrant enters (Collinson 1996). In short, readmission agreements exist to facilitate the expulsion of undocumented 'third country' nationals from states in which they are unauthorised to reside.

Unsurprisingly, research has found that these actions have thrust inequitable protection responsibility onto transit countries, while simultaneously diminishing the protection experienced by asylum seekers due to the disparities in processing systems (or lack thereof) across the region (Gerand and Pickering 2012; Fekete 2011; Gammeltoft-Hansen 2012; Schuster 2011; Lutterbeck 2009; Garlick 2006; Abell 1999; Lavenex 1998; Collinson 1996).

The European Council itself has recognised the considerable effect the intensification of protection responsibilities would have upon peripheral regions, stating that 'the implementation of asylum policies poses severe budgetary and operational problems for these countries' (Collinson 1996, 84). This is compounded by the fact that a number of countries labelled 'safe third countries' by the EU are developing nations, characterised by limited resources, porous borders, underdeveloped reception policies, political instability and often poor human rights records (Hamood 2008; Chatelard 2008; Gil-Bazo 2006; Garlick 2006; Legomsky 2003). For example, Libya, Tunisia, Morocco, Turkey and Jordan are all classified as 'safe third countries', and are thus responsible for the processing of a disproportionate number of asylum applications each year under this policy (Baldwin-Edwards 2007). Meanwhile, core EU states such as France, Germany and Belgium are safeguarded from the majority of arrivals by these peripheral states and retain the ability to forcibly return those who do make it through these exclusionary barriers.

This situation has led to a serious reduction in the safeguards (codified in the Refugee Convention) that are essential to the protection of forced migrants' human rights. In his case study of irregular migration in North Africa, Baldwin-Edwards (2007, 320) details how Italy established readmission agreements with Morocco, Tunisia and Libya in 2003 through linking development aid with migration policy. Through these agreements, Italy returned thousands of irreg-ular migrants after denying them the right to apply for asylum. Subsequently it was found that a large number of individuals expelled from Italy to Libya were later refouled to Egypt and Nigeria in breach of international law. In response to criticism of this practice, Klepp (2010) claims Italy sought to strengthen its extra-territorial controls, particularly in Libyan territorial waters, to reduce the number of asylum seekers who may arrive at its border in the future.

Through the strengthening of non-arrival regimes – operationalised in neighbouring regions – Italy was able to secure its own border and shift the burden for refugee protection back on to Libya, and was thus able to avoid future accusations of refoulement by immobilising migrants before the border.

A further challenge posed by these policies is the downstream effects they have on neighbouring regions. Many peripheral states have been forced to make policy changes that mimic their powerful neighbours. This is due to rising fears that they would be left to deal with disproportionate levels of asylum seekers, as was the case for many Central European states immediately following the breakup of the former Yugoslavia (Papadopoulou 2005). Amnesty International has argued that this process will continue to replicate itself, proposing that under increased pressure more states will be inclined to follow the agenda set by Western Europe, privileging border security over human rights, thereby putting the entire refugee protection system in jeopardy (cited in Collinson 1996, 84). Forced migrants, compelled to move, find they have less capacity to do so, leading to the paradoxical situation whereby 'Western states now acknowledge the rights of refugees but simultaneously criminalize the search for asylum' (Gibney 2005, 4).

Furthermore, research has found that these transit sites are encountering new social and political issues resulting from the rapid increase in the number of irregular migrants in their jurisdiction. According to the former Assistant High Commissioner for the Protection of Refugees, Erika Feller, 'large scale arrivals are seen as a threat to political, economic or social stability and tend increasingly to provoke hostility and violence' (Feller 2006, 514). Numerous studies have looked at the impact of this process on newly transformed transit countries (Gerard and Pickering 2012; Lutterbeck 2009; Baldwin-Edwards 2007; Zhyznomirska 2006; Papadopoulou 2005 and 2004; Kirisci 2004). Turkey is considered a prime example of this trend. The challenges it faces in trying to balance its international responsibilities to protect refugees whilst reforming its immigration policies as a condition of membership into the EU demonstrates the competing interests acting on the country. While Member States now have the power to return irregular migrants to Turkey, the lack of bargaining power has left Turkey unable to secure such agreements with its neighbouring countries such as Iraq, Iran and Egypt, whose citizens are transiting through Turkey *en route* to Europe. Kirisci (2004, 12) concludes that without adequate burden-sharing mechanisms in place, Turkey could become a buffer zone, rather than a Member State that shares benefits and responsibilities equitably.

Similar themes can be found in Papadopoulou's (2004) analysis on transit migration in Greece, and Johnson's (2013) study on the borderland between Morocco and Spain, both of which highlight the inequitable conditions forced onto these states and the negative impacts that follow. Papadopoulou (2004, 167) claims Central and Eastern European countries have come under extreme pressure in the past to reform their immigration policies in line with the desires of core EU states, arguing that 'to a large extent, the institutional framework of migration and asylum in the EU Member States is one of control and restriction'.

Yet perhaps the most pertinent example of how migration policies of the Global North can impact upon peripheral regions is in the case of Malta. Prior to 2001, the main entry point into Europe was through the Adriatic route between Albania and Italy (Lutterbeck 2009, 122). Yet efficient border control in this area diverted forced migrants through Malta, which has since witnessed a rapid increase in irregular migration. According to Lutterbeck (2009 123):

> This diversion effect shows how migration into Malta is also profoundly affected by the immigration control measures of other Southern European countries, and how plugging one hole in the EU's outer perimeter quickly leads to enhanced pressure on other parts of its external borders.

As a result, Malta – once a country of emigration – has quickly been transformed into a transit country, leading to claims that Malta is the victim of Italy's successful border closure (Lutterbeck 2009, 123). Due to Malta's new position as a prime transit route into Europe, it has come under increased pressure regarding border patrol. Unsurprisingly, Malta has been one of the most outspoken opponents to the Dublin II regulation and the principle of the 'safe third country', given the massive increase in their own protection role as a result of these agreements and its transformation into an asylum seeker buffer zone (Gerard and Pickering 2012).

One final consequence of the EU's non-arrival regime is the impact on irregular migration. Since the late 1990s, scholars have been examining the correlation between restrictive asylum policies and the growth of people smuggling operations that subvert them. Mounting research suggests that at least in regards to Europe, non-arrival regimes coupled with the dismantling of traditional migration routes has resulted in the growth of people smuggling operations, accessed by both economic migrants and asylum seekers alike (see for example Koser 2001 and 1997). As Morrison and Crosland (cited in Koser 2000, 92) state, 'the fear is that the social construction in policy agendas of all asylum seekers as illegal migrants is becoming a social reality as asylum seekers are forced to turn to traffickers in order to enter Europe and apply for asylum'.

The following section will examine a similar impulse in Australia's approach to border security, demonstrating how it has externalised its border controls to minimise the arrival of asylum seekers. In a fashion similar to the EU, the outcome of this approach can be witnessed in a multitude of negative ways: burden shifting leading to the intensification of protection responsibility thrust onto regional neighbours (in this case Indonesia), through the increase in irregular migration as asylum seekers attempt to overcome exclusionary barriers erected in transit sites, and through the decline in protection more broadly as human rights standards are avoided or curtailed in morally and legally dubious ways.

Australia's Non-Arrival Regime and Architecture of Exclusion

A review of Australia's migration and border control policies since 2001 shows that it has been engaged with the production and maintenance of its own non-arrival regime, elements of which reflect the European model. One direct parallel, for example, is the strict implementation of pre-departure screenings and carrier sanctions that have proven so effective at closing down legitimate migration pathways for potential asylum seekers. However, faced with a unique geopolitical setting and lacking the broader bargaining power of enticements such as membership into the EU, Australia has instead had to innovate creative strategies for gaining the cooperation of regional neighbours in order to suit its migration agenda. The most recognisable of these uniquely Australian tactics is the policy bundle known as the 'Pacific Solution'. Implemented in 2001 by the Coalition government, the Pacific Solution possessed all the hallmarks of a non-arrival regime; the primary architecture of exclusion being the annexation of Australia's island territories and the development of an intercept and detain model of offshore processing. The Pacific Solution allowed the government to physically intercept boats on the high seas and transfer the asylum seekers on board directly to offshore processing centres in third countries or specially designated areas outside Australia's migration zone, thus destroying people's ability to lodge protection claims in Australia.

Australia can be understood as drawing heavily on the notion of 'positive conditionality' when negotiating with third countries, in order to establish arrangements to intercept and transfer asylum seekers to Australian funded detention centres in these sovereign states. For example, Nauru and Papua New Guinea have both received handsome financial compensation for their cooperation (Grewcock 2014), while in 2014 Australia and Cambodia reached a controversial resettlement deal that would see Australia provide more than AU$40 million in aid funding on the quid-pro-quo that Cambodia permanently resettle Convention Refugees who had been processed offshore in Australian funded detention centres (University of New South Wales 2014). In each of these cases there was considerable backlash from citizens in these states, yet the economic and political capital governments gained through their acquiescence to Australia's requests proved hard to refuse, exposing an asymmetrical power relationship that echoes that of core and peripheral states across Europe.[2] Much has been written about this particular aspect of Australia's response to asylum seekers, and therefore will not be revisited here (for detailed accounts see: Briskman, Latham and Goddard 2008; Burnside 2008; Hyndman and Mountz 2008; Gordon 2007; Mares 2002 and 2007; Crock, Saul and Destyari 2006; Howard 2003).

Attention will instead be directed towards Australia's less examined interactions with Indonesia. In the Australian media, Indonesia is rarely presented as a willing partner due to it being the prime departure point for asylum seekers looking to reach Australia. Yet this framing appears ignorant of the crucial role Indonesia has played in Australia's migration agenda, which at times appears in stark opposition to its own interests.

Since the late 1990s, Australia has sought to implement a readmission agreement with Indonesia similar to those practiced across Europe. However, Indonesia has been uncompromising on its stance that it will not readmit undocumented foreign nationals into its territory, insisting that once asylum seekers pass into Australian territorial waters the responsibility for their protection is Australia's alone.[3] This position has led the Australian government to pursue extraterritorial strategies that contain asylum seekers within Indonesia, removing their ability for onward migration. This is despite the fact that Indonesia is not a signatory to the Refugee Convention, nor can it be considered a 'safe country' of first asylum given the lack of human rights protections (Kneebone 2015). According to Goodwin-Gill a minimum standard

---

[2]   Many have viewed Australia's engagement with its Pacific neighbours through a neo-colonial lens, arguing that the Pacific Solution functions through the exploitation of aid dependent, impoverished, island nations (see for example Hayden 2002; Grewcock 2014).

[3]   The Oceanic Viking and Jaya Lestari incidents serve as prime case studies of Indonesia's refusal to readmit 'third country' nations to its territory. For more information, see Missbach and Sinanu 2011.

of protection 'would appear to entail the right of residence and re-entry, the right to work, guarantees of personal security and some form of guarantee against return to a country of persecution' (Goodwin-Gill cited by UNHCR 2004, 1); factors that are currently lacking in Indonesia at present. Despite this, Australia has pursued a number of arrangements that shift the burden of refugee processing and protection onto Indonesia. Similar to the EU, Australia has used diplomatic channels (covered in a veneer of international cooperation) alongside more overtly coercive levers to achieve this goal.

Since early 2000, Australia and Indonesia have been party to a bilateral regional cooperation agreement (RCA) in partnership with the International Organisation for Migration (IOM) and their local partners, World Church Services (WCS) and the Jesuit Refugee Services (JRS) (UNHCR Indonesian Factsheet, September 2014). Under this agreement, the Australian government funds large scale projects in Indonesia in return for Indonesia's co-operation in preventing the flow of irregular migration to Australia. This is achieved by monitoring and intercepting suspected asylum seekers and referring them to the IOM for case management and care in Indonesia (Howard 2003). This arrangement was designed to prevent asylum seekers from moving irregularly from Indonesia to Australia by providing a processing system in Indonesia where individuals could have their refugee claims assessed. Since Indonesia is not a signatory to the Refugee Convention and lacks a legal framework to process these claims, the UNHCR fills this gap through a Memorandum of Understanding (MoU) with the Indonesian government (UNHCR South-East Asia 2013, 1). In accordance with regulations outlined by the Indonesian Director General of Immigration, those migrants who indicate their desire to lodge a refugee application are referred by IOM to UNHCR who 'assess these claims pursuant to its own international mandate' (Taylor and Rafferty-Brown 2010, 138). Through the RCA, Australia has also played a key role in reshaping Indonesia's immigration detention system. According to Taylor (2010), before Australia's intervention the Indonesian government's preferred policy practice was to allow people who fell within the scope of the RCA to live freely in the community, yet this penchant for using alternatives to detention was steadily replaced with a drive to detain asylum seekers in Australian funded detention centres across the archipelago.

Significantly, neither government, nor the contracting partners, have revealed the cost of this agreement (Kneebone 2015; Taylor 2009). Nonetheless, occasional indicators suggest that the sum of money invested in this process is high. In May 2014, the Australian government announced that it will provide Indonesia with a further AU$86.8 million to support stranded refugees and asylum seekers over the following three years (SUAKA 2014).

Australia has also used other multilateral forums to push for changes to Indonesia's domestic law to further its containment agenda. Under sustained economic and political pressure from Australia, Indonesia has introduced a raft of new legislation in recent years that criminalises people smuggling, increases surveillance and interceptions operations, and rapidly expands immigration detention systems (Human Rights Watch 2013; Missbach 2012; Taylor 2010; Taylor 2009).

Beyond efforts that leverage Australia's economic and political clout for cooperation in this area are a number of practices that are far more coercive and legally dubious. Prime among these is the reintroduction of the controversial 'turnback' policy in 2013, where Australian Navy and Customs officers intercept suspected asylum seekers to turn back, or physically tow boats into international waters – an action that is akin to forced readmissions to Indonesia. Shrouded in secrecy, this militarised response operating under the codename 'Operation Sovereign Borders' has been widely criticized by Indonesia, who sees it as an attack on its sovereignty, a claim boosted by revelations that Australian Navy ships were operating in Indonesia's territorial waters without authorisation (Bourke 2014). The UNHCR also objected on the basis that Australia has breached its obligations under international law to assess the protection claims of asylum seekers in its territory (Refugee Council of Australia 2014).

Further techniques used to dissuade asylum seekers from attempting onward migration from Indonesia include, the removal of all rights to apply for Protection Visas for any irregular maritime arrival, 'unless the Minister for Immigration personally intervenes to lift the bar' (Refugee Council of Australia 2017). The removal of this protection means that for many asylum seekers the UNHCR office in Jakarta is their last hope of accessing international protection despite its clear deficiencies. This move has been accompanied by a widespread advertising campaign *'No Way. You Will Not Make Australia Home'* (Laughland 2014). This 'reverse tourism' advertisement was designed to psychologically disincentivise asylum seekers from pursuing protection claims in Australia.

While far from exhaustive, the above discussion attempts to highlight just some of the extraterritorial strategies Australia pursues in order to protect itself from unwanted migration and minimise its protection obligations by shifting these to Indonesia. The consequence of this is that Australia has removed all feasible ways for asylum seekers to legally access protection in its territories. Simultaneously, these policies have contributed to the increased protection responsibility felt by Indonesia, as it is slowly transformed into one of the last places in the region where asylum seekers can have their protection claims accessed.

On the individual level, Australia's non-arrival regime is experienced by asylum seekers as a further assault on their human rights (in a manner reminiscent of the European literature). This truncation comes about through their effective immobilisation in transit states that lack the appropriate framework for their protection. In this liminal state, asylum seekers reside for many years without legal status, without government support, without civil and political rights and, most significantly, without hope of a durable outcome. Their deliberate exclusion from protection zones and relegation to areas that fall outside the international protection system means the only hope of resettlement must come through selection to a voluntary 'third country' humanitarian program – the kind responsible for the resettlement of less than one per cent of the world's refugee population annually. Unsurprisingly, it is this reality that has given rise to irregular migration between Indonesia and Australia, directly echoing the border pattern established across Europe as desperate people search for ways to seek protection. In Australia this situation has then precipitated a further 'securitised' response by the state looking to exclude asylum seekers through increasingly punitive and militaristic efforts, contributing to the further destruction of human rights.

What becomes apparent through case studies such as these is that despite the brevity of human rights legislation – recognised across most of the developed world – states are now implementing pre-emptive measures that effectively neutralise their obligations. The result of this is that the architecture of international refugee protection appears intact, despite the purposeful dismantling of almost all legal ways for asylum seekers to access such rights, delegitimising the search for asylum and exposing people to increasingly vulnerable situations in legally ambiguous spaces in the process. To overcome this situation it is imperative that states implement migration policies that reflect the unique status of asylum seekers. Furthermore, the Convention states must recognise that their duty of care stretches beyond the border of the nation-state, beginning whenever state apparatus interacts with forced migrants, be it in foreign embassies, third countries or on the high seas. This will prevent the uncoupling of deterritorialised border control and the flouting of state responsibility.

References

Abell, N.A. 1999. "The Compatibility of Readmission Agreements with the 1951 Convention relating to the Status of Refugee." *International Journal of Refugee Law* 11, no. 1: 60–81.

Baldwin-Edwards, Martin. 2005. "Migration in the Middle East and Mediterranean." *Global Commission on International Migration*, Geneva.

Baldwin-Edwards, Martin. 2007. "Between a Rock and a Hard Place: North Africa as a Region of Emigration, Immigration and Transit Migration." *Review of African Political Economy*, no. 108: 311–324.

Betts, Alexander. 2006. "Towards a Mediterranean Solution? Implication for the Region of Origin" *International Journal of Refugee Law* 18, no. 3/4: 652–676.

Bigo, Didier, Sergio Carrera, Elspeth Guild and R.B.J. Walker. 2009. "The Changing Landscape of European Liberty and Security: The Mid-term Report of the CHALLENGE Project." *International Social Sciences Journal* 59, no. 152.

Boubakri, Hassen. 2004. "Transit Migration between Tunisia, Libya and Sub-Saharan Africa: Study Based on Greater Tunis." *Migrants in Transit Countries: Sharing Responsibility for Management and Protection* Conference Paper.

Bourke, Latika. 2014. "Navy Breached Indonesian Waters Six Times under Operation Sovereign Borders, Review Finds." *ABC News*, 20 February 2014. http://www.abc.net.au/news/2014-02-19/navy-breached-indonesian-waters-six-times,-review-finds/5270478.

Briskan Linda, Chris Goddard and Susie Latham. 2008. *Human Rights Overboard: Seeking Asylum in Australia*. Melbourne: Scribe Publications.

Brouwer, Andrew and Judith Kumin. 2003. "Interception and Asylum: When Migration Control and Human Rights Collide." *Refuge* 21, no. 4: 6–23.

Burnside, Julian. 2007. "Australia's Refugee Policy." In *Yearning to Breathe Free: Seeking Asylum in Australia*, edited by Dean Lusher and Nick Haslam. Annandale: The Federation Press.

Castles, Stephen. 2003. "Towards a Sociology of Forced Migration and Social Transformation." *Sociology* 37, no. 1: 13–34.

Chatelard, Géraldine. 2008. "Iraqi Asylum Migrants in Jordan: Conditions, Religious Networks and the Smuggling Process." In *Poverty, International*

Migration and Asylum. Studies in Development Economics and Policy, edited by George Borjas and Jeff Crisp: 341–370. Basingstoke: Palgrave Mcmillan.

Collinson, Sarah. 1996. "Visa Requirements, Carrier Sanctions, 'Safe Third Countries' and Readmission': The Development of an Asylum 'Buffer Zone' in Europe'." *Transactions of the Institute of British Geographers, New Series* 21, no. 1: 76–90.

Crisp, Jeff and Nicholas Van Hear. 1998. "Refugee Protection and Immigration Control: Addressing the Asylum Dilemma." *Refugee Survey Quarterly* 17, no. 3: 1–27.

Crock, Mary, Ben Saul and Azadeh Dastyari. 2006. *Future Seekers II: Refugees and Irregular Migration in Australia*. Leichhardt: Federation Press.

Dastyari, Azadeh. 2014. "Explainer: The legal Implications of Tow-Backs." *The Conversation,* 20 January 2014. https://theconversation.com/explainer-the-legal-implications-of-tow-backs-22151.

Del Sarto, Raffaella. '2009. "Borderlands: The Middle East and North Africa as the EU's Southern Buffer Zone." In *Mediterranean Frontiers: Borders, Conflicts and Memory in a Transnational World*, edited by Dimitar Bechev and Kalypso Nicolaidis. London: Oxford University Press.

Fekete, Liz. 2011. "Accelerated Removals: The Human Cost of EU Deportation Policies." *Race and Class* 52: 89–97.

Feller, Erika. 2006. "Asylum, Migration and Refugee Protection: Realities, Myths and the Promise of Things to Come." *International Journal of Refugee Law* 18, no: 3/4: 509–536.

Francis, Angus J. 2009. "Removing Barriers to Protection at the Exported Border: Visas, Carrier Sanctions, and International Obligation." In *Sanctions, Accountability and Governance in a Globalised World*, edited by Jeremy Farrall,and Kim Rubenstein: 378–406. Cambridge: Cambridge University Press.

Gammeltoft-Hansen, Thomas. 2012. "Outsourcing Asylum: The Advent of Protection Lite." In *Europe in the World: EU Geopolitics and the Making of European Space*, edited by Luiza Bialasiewicz. Routledge.

Garlick, Madeline. 2006. "The EU Discussion on Extraterritorial Processing: Solution or Conundrum?" *International Journal of Refugee Law* 18, no. 3/4: 601–629.

Gerard, Alison and Sharon Pickering. 2012. "The Crime and Punishment of Somali Women's Extra-legal Arrival in Malta." *British Journal of Criminology* 52: 514–533.

Ghosh, Bimal. 1998. "Huddled Masses and Uncertain Shores: Insight into Irregular Migration." *International Organisation for Migration*, The Hague.

Gibney, Matthew. 2005. "Beyond the Bounds of Responsibility: Western States and Measures to Prevent the Arrival of Refugees." *Global Migration Perspectives*, no. 22. Global Commission on International Migration, Geneva.

Gil-Bazo, María-Teresa. 2006. "The Practice of the Mediterranean States in the Context of the European Union's Justice and Home Affairs External Dimension: The Safe Thirds Country Concept Revisited." *International Journal of Refugee Law* 18, no. 3: 571–600.

Gordon, Michael. 2007. "The 'Pacific Solution'." In *Yearning to Breathe Free: Seeking Asylum in Australia*, edited by Dean Lusher and Nick Haslam. Annandale: The Federation Press.

Green, Penny and Mike Grewcock. 2002. "The War against Illegal Immigration." *Current Issues in Criminal Justice* 14: 87–101.

Grewcock, Mike. 2013. "Australia's Ongoing Border Wars." *Race and Class* 54, no. 3: 10–31.

Grewcock, Mike. 2014. "Australian Border Policing: Regional 'Solutions' and Neocolonialism." *Race and Class* 55, no. 3: 71–78.

Hamood, Sara. 2008. "EU-Libya Cooperation on Migration: A Raw Deal for Refugees and Migrants?" *Journal of Refugee Studies* 21, no. 1: 19–42.

Hayden, Bill. 2002. "The Pacific solution is a fraud on us." *The Age*, 20 March 2002. http://www.theage.com.au/articles/2002/03/14/1015909883881.html.

Howard, Jessica. 2003. "To Deter and Deny: Australia and the Interdiction of Asylum Seekers." *Refuge* 21, no. 4: 35–50.

Human Rights Watch. 2013. "Barely Surviving: Detention, Abuse, and Neglect of Migrant Children in Indonesia." 23 June 2013. https://www.hrw.org/report/2013/06/23/barely-surviving/detention-abuse-and-neglect-migrant-children-indonesia.

Hyndman, Jennifer and Alison Mountz. 2008. "Another Brick in the Wall? Neo-Refoulement and the Externalisation of Asylum by Australia and Europe." *Government and Opposition* 43, no. 2: 249–269.

Jerrems, Ari. 2011, "Bordering Beyond State Boundaries: Nick Vaughan-Williams, Border Politics: The Limits of Sovereign Power. Book Review" *Borderlands e-Journal* 10, no. 1.

Johnson, Heather. 2013. "The Other Side of the Fence: Reconceptualising the "Camp" and Migration Zones at the Border of Spain." *International Political Sociology* 7: 75–91.

Kirisci, Kemal. 2004. "Reconciling Refugee Protection with Efforts to Combat Irregular Migration: The Case of Turkey and the European Union." *Global Migration Perspectives*, no. 11. Global Commission on International Migration, Geneva.

Klepp, Silja. 2010. "A Contested Asylum System: The European Union between Refugee Protection and Border Control in the Mediterranean Sea." *European Journal of Migration and Law* 12: 1–12.

Kneebone, Susan. 2005. "The legal and Ethical Implications of Extra-Territorial Processing of Asylum Seekers: Europe Follows Australia." *Seeking Asylum in Australia: 1995–2005: Experiences and Policies*, Conference paper.

Koser, Khalid. 1997. "Negotiating Entry into Fortress Europe: The Migration Strategies of "Spontaneous" Asylum Seekers." In *Exclusion and Inclusion of Refugees in Contemporary Europe*, edited by Philip Muun: 157–70. Utrecht: ERCOMER.

Koser, Khalid. 2000. "Asylum Policies, Trafficking and Vulnerability." *International Migration*: 91–111.

Koser, Khalid. 2001. "New Approach to Asylum?" *International Migration* 39, no. 6: 85–102.

Koser, Khalid. 2005. "Irregular Migration, State Security and Human Security." Global Commission on International Migration, Geneva.

Laughland, Oliver. 2014. "Australian Government Targets Asylum Seekers with Graphic Campaign." *The Guardian*, 11 February 2014 https://www. theguardian.com/world/2014/feb/11/government-launches-new-graphic-campaign-to-deter-asylum-seekers.

Lavenex, Sandra. 1998. "'Passing the Buck': European Union Refugee Policies towards Central and Eastern Europe." *Journal of Refugee Studies* 11, no. 134: 126–145.

Legomsky, Stephen H. 2003. "Secondary Refugee Movements and the Return of Asylum Seekers to Third Countries: The Meaning of Effective Protection." *International Journal of Refugee Law* 15, no. 4: 567–677.

Lutterbeck. Derek. 2009. "Small Frontier Island: Malta and the Challenge of Irregular Immigration." *Mediterranean Quarterly* (Winter): 119–144.

Mares, Peter. 2002. *Borderline: Australia's Response to Refugees and Asylum Seekers in the Wake of the Tampa.* Sydney: UNSW Press.

Missbach, Antje. 2012. "Easy Pickings: The Plight of Asylum Seekers in Indonesia." *Asian Currents, the Asian Studies Association of Knowledge*: 1–3.

Missbach, Antje and Frieda Sinanu. 2011. "'The Scum of the Earth?' Foreign People Smugglers and their Local Counterparts in Indonesia." *Journal of Current Southeast Asian Affairs* 30, no. 4: 57–87.

Morrison, John and Beth Crosland. 2000. "The Trafficking and Smuggling of Refugees: The End Game in European Asylum Policy?" Final Draft Report for UNHCR, Working Paper. No. 39. http://www.unhcr.org/3af66c9b4.pdf.

Papadopoulou, Aspasia. 2004. "Smuggling into Europe: Transit Migrants in Greece." *Journal of Refugee Studies* 17, no. 2: 167–184.

Papadopoulou, Aspasia. 2005. "Exploring the Asylum-Migration Nexus: A Case Study of Transit Migration in Europe." *Global Migration Perspectives*, no. 23. Global Commission on International Migration, Geneva.

Pirjola, Jari. 2009. "European Asylum Policy, Inclusion and Exclusions under the Surface of Human Rights Language." *European Journal of Migration and Law* 11, no. 4: 347–366.

Refugee Council of Australia. 2014. "UN High Commissioner Criticises Australia's 'Strange' Obsession with Boat." http://www.refugeecouncil.org. au/n/mr/140618_UNHCRNGO.pdf.

Refugee Council of Australia. 2017. "Recent Changes in Australian Refugee Policy." https://www.refugeecouncil.org.au/publications/recent-changes-australian-refugee-policy/ .

Rodenhauser, Tilman. 2014. "Another Brick in the Wall: Carrier Sanctions and the Privatization of Immigration Control." *International Journal of Refugee Law* 26, no. 2: 223–247.

Schuster, Liza. 2011. "Turning Refugees into 'Illegal Migrants': Afghan Asylum Seekers in Europe." *Ethics and Racial Studies* 34: 1392–1407.

SUAKA. 2014. "Funding for Regional Cooperation on Refugees and Asylum Seekers in Indonesia Must be Directed to Protection Needs." http://aprrn.info/ funding-for-regional-cooperation-on-refugees-and-asylum-seekers-in-indonesia-must-be-directed-to-protection-needs/.

Taylor, Jessie. 2009. *Behind Australian Doors: Examining the Conditions of Detention of Asylum Seekers in Indonesia.* https://www.safecom.org.au/pdfs/ behind-australian-doors-examining-the-conditions.pdf.

Taylor, Savitri and Bryanna Rafferty-Brown. 2010. "Waiting for Life to Begin: The Plight of Asylum Seekers Caught by Australia's Indonesian Solution." *International Journal of Refugee Law* 22, no. 4: 558–592.

Taylor, Savitri. 2010. "Australian Funded Care and Maintenance of Asylum Seekers in Indonesia and Papua New Guinea: All Care but No Responsibility." *UNSW Law Journal* 33, no. 2: 337–359.

United Nations High Commissioner for Refugees (UNHCR). 2001. "The Scope and Content of the Principle of Non-Refoulement: Opinion." http://www. unhcr.org/en-au/publications/legal/419c75ce4/refugee-protection-international-law-scope-content-principle-non-refoulement.html?query=non-refoulement.

United Nations High Commissioner for Refugees (UNHCR). 2013. "South-East Asia '2013 UNHCR Regional Operations Profile- South-East Asia." http://www.unhcr.org/pages/4b17be9b6.html.

United Nations High Commissioner for Refugees (UNHCR). 2014. "Indonesian Fact Sheet." http://www.unhcr.org/50001bda9.pdf.

University of New South Wales (UNSW). 2014. *Fact Sheet: The Cambodia Agreement*, Andrew and Renata Kaldor Centre for International Refugee Law. http://www.kaldorcentre.unsw.edu.au/sites/kaldorcentre.unsw.edu.au/files/cambodia_agreement_fact_sheet_0.pdf.

Weber, Leanne. 2006. "The Shifting Frontiers of Migration Control." In *Borders, Mobility and Technologies of Control*, edited by Sharron Pickering and Leanne Weber. Dordrecht: Springer.

Zhyznomirska, Lyubov. 2006. "Externalities of the EU Immigration and Asylum Policy: The Case of Ukraine." *Review of European and Russian Affairs* 2, no. 2: 30–55.

10

Containment Practices of Immobility in Greece

ANDRIANI FILI

Huysmans (2006) argues that the process of securitising migration is comprised of three themes: internal security, cultural identity and welfare. These three themes are not only evident internationally (Bosworth and Guild 2008) but have been central to Greek immigration (detention) policy since the early 1990s, when the sudden influx of – mostly undocumented – migrants sparked the adoption of restrictive state policies and a rapid increase in anti-immigration attitudes (Karyotis 2012). The public discourse on mobility in Greece has become marked by a toxic combination of internal securitisation and racism, as politicians of all parties raise concerns about links between the undocumented, rising crime, urban degradation and widespread hardship.[1] Immigration, moreover, is characterised as a challenge to conceptions of Greek national identity in public perception, too, thus explaining the continuing rise of xenophobia and anti-immigrant rhetoric (Voutira 2013). Immigration, finally, has traditionally been seen as threatening the welfare of Greek citizens in austerity-ridden Greece (Karamanidou 2016). In tandem with hostile representations of immigrants and refugees has been the evolution of Greek immigration policies, which have mainly been dealing with immigration as a necessary evil (Triantafyllidou 2009). Hence it is clear that *'the securitisation of migration has both explicitly and implicitly made borders more selective and targeted in their policing of irregular migrants'* (Gerard and Pickering 2013). In this context, irregular entry in Greece is a crime in itself, punishable with at minimum a three-month imprisonment and a fine of no less than 1,500 euros [Greek Law 3386/2005, Art. 83(1)].

However, this form of punishment is rarely enforced. Instead, the blanket

---

[1]   For a discussion on how the securitisation of immigration was hijacked by the far right see Lazaridis and Skleparis 2015.

administrative detention of all irregular migrants that have either crossed irregularly or remained in Greece without a legal status has taken place across the country for a number of years (Triantafyllidou et al. 2014); punishment in relation to border control is not explicit but is enacted through administrative policies and practices (Bosworth and Guild 2008; Gerard and Pickering 2014). This goes hand-in-hand with Greece's policy of deporting unwanted population from its territory. Indeed, for far too long, Greece has sought to reduce rates of irregular immigration by relying increasingly on detaining and deporting the immigrant 'other' (Furman et al. 2016).[2] Despite growing evidence that these policies have never borne the intended results, they have been excessively employed to the detriment of human lives (Angeli et al. 2014) with the pretence of these policies being the result of the hospitable feelings of the Greek people.

The Greek notion of hospitality (*filoksenia*) has more than often appeared in official rhetoric as a national virtue and a generous offer to irregular migrants in order to refute numerous accusations regarding the conditions in the country's detention centres (Rozakou 2012). '*[This is] a project that makes us proud of the level of filoksenia (hospitality) that our country offers to illegal immigrants who stay here until their return to their country of origin*', said then Minister of Public Protection, Prokopis Pavlopoulos, at the inauguration of a detention centre on the island of Samos (Rozakou 2012). In the same line of thought, pre-removal detention centres have been euphemistically called 'closed hospitality centres' (Hellenic Republic 2012). More recently, the Greek government has built hotspots on five islands (Samos, Chios, Lesbos, Kos, Leros) at the sea border between Turkey and Greece, which deal with large influxes. The hotspots were ordered by the European Union (EU) to manage exceptional migratory flows. However, when the Greek Defence Minister, Panos Kammenos, announced their long-stalled creation, he claimed that they were ready to '*function and welcome refugees*' (Ekathimerini 2016).

Refugees and migrants, though, feel nothing like welcome. Instead, there are a number of human rights organisations' accounts that report hopelessness and despair (Human Rights Watch 2016; Amnesty International 2016). Does this constitute a hospitality crisis? Or has the rhetoric around hospitality been employed purely to reaffirm state sovereignty through the ultimate control of the 'other' in immigration detention centres? Prompted by these questions, this chapter will attempt to lay out the primary characteristics of the Greek

---

[2]   In the study of people who cross borders extra-legally, defining 'the immigrant' is a process of exclusion or inclusion enacted by states, often involving racial 'othering' (Kofman et al. 2000, 8; Mountz 2010). There have been a number of studies in Australia (Grewcock 2009) and in the US (Bosworth and Kaufman 2011), that point to the fact that the treatment of immigrants and asylum seekers reflects entrenched cultural and political xenophobic othering.

detention system over the past few years (for more on this see Bosworth and Fili 2015). In doing so, it will claim that detention practices have been legitimated through interlinked discursive strategies: a narrative of deterrence; the rationalisation of deportation as an opposition to the imagery of invading hordes and hungry masses; and the denial of both policies' racialised nature.

The Politics of Detention

For a number of years, detention was Greece's main policy in the manage-ment of irregular arrivals (Triantafyllidou et al. 2014). It was predicated upon two simple ideas. The first one was the narrative of deterrence, signalling at the same time an investment in safeguarding Greece's porous borders and a focus on 'humanely acceptable deficiencies in detention centres'.[3] Internationally, the securitisation of migration applies theories of deterrence in attempts to control and influence the mobility of irregular migrants. Migration, in this context, is constructed as a rational choice to be 'deterred by rapidly expanding preventative infrastructures' (Bosworth and Guild 2008, 711). Indeed, in 2012, the Greek government completed a 10.5km fence along the most transited part of its land border with Turkey,[4] and deployed almost 2,000 additional border guards (Pallister-Wilkins 2015). The measures proved effective in discouraging immigrants or smugglers. However, it redirected the flows back to the Greek islands increasing the death toll in the Aegean. In addition to hardening the external border, resourceful Greek police and coastguard have employed over the years, a number of pre-emptive measures to control movements across the borders with neighbouring Turkey, including illegal deportations and pushbacks.

Required to secure its border with Turkey on behalf of all of Europe, Greece did so under conditions of financial privation and surging xenophobia, without contravening the human rights standards expected of EU members. '*We have to make their lives miserable, otherwise they will be under the impression that coming to Greece they will be free to do what they want*', the Head of Greek Police advised his officers (Demetis 2016). From this view, faced with the prospect of prolonged stays inside a Greek detention centre under deplorable conditions, irregular migrants will be discouraged from making the perilous

---

[3]   When asked about the living conditions of Amygdaleza detention centre, Mr. Dendias, the Minister of Public Protection was clear: 'We make sure we follow European standards. However, conditions are not ideal, this is not a hotel. The logic is that 'humanely acceptable deficiencies' will force irregulars out of Greece' (Autopsia 2012).

[4]   At a time of severe cuts in public spending, Greece completed the construction of the fence with national funds because the European Commission denied money and support for the project.

journey to Greece. Indeed, as a number of legal rulings and non-governmental organisation (NGO) reports made quite clear, many of the Greek facilities fail to meet basic standards of care and are mainly defined by arbitrariness, sheer overcrowding and poor conditions (European Committee for the Prevention of Torture and Inhuman or Degrading Treatment of Punishment (CPT) 2012; Human Rights Watch 2008; Amnesty International 2010 and 2012; Médecins Sans Frontières (MSF) 2014). The current so-called 'refugee crisis'[5] that has played out in the Aegean as the main gateway to Europe, however, proves that any focus on deterrence, either in the form of fencing and gatekeeping (Triantafyllidou and Ambrosini 2011) or by making detention facilities unliveable, is wilfully ignorant of the kinds of factors propelling people to move in the first place and, thus, completely ineffective.

The second legitimating basis for detention was deportation. As former Minister of Citizen's Protection, Nikos Dendias, stated: 'Our aim is that every illegal migrant, unless the competent authorities decide that he is entitled to international protection, will be detained until he is returned to his home country' (Ministry of Citizen Protection 2013). In this line of thought, the detention infrastructure formed the linchpin for the successful implementation of returns. This was further supported by an advisory opinion of the Greek Legal Council that allows authorities to prolong detention beyond the 18-month limit until the detainee has consented to be returned (European Council on Religion and Ethics (ECRE) 2014). Under this framework, Greece launched a massive operation to arrest and detain all irregular migrants in the Greek territory, ironically labelled 'Operation Xenios[6] Zeus', referring to the ancient Greek God Zeus to once again symbolise hospitality to and patronage of foreigners (Human Rights Watch 2013). Once the number of arrestees started exceeding the number of places available, the government engaged in a large-scale investment in pre-removal detention establishments to increase the return rate.[7] Nonetheless, the policy proved to be far from successful. In fact, between 2008 and 2013, Greece issued 491,411 orders to leave, of which only 24.5 per cent on average were enforced. These orders are rarely enforced with a judicially approved deportation proceeding because most irregular migrants lack the travel documents to leave the country legally. In 2014, in the midst of its worst economic crisis and given the extreme costs of forced returns (Ageli et al. 2014), the Greek government ceased all deportations. However, this was not accompanied by a reduction in the number of detainees as one would expect; in fact, the detainee population continued to increase (Asylum Information Database (AIDA) 2015).

---

[5]   In 2015 the UN refugee agency declared an emergency inside the EU, and the EU deployed its own humanitarian response unit inside Europe for the first time.

[6]   Xenios refers to the ancient Greek concept of hospitality.

[7]   See Report of the Special Rapporteur on the human rights of migrants, Mission to Greece, 18 April 2013.

Arguably, then, the Greek detention policy has been based on a flimsy foundation, as the Greek state has managed neither to curb arrivals nor remove the undesirable population. Nevertheless, detention practices, employed in the most capricious and arbitrary manner (Majcher and Flynn 2014), remained unchallenged, highlighting their deeply racialised nature (Bosworth et al. forthcoming). 'The migrant from the ex-Soviet Union that goes to Sweden has some kind of level. Greece gets migrants from Bangladesh, Afghanistan who have a different culture; they belong to a different world. That's our misfortune' (Ekatihimerini 2014), exclaimed former Minister of Public Protection, Nikos Dendias, about the quality of detainees. Similarly, a detention officer at Petrou Ralli detention centre claimed in response to a question about women detainees: 'They are not able to freely move around, they can't talk to anyone, they just come to Greece and become slaves. So in a way in here [detention centre] they have a better life, because we feed them and provide them with accommodation.'[8] Hence, detention is heavily invested in 'civilising' tropes and gendered moralities. It provides another, potent opportunity not only to reject, but to demean and diminish racially othered peoples.

In this kind of discourse, the provision of 'shelter' to undocumented migrants by the Greek state was considered as a marker of a civilised state (us) pitted against uncivilised masses (them) (Bosworth et al. forthcoming 2018), a timeless persuasive technique that helps define any issue in security terms (Karyotis 2012). In this context, there were frequent announcements about pending reforms aimed at increasing the detention estate, which all the same was not a small one to begin with. Up until 2015, there were 9 pre-removal/detention centres, two screening centres in Samos and Chios in the Aegean, two first reception centres in Orestiada on the mainland border with Turkey and Lesbos at the sea border with Turkey, in addition to a number of border guards and police stations, with a known capacity for around 5,000 (Majcher and Flynn 2014).

The growing activist movements against detention, racism and fascism, though strong, could not reach beyond their own circles, which did not yet have any political capital. The paradox of the Greek detention policy was not lost on detainees either. 'We are buried alive here. This is like a mass grave ... but we are not animals, we are humans and we have human rights, no?' male detainees at the Athens International airport detention facility pronounced firmly (Fili 2013). In this framework, forms of resistance flourished. In some instances, it was spontaneous, triggered by an incident of violence, and in others it was organised in advance. Detainees often engaged

---

[8]   The interview was conducted by the author under the project 'Border Policing: Gender, Human Rights & Security' funded by the Australian Research Council.

in hunger strikes and self-harm. Others issued statements, with the support of human rights organisations, against detention practices (Infomobile n.d.). The voices that demanded a change in the detention system grew stronger every day.

Resistance to Change

In February 2015, the new left-wing government assured Greek citizens that immigration detention centres belonged to the past, committing to its election pledge to reverse anti-immigrant policies of the previous right-wing government (AIDA 2015). To this effect, it formed a new Immigration Policy Ministry under the Ministry of Internal Affairs. At a visit to the infamous Amygdaleza pre-removal detention centre (Angeli and Triantafyllidou 2014), following the suicide of a Pakistani detainee, then Deputy Minister of Citizen's Protection, Yannis Panousis, said 'I am here to express my embarrassment. We are done with detention centres' (Ekathimerini 2015). Indeed, in March 2015, the government started evacuating this centre at a rate of 30 migrants per day (Chrysopoulos 2015), amid great fanfare about the humanitarian face of the new era and, to its credit, despite fervent opposition not only by other parties but also by local residents. The aim was to close down the centre within 100 days, and other centres as soon as possible. It was a moment much celebrated by NGOs and human rights organisations, as this was the first time a member of a Greek government spoke openly about what was going on inside detention facilities (Kathimerini 2015).

The Greek government's plan was further accompanied by the announcement of a range of measures that presented an important step towards reducing the use of immigration detention in Greece (Ministry of Citizen Protection 2015). The announcement included the revocation of the Ministerial Decision allowing for detention beyond 18 months, and the immediate release of persons concerned. Furthermore, action would be taken in order to put in place open reception centres instead of detention facilities. The announcement also noted that alternatives to detention would be implemented for the first time, the maximum period of detention would be limited to six months, and persons belonging to vulnerable groups as well as asylum seekers would be immediately released.

Indeed, in the following months, the detained population shrunk from around 7,000 to a few hundred (Aitima 2016). A year later, in March 2016, pre-removal detention centres were back again reaching their full capacity, and Greece was fast becoming a containing space of the thousands of refugees trapped in its islands and mainland (Aitima 2016). How can this turnaround be explained?

Containing Immobility

In June 2015, at the same time as the Greek government was negotiating a new bail out deal with Europe, there was a general understanding that the boats would not stop coming. Indeed, over the summer of 2015, the numbers escalated, reaching their peak in October with 218,394 new arrivals (United Nations High Commissioner for Refugees (UNHCR) n.d.a.). However, the government did not have the resources to deal with the enormous task of registering and managing the incoming population. For example, during the summer there were only four representatives of the First Reception Service to register new arrivals on Lesbos, the island which received thousands per day (UNHCR n.d.c.). In an attempt to put more pressure on the EU to pour in more funds, members of the government threatened to unleash a wave 'of millions of economic migrants' on Europe unless the EU helped Greece financially (Waterfield and Bruno 2015). Unofficially, though, the wave-through approach had already started. Operating in a state of legal limbo and with an overwhelmed system, due to severe staff shortages, Greek officials neither registered nor fingerprinted most of the new arrivals (Greek Council for Refugees 2015). Near the end of the summer, the police that were responsible for managing the closed reception centres on the islands opened the gates due to their incapability to provide food to all the detainees[9].

Rather than trying to impede movement like in the past, the focus was now on speeding up the flow to avoid congestion on the islands. Hence, the number of immigrant and asylum seeker detainees remained very low. The Greek government did not just turn a blind eye to this practice, but was actively involved by chartering ferries to take people from the islands where they land (Spathopoulou 2016), to Athens and buses to take them to train stations so they could continue their journey to Northern Greece. The idea was that they would eventually leave Greece to reach their desired destinations. However, in lack of a sustainable plan, this resulted in refugees and migrants congregating in squares in Athens, where the number of people sleeping rough swelled dramatically. The huge makeshift camp in Idomeni, Greece's border with the Former Yugoslav Republic of Macedonia (FYROM), which the Greek Interior Minister, Panagiotis Kouroumblis, called 'modern-day Dachau' (Worley and Dearden 2016), was constructed by the Doctors Without Borders (*Médecins Sans Frontières*) and other NGOs to hold those who were waiting to cross the border to continue their journeys through the Balkans to Northern Europe. However, the idea of people being waved through was not welcomed by the countries on the receiving end of the flow (European Commission 2016b), isolating Greece from its neighbouring countries, as evidenced by its

---

[9]   This is mainly based on anecdotal evidence drawn from my experience as an NGO worker at the time.

exclusion from the Visegrad and Austria summit which were convened to discuss the handling of the 'refugee crisis' (Deutsche Welle 2016). The message from this summit was clear: Greece is responsible to stop the flow, otherwise plans will be enforced to tighten border controls, including closing borders, on the Balkan route.

The European agenda for immigration, thus, focused on deterrence at all costs, and greater mobilisation of border control. Drawing on this, the European Commission developed the idea of the 'hotspot approach.' (European Commission n.d.). The aim was to help slow the flow of migrants heading to the north, and mitigate security risks by swiftly identifying, registering, and fingerprinting all arrivals in Italy and Greece, as 'hotspots' were considered key to securing the EU's external borders (European Commission 2016c). Furthermore, in late January, the EU gave Greece a three-month ultimatum to stop migrants crossing from Turkey, or else the country would be banned from the borderless Schengen area (European Commission 2016b). Austria and several Balkan countries were determined to stop migrants passing through by building rows of fences, and FYROM sealed its southern border with Greece. With the end of the wave-through approach, thousands of migrants were stranded in Greece.

Amid EU pressure to deal with mass mobility, and with just few of the resources pledged by the EU actually coming through, the available evidence shows that confinement and detention are once again employed as an accommodation strategy for the rising number of refugees and migrants[10]. In the beginning of 2016, the government started detaining nationals of North African countries followed by nationals of Pakistan and Bangladesh, separating once more between bona fide refugees and economic migrants (Aitima 2016). At the same time, the authorities started to arrest nationals of other countries, including Afghans, holding expired police documents. In a just a few months, the number of detainees increased significantly (Aitima 2016). In February 2016, the five long-delayed 'hotspot' centres opened on the islands of Lesbos, Chios, Leros, Samos, and Kos in order to cope with a relentless flow of people landing from Turkey (Antonakaki et al. 2016).

Under the EU-Turkey deal, which came into force on 20 March 2016, people arriving on the Greek islands are immediately detained for 20 days in these hotspots in order to be individually assessed by the Greek authorities. Following the 20 days' period, they are released but have to remain on the island, thus further restricting their movement. Anyone who does not apply for

---

[10]   It is important to note that the borders for nationalities other than Syrians, Afghans and Iraqis closed on December 2015 and the borders for Afghans closed on February 2016.

asylum will be sent back to Turkey, as will anyone whose claim is rejected. Implementation of the deal has presented Greece with two challenges: first, the legal challenge of presenting Turkey as a safe 'third country' in order to expedite returns. Second, to separate between those already trapped in Greece and new arrivals, as the fate of the former group is not addressed by the deal. As for the former, the Greek government amended its asylum legislation in a fast-track legislative procedure to modify the structure of the Asylum Appeals Committees, raising concerns about the independence and impartiality of the new body (for more on this see Gkliati 2016). The latter challenge was addressed by emptying Greek islands of all those who crossed over from Turkey prior to the deal and transforming the much vaunted open hotspots into massive police-run detention centres to host newcomers. The amended legal framework of first reception procedures (3907/2011) further clarifies that migrants are subject to restriction of freedom of movement within the premises of these centres.

Within a few months, Greece was transformed from a fast lane to a grim waiting room. At the moment, there are more than 50 emergency reception sites[11] and five hotspots, as well as a number of informal sites, spread all over Greece, operating with capacity for around 60,000 people (UNHCR n.d.a). In addition to these new facilities, Greece continues to use a number of pre-removal detention centres, older dedicated detention facilities, and numerous border guard and police stations. For example, pre-removal detention centres like Amygdaleza and Corinth, the closure of which was celebrated in the presence of the media at the beginning of the government's term of office, have now been re-opened. According to a report released in October 2016 (Aitima 2016) drawing on a project that involved monitoring visits to detention centres in Greece, there are still long-standing systemic problems, no different to what human rights organisations have castigated Greece for in the past. In fact, they arise from a well-known mixture of pleasing the EU, appeasing their native citizens, and attempting to deter prospective arrivals. Based on 31 monitoring visits to detention centres conducted over one year, the analysis of 277 individual cases and interviews with competent authorities the research team observed, among others, the use of inappropriate detention areas, lack of outdoor time, recreational activities and interpretation services, inadequate healthcare, social and psychological support, detention of minors and seriously ill persons and the sheer lack of information regarding the case. Furthermore, Amnesty International at a press meeting in October 2016 claimed that detention conditions on the islands are purposefully bad to deter prospective arrivals, alluding to former practices described above (Huffington Post Greece 2016).

---

[11] Migration ministry bulletins list 39 camps, some of which are empty; others are mothballed and others still are in the planning phase but do not appear on the list (Howden and Fotiadis 2017).

Refugee camps, too, are full or host to a range of problems. Almost half of the new sites were created in under ten days, some in very remote locations with little to no access to legal aid, limited access to services and support, and hardly any information offered about their status. Conditions in most open centres fall below international humanitarian standards, to the point where some have been characterised as even 'unfit for animals' (Human Rights Watch 2016). What is more, access to asylum is severely impeded. The Greek army[12] has played a lead role in setting up most of the facilities covering mainly catering services, receiving complaints not just about the quality of the food but also due to the rumours of corruption following the deals made with the catering companies.[13]

All the above have long been a source of intense criticism from both domestic and international observers, as well as the subject of numerous cases at the European Court of Human Rights. What is relatively new, however, is the level of advanced confusion that is taking shape on the ground, reflecting the confused and improvised nature of reactive (EU) immigration policies and their implementation. Who is detained, where, for what reasons, and for how long, are issues that no one knows. Your quality of life depends on where you have been placed, and where you have been placed is down to luck. It is also unclear as to which part of the government is responsible for running open and closed facilities. Even the Action Plan presented by the Greek authorities in the beginning of March 2016 lacks information on the authorities responsible for the implementation of certain actions and for monitoring the implementation of those actions (European Commission 2016a).

While not all facilities used to confine people at the moment are detention centres per se, the line between open accommodation and confinement often becomes difficult to draw in practice. The spatial logic of refugee camps being as remote as possible (Zeveleva 2017), together with severely restricted access to the asylum process in these places, render most people inside them immobile[14] in overcrowded and unhygienic conditions. Still, refugees are not only stuck inside camps; under the EU-Turkey deal and in view of walls being literally and metaphorically built across Europe they are also physically prevented from leaving Greece[15]. As this form of containment is neither reasonable nor proportionate to a government objective, because these

---

[12] $74 million was added to the defence ministry budget for refugee support.

[13] Internal NGO migration brief.

[14] This is not to say that people are discouraged from finding ways to move but that this is now more time-consuming and riddled with a number of challenges.

[15] In stark opposition to this framing refugees and migrants across Greece find ways to circumvent containment practices and, albeit in smaller numbers, manage to leave Greece. However, this means that they increasingly depend on smuggling networks and attempt risky journeys.

people cannot be expelled, it can be argued that, in essence, the government resorts to arbitrary and illegitimate detention of refugees on Greek soil.

As a recent report by the European Council on Refugees and Exiles argues, there is little official clarity as to what can be presented as detention facilities or reception structures in Greece (ECRE 2016). It is explained that the highly misleading representation of the country's reception capacity, including detention places, can be attributed to the effort to reach the EU target of 30,000 reception places and satisfy other Member States. At the same time, the number of detainees is wrongly presented as smaller than the actual one, failing to include the number of people detained in hotspots. This is further reflected in another report by the Global Detention Project (2015), which aimed to obtain a true picture of the number of migrants and asylum seekers being held in detention around the world. Greece failed to provide complete information on the names and locations of detention centres and offered invalid answers to questions about the number of (asylum seeker) detainees and the number of minors in detention. Greek authorities did not include the many police stations, where migrants are known to be detained, thus, invisibilising a great number of detainees and directed the researchers to a website that contains limited information in order to avoid directly responding to questions (Hellenic Police n.d.). In effect, Greece's detained migrants are going uncounted and hence unaccounted for.

Conclusion

For a number of years, the Greek government blamed the lack of infra-structure, organisation, capital and the intrinsic pressures of its geographical position for Greece's difficulty in managing borders and effectively dealing with migrant populations. The narratives of crises, which have been employed since 2009, only grant moral legitimacy to Greece's continued political, legal, and financial margin within Europe (Mantanika 2014). In this context of yet another crisis, Greece soon became a space of humanitarian intervention where governmental and nongovernmental, security, humanitarian and human rights actors co-operate to respond to 'humanitarian crises'. In a situation of endless emergency, people on the move were kept apart and out of sight, while the care dispensed was designed to control, filter and confine.

With a floundering political leadership, unable to find solutions to anything at all, and with a downward spiralling economy and pressure from the EU to employ mechanisms of repressive immigration control, it comes as no surprise that the Greek government succumbed to models of encampment and abandoned its humanitarian and leftist ideals that were its flagship for almost a year ago. While some remodelling has been observed recently, this chapter argues that containment practices of immobility in Greece are enduring in time and employed by all governing parties. 'This refutes a left-right dichotomy and points to the racialised dynamics of immigration control, informed by dominant and shared discourses of securitization and illegalization of migrants' (Karamanidou 2016). As the Minister of Immigration Policy, Giannis Mouzalas, asserted 'there can be no immigration policy without closed hospitality centres' (Georgiopoulou 2016) allegedly to reduce criminal rates among immigrants and asylum seekers. What lies ahead for the migrants and refugees who arrive on Greece's shores remains to be seen; yet, the reality on the ground points to a looming bleak future that will focus on the expansion of containment practices. In January 2017, the government, in the spirit of the EU-Turkey deal, announced the construction of new closed detention centres for the arriving population that does not conform to a refugee profile. The multiple crises that Greece is dealing with have fallen from view in the rest of Europe. It is now time to raise our voices for the people who have an inalienable right to live somewhere safely.

References

Asylum Information Database (AIDA). 2015. "An Edn to Indefinite Immigration Detention in Greece?" 16 February 2015. http://www.asylumineurope.org/news/25-05-2017/end-indefinite-immigration-detention-greece.

AITIMA. 2016. *Forgotten: Administratively detained irregular migrants and asylum seekers*. Athens: AITIMA.

Amnesty International, *Greece: Irregular Migrants and Asylum-Seekers Routinely Detained in Substandard Conditions*. London: Amnesty International, 2010.

Amnesty International. 2012. *Greece: The End of the Road for Refugees, Asylum-Seekers and Migrants*. London: Amnesty International.

Amnesty International. 2016. *Trapped in Greece: An avoidable refugee crisis*. London: Amnesty International.

Angeli, Danai and Anna Triantafyllidou. 2014. *Is the indiscriminate detention of irregular migrants a cost-effective policy tool? A case-study of the Amygdaleza Pre-Removal Center.* Midas Policy Brief, Athens: ELIAMEP.

Angeli, Danai, Angeliki Dimitriadi, and Anna Triantafyllidou. 2014. "Assessing the Cost-effectiveness of Irregular Immigration Control Policies in Greece." *Midas Report*. Athens: ELIAMEP.

Antonakaki, Melina, Bernd Kasparek, and Georgios Maniatis. 2016. "Counting, Channelling, and Detaining: The Hotspot Center Vial in Chios, Greece." *Society + Space*. http://societyandspace.org/2016/11/29/counting-channelling-and-detaining-the-hotspot-center-vial-in-chios-greece/.

Autopsia. 2012. Alpha Channel 04th October. http://www.alphatv.gr/Microsites/Autopsia/Shows/04-10-2012.aspx.

Bosworth, Mary and Mhairi Guild. 2008. "Governing Through Migration Control: Security and Citizenship in Britain." *British Journal of Criminology* 48, no. 6: 703–719.

Bosworth, Mary and Emma Kaufman. 2011. "Foreigners in a Carceral Age: Immigration and Imprisonment in the United States." *Stanford Law and Policy Review* 22, no. 2: 429–454.

Bosworth, Mary and Andriani Fili. 2015. "Immigration Detention in Britain and Greece." In *Detaining the Immigrant Other: Global and Transnational Issues*, edited by Douglas Epps and Rich Furman. Oxford: Oxford University Press.

Bosworth, Mary, Andriani Fili and Sharron Pickering. 2017. "Women and Border Policing at the Edges of Europe." *Journal of Ethnic and Migration Studies*. https://doi.org/10.1080/1369183X.2017.1408459.

Chrysopoulos, Phillip. 2015. "Migrants from Amygdaleza Detention Center Released in Athens." *Greek Reporter*. 2 May 2015. http://greece.greekreporter.com/2015/03/02/migrants-from-amygdaleza-detention-center-released-in-center-of-athens/

Demetis, Christos. 2013. "Αρχηγός ΕΛ.ΑΣ για Μετανάστες: 'Να τους Κάνουμε το Βίο Αβίωτο" [Greek Police for Migrants: (We should) Make Their Lives Insufferable] News247, 20 December 2013. http://news247.gr/eidiseis/koinonia/arxhgos-el-as-gia-metanastes-na-toys-kanoyme-to-vio-aviwto.2561326.html.

Deutsche Welle. 2016. "Austria Hosts Balkan Refugee Conference without Greece." 24 February 2016. http://www.dw.com/en/austria-hosts-balkan-refugee-conference-without-greece/a-19069784.

European Council on Religion and Ethics (ECRE). 2014. *Weekly Bulletin of 4 April 2014.* http://www.asylumineurope.org/news/07-04-2014/greek-state-legal-council-justifies-detention-pending-removal-beyond-18-month-limit.

Ekatihimerini. 2014. *"Dendias Criticizes Dublin Regulation, Says Quality of Undocumented Immigrants Is 'Tragic'"*. 30 January 2014. http://www.ekathimerini.com/157413/article/ekathimerini/news/dendias-criticizes-dublin-regulation-says-quality-of-undocumented-immigrants-is-tragic.

Ekathimerini, 2015. "Migrant Centers to Be Shut Down After Suicide". 14 February 2015. http://www.ekathimerini.com/167320/article/ekathimerini/news/migrant-centers-to-be-shut-down-after-suicide.

Ekathimerini. 2016. "Four of Greece's five 'hotspot' migrant centres ready, says Kammenos". 16 February 2016. http://www.ekathimerini.com/206027/article/ekathimerini/news/four-of-greeces-five-hotspot-migrant-centres-ready-says-kammenos.

European Commission. 2016a. *Communication from the Commission to the Council: Assessment of Greece's Action Plan to remedy the serious deficiencies identified in the 2015 evaluation on the application of the Schengen acquis in the field of management of the external border.*

https://ec.europa.eu/home-affairs/sites/homeaffairs/files/what-we-do/policies/europeanagenda-migration/proposal-implementationpackage/docs/20160412/communication_assessment_greece_action_plan_en.pdf.

European Commission. 2016b. *Commission adopts Schengen Evaluation Report on Greece and proposes recommendations to address deficiencies in external border management.* Strasbourg, 2 February 2016. https://ec.europa.eu/malta/news/commission-adopts-schengen-evaluation-report-greece-and-proposes-recommendations-address_en.

European Commission. 2016c. *Implementing the European Agenda on Migration: Progress on Priority Actions.* http://europa.eu/rapid/press-release_IP-16-271_en.htm.

European Commission. n.d. "The Hotspot Approach to Managing Exceptional migratory Flows." https://ec.europa.eu/home-affairs/sites/homeaffairs/files/what-we-do/policies/european-agenda-migration/background-information/docs/2_hotspots_en.pdf.

European Committee for the Prevention of Torture and Inhuman or Degrading Treatment of Punishment (CPT). 2011. *Report to the Government of Greece on the Visit to Greece carried out by the CPT from 19 to 27 January 2011*. Strasbourg: Council of Europe, 2012.

Fili, Andriani. 2013. "The Maze of Immigration Detention in Greece: A Case Study of the Airport Detention Facility in Athens." *Prison Service Journal*, no 205.

Furman, Rich, Douglas Epps, and Greg Lamphear, eds. 2016. *Detaining the Immigrant Other: Global and Transnational Issues*. Oxford: Oxford University Press.

Georgiopoulou, Tania. 2016. "Κλειστά Κέντρα Φιλοξενίας για Μετανάστες" [Closed Detention Centres for Migrants]. *Kathimerini*. 13 November 2016. http://www.kathimerini.gr/883382/article/epikairothta/ellada/kleista-kentra-filo3enias-gia-metanastes.

Gerard, Alison, and Sharron Pickering. 2013. "Crimmigration: Criminal Justice, Refugee Protection and the Securitisation of Migration." In *The Routledge Handbook of International Crime and Justice Studies*, edited by Bruce Arrigo and Heather Bersot. Routledge: London.

Gkliatsi, Mariana. 2016. "Greece Creates New Asylum Committees after Decisions Blocking Returns Under the EU-Turkey Deal." *Leiden Law Blog*. 5 August 2016. http://leidenlawblog.nl/articles/greece-creates-new-asylum-appeals-committees.

Global Detention Project. 2015. *The Uncounted: Detention of Migrants and Asylum Seekers in Europe*. Geneva: Global Detention Project.

Greece: Law No. 3386/2005, Codification of Legislation on the Entry, Residence and Social Integration of Third Country Nationals on Greek Territory [Greece], June 2005. http://www.refworld.org/docid/4c5270962.html

Greece: Law No. 3907 of 2011 on the establishment of an Asylum Service and a First Reception Service, transposition into Greek legislation of Directive 2008/115/EC "on common standards and procedures in Member States for returning illegally staying third country nationals" and other provisions. [Greece], 26 January 2011. http://www.refworld.org/docid/4da6ee7e2.html

Grewcock, Michael. 2009. *Border Crimes: Australia's War on Illicit Migrants.* Sydney: Institute of Criminology.

Hellenic Police. n.d. "Statistic Data on Illegal Immigration." http://www. astynomia.gr/index.php?option=ozo_ content&perform=view&id=24727&Itemid=73&lang=EN.

Hellenic Republic. 2012. *Press Release on the Meeting between the Political Leadership of the Ministry of Citizen Protection and the Leadership of the Hellenic Police with Representatives of Immigrant Organizations, April. Athens.* http://www.yptp.gr/index.php?option=ozo_ content&perform=view&id=4215&Itemid=540&lang=EN.

Howden, Daniel and Apostolos Fotiadis. 2017. "The Refugee Archipelago: The Inside Story of What Went Wrong in Greece." *Refugees Deeply*, 6 March 2017. https://www.newsdeeply.com/refugees/articles/2017/03/06/the-refugee-archipelago-the-inside-story-of-what-went-wrong-in-greece.

Human Rights Watch. 2008. *Stuck in a Revolving Door: Iraqis and Other Asylum Seekers and Migrants at the Greece/Turkey Entrance to the European Union.* New York: Human Rights Watch.

Human Rights Watch. 2016. *Greece: Refugee "Hotspots" Unsafe, Unsanitary.* New York: Human Rights Watch. https://www.hrw.org/news/2016/05/19/ greece-refugee-hotspots-unsafe-unsanitary.

Huffington Post Greece. 2016. "Διεθνής Αμνηστία: Οι συνθήκες διαβίωσης των προσφύγων παραμένουν σκόπιμα άσχημες. Το θέμα είναι πολιτικό και όχι οικονομικό" [Amnesty International: Refugees' Living Conditions Deliberately Remain Bad]. 18 October 2016. http://www.huffingtonpost.gr/2016/10/18/ metanasteutiko_n_12540288.html.

Huysmans, Jef. 2006. *The Politics of Insecurity, Fear, Migration and Asylum in the EU.* London: Routledge.

Infomobile. n.d. "Hunger Strikes". http://infomobile.w2eu.net/resistance/ hunger-strikes/

Karamanidou, Lena. 2016. "Violence against Migrants in Greece: Beyond the Golden Dawn." *Ethnic and Racial Studies* 39, no. 11: 2002–2021.

Kofman, Eleonore, Annie Phizacklea, Parvati Raghuram and Rosemary Sales. 2000. *Gender and International Migration in Europe.* London: Routledge.

Karyotis, Georgios. 2012. "Securitization of Migration in Greece: Process, Motives, and Implications." *International Political Sociology* 6, no. 4: 390–408. doi: 10.1111/ips.12002.

Kathimerini. 2015. "Ριζικές Αλλαγές στα Κέντρα Κράτησης Ανακοίνωσαν Πανούσης-Χριστοδουλοπούλου" [Panousis-Christodoulopoulou Announced Fundamental Changes to Detention Centres]. 17 February 2015. http://www. kathimerini.gr/804014/article/epikairothta/politikh/rizikes-allages-sta-kentra-krathshs-anakoinwsan-panoyshs-xristodoylopoyloy.

Lazaridis, Gabriella and Dimitris Skleparis. 2016. "Securitization of Migration and the Far Right: The Case of Greek Security Professionals." *International Migration* 54, no.2: 176–192. doi:10.1111/imig.12219.

Majcher, Izabella and Michael Flynn. 2014. *Immigration Detention in Greece.* Geneva: Global Detention Project.

Mantanika, Regina. 2014. "Confinement Practices Of Undocumented Migrants At The Borders Of Europe. The Case of Greece." In *The EU, Immigration and the Politics of Imimmigration Detention*, edited by Michella Ceccorulli and Nicola Labanca, 109–127. Abingdon and New York: Routledge.

Médecins Sans Frontières (MSF). 2014. *Invisible Suffering: Prolonged and Systematic Detention of Migrants and Asylum Seekers in Substandard Conditions in Greece.* Athens: MSF.

Ministry of Citizen Protection. 2013. "Press Release." 11 August 2013. http:// www.yptp.gr/index.php?option=ozo_content&lang=GR&perform=view&id=4736&Itemid=579.

Ministry of Citizen Protection. 2015. "Press Release." 17 February 2015. http://www.mopocp.gov.gr/index.php?option=ozo_content&lang=&perform=view&id=5374&Itemid=607.

Mountz, Alison. 2010. *Seeking Asylum: Human Smuggling and Bureaucracy at the Border,* Minneapolis: University of Minnesota Press.

Pallister-Wilkins, Polly. 2015. "The Humanitarian Politics of European Border Policing: Frontex and Border Police in Evros." *International Political Sociology* 9, no. 1 53–69.

Rozakou, Katerina. 2012. "The Biopolitics of Hospitality in Greece: Humanitarianism and the Management of Refugees." *American Ethnologist* 39, no. 3: 562–577.

Spathopoulou, Aila. 2016. "The Ferry as a Mobile Hotspot: Migrants at the Uneasy Borderlands of Greece." Society and Space. http://societyandspace. org/2016/12/15/the-ferry-as-a-mobile-hotspot-migrants-at-the-uneasy-borderlands-of-greece/.

Triantafyllidou, Anna. 2009. "Greek Immigration Policy at the Turn of the 21st Century. Lack of Political Will or Purposeful Mismanagement?" *European Journal of Immigration and Law* 11: 159–177.

Triantafyllidou, Anna and Maurizio Ambrosini. 2011. "Irregular Immigration Control in Italy and Greece: Strong Fencing and Weak Gate-Keeping Serving the Labour Market." *European Journal of Immigration and Law* 13: 251–273.

Triantafyllidou, Anna, Danai Angeli and Angeliki Dimitriadi. 2014. *Detention As Punishment: Can Indefinite Detention Be Greece's Main Policy Tool To Manage Its Irregular Migrant Population?* Midas Policy Brief. Athens: ELIAMEP.

UN Human Rights Council. 2013. *Report of the Special Rapporteur on the human rights of migrants, Addendum: Mission to Greece*, 18 April 2013, A/ HRC/23/46/Add.4. http://www.refworld.org/docid/51b983ab4.html.

United Nations High Commissioner for Refugees (UNHCR). n.d.a "Sites in Greece". http://rrsesmi.maps.arcgis.com/apps/MapSeries/index. html?appid=d5f377f7f6f2418b8ebadaae638df2e1

United Nations High Commissioner for Refugees (UNHCR). n.d.b. "Snapshot Greece statistics" United Nations High Commissioner for Refugees. https:// data2.unhcr.org/en/documents/details/46440.

United Nations High Commissioner for Refugees (UNHCR). n.d.c. "Snapshot Lesbos Statistics." United Nations High Commissioner for Refugees. https:// data2.unhcr.org/en/documents/details/46441.

Voutira, Eftihia. 2013. "Realising 'Fortress Europe': 'Managing' Migrants and Refugees at the Borders of Greece." *Social Sciences Review* 140/141: 57–69.

Waterfield, Bruno. 2015. "Greece's Defence Minister Threatens to Send Migrants Including Jihadists to Western Europe" *The Telegraph*. 9 March 2015. http://www.telegraph.co.uk/news/worldnews/islamic-state/11459675/Greeces-defence-minister-threatens-to-send-migrants-including-jihadists-to-Western-Europe.html.

Worley, Will and Lizzie Dearden. 2016. "Greek Refugee Camp Is 'As Bad As a Nazi Concentration Camp', Says Minister" *The Independent*. 18 March 2016. http://www.independent.co.uk/news/world/europe/idomeni-refugee-dachau-nazi-concentration-camp-greek-minister-a6938826.html.

Zeveleva, Olga. 2017. "Biopolitics, Borders, and Refugee Camps: Exercising Sovereign Power Over Nonmembers of the State." *The Journal of Nationalism and Ethnicity* 45, no. 1: 41–60.

11

Solidarities in Migration

ANITTA KYNSILEHTO

The contemporary migration regime is highly unequal, leaving the majority of people in the world without real access to official channels of migration. Over the past years, asylum has been attested as being in crisis (see for example Zetter 2015; Väyrynen et al. 2017, 9). The increased number of asylum seekers that arrived in Europe in 2015 concretely demonstrated this political crisis (Kynsilehto 2017), leaving thousands to struggle over basic rights and to exercise the very right to ask for asylum that is endorsed in various human rights treaties. Undocumented or irregular migration in particular is perceived as a problem by established society. Irregularity is also a severe problem for people who are themselves in an irregular situation due to their lack of access to basic rights such as accommodation, healthcare, education and work. Moreover, uneven practices by states to provide basic services for people on the move create a necessity for civil society in a large sense – comprising not only non-governmental organisations but also more informal groups – to engage in diverse forms of everyday solidarity. Many associations including registered organisations with paid staff, those operating on a voluntary-work basis, as well as formal and informal networks of organisations and individuals across local, national and transnational scales engage with people on the move in order to provide greatly needed everyday assistance, information and human contacts. I call these people and organisations 'solidarity actors'.

In this chapter, I discuss examples of different types of solidarity action, both those with more humanitarian orientation and those geared towards advocacy and making political claims that seek to challenge the status quo. The latter are often also further divided between legalistic human rights argumentation and more explicitly political claims. However, I argue that these distinctions are becoming increasingly difficult to uphold due to the striking inequalities that actors at all levels witness on a daily basis, and the radical undermining of human rights frameworks. Most of these forms of activism comprise links across localities and countries, even continents. Solidarity networks are thus transnational and translocal. Moreover, individual solidarity actors often engage in different types of parallel and overlapping networks, formal and more informal ones, and interlinked networks exchange information, best practises and critiques of the status quo at different levels.

This chapter has a two-fold aim. Firstly, it discusses diverse forms of acting together in solidarity for, with and by migrants. Secondly, it will address the question of politics within these forms of acting together. These politics concern access to information, knowledge production and the possibilities of being mobile in order to engage in solidarity action. The chapter draws on insights from my own on-going multi-sited ethnographic research at different borders around the Mediterranean Sea, and my long-term engagement in transnational migrants' rights advocacy. The chapter begins by addressing variegated spaces and times of solidarity activism and includes the issue of sustainability of movements. It introduces an example and innovative mechanism that combines technical academic knowledge to activist practice, and then moves to critical practices and politics of movements. A final section will address the tendency of criminalising solidarity action that seeks to impede contact between privileged actors and people on the move.

Spaces and Times of Solidarity Activism

The phenomenon of solidarity activism is by far not new: many locations, such as the Sonoran desert between the US and Mexico (see for example Doty 2006; Cabrera and Glavac 2010; Squire 2014), and the town of Calais (Laacher 2002; Rygiel 2011) by the English Channel are well-known examples of border locations where solidarity actors have engaged for years to provide food, water and clothes for people transiting these sites. In some of these sites, more or less permanent forms of dwelling are established in the margins of towns, in the fields or forests, where shelters can be built before journeys are to continue. Based on long-term observations at different refugee camps and informal sites, Michel Agier argues:

> Other spaces emerge, in this age of globalization and local interventions by the "international community", and these become sites of political expression of a new type, which are invented and acted out in and on the limits (Agier 2011, 155).

'Enforcement archipelago' (Mountz 2011) refers to the use of islands to enact border control at a distance, with Nauru and Christmas Island as well-known cases for the Australian externalisation efforts, and Guam as one example of similar practice by the United States. In the Mediterranean, Lampedusa has become a highly symbolic site (Friese 2010; Cuttitta 2014) together with the

Aegean Islands, of which Lesbos became the most mediatised in 2015 – even though these forms of mobilities and parallel solidarities are far from being new there either (Trubeta 2015). As the islands are located at a distance from the mainland, being stuck on an island does not always need to denote being locked into a detention unit, though this is often an additional measure used. The remote location already necessitates some form of help, usually a written document, so that the person who entered irregularly can leave the island. In the Greek context, it was for a long time impossible to even apply for asylum on the islands, leaving the capital city Athens as the only location where an asylum claim could be lodged. As a peculiar practice, one needed a removal order to leave an Aegean island, take a ferryboat to Athens, and figure out whether applying for asylum in Greece could be an option (Worldwide Movement for Human Rights (FIDH), Migreurop and Euro-Mediterranean Human Rights Network (EMHRN) 2014, 75–77). While waiting, immediate assistance and human contacts by solidarity actors were highly needed.

For many people seeking asylum in the European Union (EU), Greece did not seem a feasible option. Many decided to continue their journeys towards other EU Member States, which turned the harbour city of Patras into a hub for people who sought a possibility to cross to Italy (Yaghmaian 2006; Lafazani 2013). Over the course of 2015, with the spotlight turned on the so-called Balkan route, the tiny village of Idomeni at the border between Greece and Macedonia became known to the wider public. Since mid-November 2015, it became a stage for successive closures and openings of the border, first with only people of Afghan, Iraqi and Syrian nationalities allowed to cross, then closing to everyone (based on the author's on-site visit to Idomeni, 21 November 2015; see also Amnesty International 2016).

With the gradual closing of the border, Idomeni began to host an increasingly permanent form of a makeshift camp that was never established and opened as a refugee camp in a formal sense, despite the presence of several international organisations such as the UN Refugee Agency (UNHCR) and Médicins Sans Frontières (Doctors without Borders [MSF]) since early on. After the border was closed completely, during the spring months of 2016, some 14,000 people ended up blocked in Idomeni (Al Jazeera 2016). The UNHCR issued a call saying that the situation was escalating day by day into a full-blown humanitarian crisis, and tension escalated as people grew increasingly frustrated for being blocked in the middle of fields and on the railroad linking the two countries (UNHCR 2016a). On Monday, 14 March 2016, hundreds if not thousands of people grew tired of waiting at the border. They decided to go past the border construction consisting of barbed wire fences and Macedonian military onto the other side of the border. Walking through woods and crossing a river, they made their way into the territory of

Macedonia. Many ended up detained once in Macedonia, and some eighty journalists and solidarity advocates who had accompanied them were arrested for illegal border crossing. Three people from Afghanistan drowned in the river, one of them a pregnant woman. The people were returned to the Greek side of the border and the frustration caused by the uncertainty continued to grow (BBC 2016). As one result of the mounting tension, on 10 April 2016 police forces from the Macedonian side fired tear gas and rubber bullets at refugees protesting at the border, leaving not even young children unaffected (Reuters 2016).

The unrest at the border in Idomeni was happening while the EU leaders were hastily preparing the second summit with Turkey to complete the deals, especially the deal from the week before, the week of 7 March 2016, by which Turkey accepted that the EU would return people arriving irregularly to the islands. If there were Syrians among the returnees, the EU states would readmit another Syrian via legal avenues (BBC 2016). A legal framework was not disclosed that would formally render the push-backs possible, nor was it revealed how these exchanges would be organized in practice. In monetary terms, the EU would pay an additional 3 billion euros to Turkey in addition to the already agreed 3 billion in support, for Turkey to continue to host refugees and to cooperate in impeding them from leaving the country by irregular means. Human rights groups and solidarity advocates have called these deals the biggest concerted operation of human trafficking ever seen.

> Twists and turns of European border politics and overall approach to migrants and refugees is closely followed by people on the move. One of these twists, negotiations concerning the deal between the EU and Turkey, was subject to many questions at Elleniko camp in the outskirts of Athens, Greece. The camp is a combination of a former airport terminal and sports grounds constructed for the 2004 Olympic Games, namely a basketball hall and an ice hockey rink. These facilities host some 5000 people of diverse nationalities with new people arriving from the islands on a daily basis. It is an open facility with a police presence and private security outside, with people able to come and go, the minimum of structured activity by voluntary groups and a couple of formal organisations. There is a lack of security especially in the night-time. The people staying here are waiting for something to happen, being blocked from continuing further, uncertain of what might happen while waiting, and terrified of the possible outcome of the deal that is being negotiated with Turkey. Serious faces, posing questions that no-one can answer, at least for now. (Extract from field notes, Athens, March 2016)

In Europe, with increased numbers of arrivals coupled with the further tightening of access to asylum and other forms of legalising one's residence, as well as curbing legal channels of access to territory such as via family reunification, it is likely that there will be more people than ever in need of regularisation and other means for day-to-day survival, such as accommodation, food and sanitation. Much of the daily assistance to both new arrivals and those who arrived some time ago is provided by associations and individuals in a voluntary, sometimes ad hoc manner as has been manifested in 2015 and onwards, with the country case of Greece continuing as the most exposed arena of the desperate need for help. As the unrest at the border between Greece and Macedonia illustrates, the lack of official response to the plight of the people on the move calls for an enhanced response by differently positioned civil society actors – not only to respond to immediate needs, but to maintain relations as peaceful as possible. This engagement is thus indispensable, both in terms of accessing basic rights as well as for the contribution of this work towards societal peace. Yet it can be very tiresome and consuming for those who are engaged in such work, especially in contexts where the need for such engagement is already known to be long-term.

In many of the most exposed 'hubs', there is a need for ensuring sustainability of activities that often signifies a need for long-term commitment. In long exposed 'hubs' such as Calais, Lesbos or Oujda at the border between Algeria and Morocco, six to seven years of experience in the local context count as a short-term commitment for some actors in the field. As an example, I met a middle-aged woman at a food delivery point for migrants in Calais in January 2010 and asked whether she had been volunteering for a long time with people on the move. She replied: 'No, not for a long time, just for six, seven years'. I have heard similar remarks at each site I have visited, from people for whom engagement with people on the move has become a part of their everyday life. Indeed, it has become such a naturalised part of everyday life that one does not even recognise the time that passes. There is a need to learn from these longer-term experiences while developing new practices and ways of engagement.

For those who come to help for either shorter or longer periods of time, appreciating local knowledge and remaining sensitive to learning local dynamics and practices of working in the local context are important. This is a recurrent theme, both as a modality of critique and as something to be highlighted in more neutral terms that I have encountered at various sites where both locals and internationals are working on similar issues. An abundance of critiques have addressed the dynamics between big international organisations and international non-governmental organisations that employ and import expatriate staff in a particular context (Harrell-Bond 1985).

This is a theme that more informal groups and engaged individuals also seek and need to remember when engaging in a context they – or we, as I consider my own positionality as much as that of any other – are not fully familiar with: to listen and learn from local dynamics, and to fully appreciate the knowledge and skills of those already present, including foremost those whose fate is at stake.

Innovative Practices of Alert

Solidarity networks create innovative practices in all areas where states are constantly failing their connected responsibilities. One of these areas is the on-going tragedy at sea borders. As a well-known example, the Mediterranean Sea has been a stage for increasing numbers of deaths at sea over the years, in particular since the signature of the Schengen Accords and, consequently, the establishment of a strict visa regime (European Commission n.d.) that has sought to separate the two shores since the early 1990s. The mobility of citizens from the northern shore of that sea is enabled, whilst that of a large majority of the southerners, both from coastal states as well as further on south- and eastwards, is in actual fact blocked via official venues. This uneven access to mobility has forced many to use very dangerous means for crossing the border that have resulted in ever increasing numbers of deaths. At the same time, there has been a multiplication of surveillance mechanisms at sea that have not been able to bring down the number of casualties which continue to increase (International Organisation for Migration 2017). In the midst of developments of what was labelled as the Arab Spring in 2011, a famous event took place. The 'Left to die' case concerned a vessel that had departed from Libya and was drifting at sea for 14 days with all eyes watching, including international media, a NATO operation that was going on against the Gaddafi regime, and all the existing surveillance in place by the European Border Agency Frontex and national coast guards of the Mediterranean coastal states. Sixty-three people died on board (see Forensic Architecture n.d.).

Awareness of these tragedies and the failure of states to respond adequately triggered a response by concerned individuals around the Mediterranean Sea and further in Europe. The Watch the Med initiative is one of the results from this concern. This initiative has created an alarm phone that provides an emergency number that functions 24/7, is ran by volunteers, and covers the Central, Eastern and Western Mediterranean 'corridors'. The idea is to localise the migrant boat in distress and contact the coast guard responsible to come and perform a search and rescue operation for the passengers. Thus, the idea is to give such specific details that the coast guards can no longer claim that they were not aware of the boat in distress. If they fail to act, the case is rendered public and disseminated widely in the media. Through this practice, the activists are using new technologies to perform a 'disobedient gaze' (Pezzani and Heller 2013) to the maritime areas that have become increasingly lethal over the past years. This disobedient gaze refuses to remain silent when obvious abuses and neglect happen and, instead, the constant search for information is used to render responsible those officials that are not fulfilling their search and rescue (SAR) responsibilities.

Critical Practice and the Politics of Acting in Solidarity

Solidarity acts are often enacted by people endowed with various degrees of privilege compared to those in a less privileged position (see for example Rozakou 2016). These positionalities and privileges are far from being fully static: they are somewhat fluid, and they may concern the legal status in a given country, socio-economic means, or access to information and funding. Increasingly, people on the move also take ownership of their struggles by engaging in new forms of solidarity (also Bredeloup 2013). In Morocco, for example, sub-Saharan migrants' groups and associations began to emerge in 2005. First they were largely established and promoted by people without a residence status, and not officially recognised as organised civil society by the Moroccan state. By claiming their space and gaining visibility through sit-ins and public marches, especially in the capital city, Rabat, they made themselves heard. Different ethnic and national groupings organised in nation-wide Councils. Parallel to these developments, and to a large extent with the same people involved, a migrant section was established as a part of the trade union Organisation Démocratique du Travail (ODT) in 2012. The regularisation campaign in 2014 that theoretically targeted people living in migrant 'ghettos' but in fact enabled a wide category of people, such as foreign students, to regularize their statuses, in parallel with the enabling of foreign residents to legally establish associations in Morocco, contributed to creating a firm ground for migrant organisations to begin formal operations, including competition over funds.[1]

Diversely positioned noncitizens acting in solidarity often advance even more diverse claims compared to those advocated by, say, undocumented migrants identifying as such, or other movements that are geared towards the claim for a general legalisation (Nicholls 2010; Robertson 2015). In other words, migrant groups may remain even more respectful of state sovereignty and the state's ensuing claim of protecting its borders and territory, and choosing those it allows to enter and stay, than groups that advocate for solidarity with everyone, including the right to free movement. Moreover, based on her work with Bulgarian migrants' associations in Turkey, Zeynep Kaşlı (2016) reminds

---

[1]   This part draws on the author's fieldwork in Morocco.

us that migrants' networks helping the newly arrived and undocumented migrants are not free from the power struggles and profit-making that exploits the vulnerability of those co-ethnics without access to accurate information and legal status.

The central paradox in humanitarian work that Ilana Feldman calls its endemic challenge; that is, the requirement to abstain from taking a political stance and to push 'to keep people alive but entirely incapable of changing the conditions that have put them at such great risk' (Feldman 2008, 139). This internalised requirement for being apolitical is more and more overtly challenged, even by organisations that have thus far kept relatively silent or, to say the least, have been more ambiguous in their critiques of state actions. One example could be the UNHCR's refusal to transport people to detention centres in the Aegean islands, explained by the Refugee Agency's unwillingness to be party to practices that breach international human rights commitments (UNHCR 2016b).

Well-intended humanitarian action and solidarity engagement includes difficult questions that need to be resolved in the course of action. Much critique has been written on the actions of international organisations (see for example Harrell-Bond 1985; Verdirame and Harrell-Bond 2005; Agier 2011), international non-governmental organisations (Terry 2002; Fassin 2011), and researchers as activists amongst other forms of participation (see for example Askins 2009; Darling 2014). Critical engagement is emerging also on and within social movement-types of responses to humanitarian crisis situations, even if this is again more difficult, knowing that the individuals in question invest their own time and money to alleviate the suffering of those considered 'beneficiaries' in the organisational jargon or 'friends' to highlight the shared humanity. All these responses embody divergent political stances with regards to the right to mobility and with regards to the takes on state action; that is, whether the role of the state is seen as something to be supported, or as something the very existence of which is to be put into question.

In 2015, in the midst of what has been labelled a refugee crisis, more people than before woke up to the catastrophic conditions at many border sites, and deficiencies in the official reception of the newly arrived. They felt compelled to do something concretely. Many engaged in solidarity groups in their own countries and neighbourhoods, whereas others travelled long distances to come and help in the most exposed sites where help was needed, such as the Aegean islands in Greece, at different 'hubs' along the so-called Balkan route, or in Calais on the shore of the English Channel. These acts of solidarity became highly visible in traditional and social media alike. Alongside celebrating the drive of people to contribute their time and skills for the sake of others in need, these movements have triggered many questions which are being answered in the midst of events. Some of these questions concern the need for organising the acts in the best possible way to respond to multiple needs. Drawing on his work with ad hoc volunteer groups and more established organisations in Rome, Nando Sigona gives the example of donations: 'it was all too easy to end up with millions of Xmas jumpers in a warehouse, when that positive energy should have been channelled else-where' (Sigona and Bechler 2016). Similar examples have been echoed throughout the peak months of 2015, and networks that organise collections seek to specify the needs in terms of sizes and kinds of clothes, shoes and other items to orientate those giving donations.

Other questions, in line with critical humanitarianism, concern the parallel phenomena created along the way, such as 'holidarity' and 'voluntourism' (see ReflActionist Collective 2016). This refers to the fashionable act of engaging in movements during one's vacations, and the different capabilities of differentially positioned people to engage in solidarity activities, especially further away from home. That is, the necessity to address the inherent and complex inequalities embedded in the system where some have the suitable identity documents, necessary financial means and flexibility with time schedules to engage in different types of solidarity acts, and others not. In the accelerating speed of political developments that in many ways has started to resemble a third world war, it may be difficult to take the distance needed to reflect upon and analyse the actions undertaken (see for example Coleman 2015). However, as much as this reflection could be integrated into the course of action, not as a paralysing idea but as something that would be helpful in making the practices more equitable, it is likely to benefit the solidarity movements' work in the long run.

Criminalising Solidarity

An important and worrying phenomenon is the harassment of solidarity actors and other activists in many contexts. In France, for example, solidarity actions have been sought to be criminalised for years under the pretext of fighting human smuggling, as 'facilitating irregular movement and stay' (Worldwide Movement for Human Rights (FIDH) and World Organisation Against Torture (OMCT) 2009; Euro-Mediterranean Human Rights Network (EMHRN) 2011, 14). Fear is a well-known way to control others (see for example Koskela 1997), and fear is a means by which governments that are unfriendly, even hostile to migrant causes and civil disobedience, seek to exert control over people willing and committed to this struggle. These authorities do it following a logic that is not quite so distant from violent factions that seek to challenge this authority, using these means to maintain an illusion of control (Brown

2010) in a global context that is beyond anyone's control.

The requirement for each person who comes to the Greek islands to help refugees to register (Secretariat General for the Aegean and Island Policy 2016) was introduced in order to have an idea of who actually came and worked with refugees. The continuing arrival of boatloads of people over the summer, autumn and winter months incited many people across the globe to engage with the plight of refugees. Some eighty non-governmental organisations arrived on the island of Lesbos, together with more informal groups and countless individuals for different periods of time (Nianias 2016). While each was willing to help, and their engagement and contribution valorised, the public authorities needed some organisation to these comings and goings. The registration process then introduced is to be done with municipal authorities, to get a global idea of who is present and engaging with people in a vulnerable position. This requirement was not fully innocent either. Early on, there were rumours about the border agency Frontex being involved in registering solidarity actors in the Greek islands.[2] An obvious question in this regard is what their involvement exactly is and why they are implicated? For what purpose are they involved in registering people who come to do voluntary work? Given the security-focused mandate of the agency, the purpose of likely intelligence-gathering. This rang the bell of criminalising solidarity, as has been the case in different locations, notably in Northern France where charges have been raised for years against those who consider it their moral duty to help others in need.

Concluding Words

Differentially positioned solidarity actors – associations, networks, individuals – are in a very problematic situation. Fundamental rights that were imagined as already shared values, at least by the state parties that have signed and ratified legally binding commitments such as the Convention of 1951 and its additional protocol at full, are put into question from different directions. Thus, commitments that have been imagined as givens, on the rhetorical level at least if not in practice, are being violated more and more openly. Moreover, solidarity actors need to ask themselves – indeed, we need to ask ourselves, as I feel implicated in this framework through my various academic and non-academic commitments – with whom do we solidarise and how do we express this in practice, in a volatile context where networks and movements are in a constant process of movement? These questions go beyond the impact analyses in the humanitarian and development industries' project logics. What moves us towards acting in solidarity and, consequently, what does this do to the various formations, temporary or more permanent ones,

---

2   Drawing on the author's exchanges with solidarity groups.

thus constituted? Also needed is alertness towards the impact of the solidarity acts in the lives of those towards whom these acts are geared. It is not a schematic understanding of impact in quantifiable terms we need, we must assess this question more broadly, accounting for the qualitative 'changes' or 'moves', however temporary and volatile they might be. Solidarity ties form and sometimes dissolve with new information and new urgencies. Not everyone can physically go and work for weeks or months in order to provide help where it is needed the most, be it for financial reasons, family commitments, emotional capacity or other reasons. For this reason we need to acknowledge these are not the only available ways to 'do something', to act in solidarity. Every encounter counts. Everyone is needed.

References

Agier, Michel. 2011. *Managing the Undesirables: Refugee Camps and Humanitarian Government*. Cambridge: Polity.

Al Jazeera. 2016. "Greece Refugee Crisis: Border Area at Breaking Point." 6 March 2016. http://www.aljazeera.com/news/2016/03/refugee-crisis-greek-governor-urges-state-emergency-160305130622083.html.

Amnesty International (AI). 2016. *Trapped in the EU's New Refugee Camp: Greece*. https://www.amnesty.org/en/latest/campaigns/2016/04/trapped-eu-new-refugee-camp-greece/.

Askins, Kye. 2009. "'That's Just What I Do': Placing Emotion in Academic Activism." *Emotion, Space and Society* 2: 4–13.

BBC. 2016. "Migrant Crisis: Hundreds Cross from Greece to Macedonia." 14 March 2016. http://www.bbc.com/news/world-europe-35805010.

Bredeloup, Sylvie. 2013. "Circumstantial Solidarities and the Transformation of Migratory Networks." *Journal of Intercultural Studies* 34: 517–32.

Cabrera, Luis and Sonya Glavac. 2010. "Minutemen and Desert Samaritans: Mapping the Attitudes of Activists on the United States' Immigration Front Lines." *Journal of Ethnic and Migration Studies* 36: 673–95.

Coleman, Lara Montesinos. 2015. "Ethnography, Commitment, and Critique: Departing from Activist Scholarship." *International Political Sociology* 9 (2015): 263–280.

Cox, Laurence. 2009. "'Hearts with one purpose alone'? Thinking personal sustainability in social movements." *Emotion, Space and Society* 2: 52–61.

Cuttitta, Paolo. 2014. "Borderizing the Island: Setting and Narratives of the Lampedusa Border Play." *ACME: An International E-Journal for Critical Geographies* 13: 196–219.

Darling, Jonathan. 2014. "Emotions, Encounters and Expectations: The Uncertain Ethics of 'The Field'. *Journal of Human Rights Practice* 6: 201–12.

Doty, Roxanne Lynn. 2006. "Fronteras Compasivas and the Ethics of Unconditional Hospitality." *Millennium* 35: 53–74.

Euro-Mediterranean Human Rights Network (EMHRN). 2011. *Calais, the Violence of the Border: Fact-finding Mission in Calais and Paris 25 January–2 February 2010*. https://euromedrights.org/wp-content/uploads/2018/03/Calais-the-violence-of-the-border-fact-finding-mission-EN.pdf

European Commission. n.d. *Schengen Area*. http://ec.europa.eu/home-affairs/what-we-do/policies/borders-and-visas/schengen_en.

Fassin, Didier. 2011. *Humanitarian Reason: A Moral History of the Present*. Berkeley: University of California Press.

Feldman, Ilana. 2008. "Difficult Distinctions: Refugee Law, Humanitarian Practice, and Political Identification in Gaza." *Cultural Anthropology* 22: 129–69.

Forensic Architecture. n.d. "The Left-to-Die Boat." Accessed 4 September 2016. http://www.forensic-architecture.org/case/left-die-boat/.

Friese, Heidrun. 2010. "The Limits of Hospitality: Political Philosophy, Undocumented Migration and the Local Arena." *European Journal of Social Theory* 13: 323–341.

Harrell-Bond, Barbara. 1985. *Imposing Aid. Emergency Assistance to Refugees*. Oxford: Oxford University Press.

International Organisation for Migration (IOM). 2017. *Missing Migrants Project*. https://missingmigrants.iom.int/mediterranean.

Kaşlı, Zeynep. 2016. "'Who Do Migrant Associations Represent? The Role of 'Ethnic Deservingness' and Legal Capital in Migrants' Rights Claims in Turkey." *Journal of Ethnic and Migration Studies*.

Koskela, Hille. 1997. 'Bold walk and breakings': Women's spatial confidence versus fear of violence." *Gender, Place and Culture* 4: 301–19.

Kynsilehto, Anitta. 2017. "Mobilities, Politics and Solidarities." *Peace Review: A Journal of Social Justice* 29: 48–54.

Laacher, Smaïn. 2002. *Après Sangatte…Nouvelles Immigrations, Nouveaux Enjeux*. Paris: La Dispute.

Lafazani, Olga. 2013. "A Border within a Border: The Migrants' Squatter Settlement in Patras as a Heterotopia." *Journal of Borderlands Studies* 28: 1–13.

Mountz, Alison. 2011. "The enforcement archipelago: Detention, haunting, and asylum on islands." *Political Geography* 30: 118–28.

Nianias, Helen. 2016. "Refugees in Lesbos: Are There Too Many NGOs on the Island?" *The Guardian*, 5 January 2016. https://www.theguardian.com/global-development-professionals-network/2016/jan/05/refugees-in-lesbos-are-there-too-many-ngos-on-the-island.

Nicholls, Walter J. 2011. "Fragmenting Citizenship: Dynamics of Cooperation and Conflict in France's Immigrant Rights Movement." *Ethnic and Racial Studies* 36: 611–31.

Pezzani, Lorenzo and Charles Heller. 2013. "A disobedient gaze: strategic interventions in the knowledge(s) of maritime borders." *Postcolonial Studies* 16: 289–98.

ReflActionist Collective. 2016. "Beyond Voluntourism and Holidarity? White German Activists on the 'Balkanroute' – (Self)Reflections." Blog post 18 June 2016. https://reflactionistcollective.noblogs.org/post/2016/06/18/beyond-voluntourism-and-holidarity/.

Reuters. 2016. "Greece Condemns Macedonia Tear Gas and Rubber Bullets Against Migrants." 10 April 2016. http://www.reuters.com/article/us-europe-migrants-greece-teargas-idUSKCN0X70CD.

Robertson, Shanthi. 2015. "Contractualization, Depoliticization and the Limits of Solidarity: Non-Citizens in Contemporary Australia." *Citizenship Studies* 19: 936–50.

Robinson, Fiona. 2011. "Stop Talking and Listen: Discourse Ethics and Feminist Care Ethics in International Political Theory." *Millennium: Journal of International Studies* 39: 845–860.

Rozakou, Katerina. 2016. "Socialities of Solidarity: Revisiting the Gift Taboo in Times of Crises." *Social Anthropology* 24 (2016): 185–199.

Rygiel, Kim. 2011. "Bordering Solidarities: Migrant Activism and the Politics of Movement and Camps in Calais." *Citizenship Studies* 15: 1–19.

Secretariat General for the Aegean and Island Policy. 2016. http://statewatch.org/news/2016/mar/greek-registering-all-volunteers-and-NGOs.pdf.

Sigona, Nando and Rosemary Bechler. 2016. "On 'Superdiversity' In a Crisis Mood." *OpenDemocracy*. 25 July 2016. https://www.opendemocracy.net/Can-europe-make-it/nando-sigona-rosemary-bechler/on-superdiversity-in-crisis-mood.

Squire, Vicki. 2014. "Desert 'trash': Posthumanism, Border Struggles, and Humanitarian Politics. *Political Geography* 39: 11–21.

Terry, Fiona. 2002. *Condemned to Repeat?: The Paradox of Humanitarian Action.* Ithaca: Cornell University Press.

Trubeta, Sevasti. 2015. "'Rights' in the Grey Area: Undocumented Border Crossers on Lesbos." *Race & Class* 56: 56–72.

UNHCR. 2016a. *Greece amid Disarray in Europe over Asylum.* Accessed 16 March 2017. http://www.unhcr.org/news/briefing/2016/3/56d564ed6/unhcr-warns-imminent-humanitarian-crisis-greece-amid-disarray-europe-asylum.html.

UNHCR. 2016b. *UNHCR Redefines Role in Greece as EU-Turkey Deal Comes into Effect.* Briefing Notes, 22 March 2016. Accessed 20 April 2016. http://www.unhcr.org/56f10d049.html.

Verdirame, Guglielmo and Barbara Harrell-Bond. 2005. *Rights in Exile: Janus-faced Humanitarianism.* Oxford: Berghahn.

Väyrynen, Tarja, Eeva Puumala, Samu Pehkonen, Anitta Kynsilehto and Tiina Vaittinen. 2016. *Choreographies of resistance: Mobile bodies and relational politics.* Lanham, MD, and London: Rowman & Littlefield.

Worldwide Movement for Human Rights (FIDH) and World Organisation Against Torture (OMCT). 2009. *Délit De Solidarité: Stigmatisation, Répression et Intimidation des Défenseurs des Droits des Migrants.* https://www.fidh.org/IMG/pdf/obsfra11062009.pdf.

Worldwide Movement for Human Rights (FIDH), Migreurop and Euro-Mediterranean Human Rights Network (EMHRN). 2014. *Frontex between Greece and Turkey: At the Border of Denial.* http://www.frontexit.org/en/docs/49-frontexbetween-greece-and-turkey-the-border-of-denial/file.

Yaghmaian, Behzad. 2006. *Embracing the Infidel: Stories of Muslim Migrants in their Journey West.* New York: Bantam Dell.

Zetter, Roger. 2015. *Protection in Crisis: Forced Migration and Protection in a Global Era.* Washington, D.C.: Migration Policy Institute.

12

Solidarity Beyond the State in Europe's Common European Asylum System

VALSAMIS MITSILEGAS

The increase in the flows of asylum seekers towards the European Union (EU) in recent years has re-awakened the discussion over the meaning, extent and limits of the principle of solidarity in European asylum law. In view of this politically sensitive and ongoing discussion, this contribution aims to assess the legal meaning of solidarity in the Common European Asylum System. I will attempt to demonstrate that the evolution and content of the principle of solidarity in both EU primary and secondary law is predominantly state-centred, with claims of solidarity being advanced primarily with states as reference points and as beneficiaries. I will aim to demonstrate the limits of this state-centred approach to solidarity, both in terms of ensuring effective protection of the rights of asylum seekers and refugees and in terms of achieving an efficient and well-functioning European asylum system. I will advocate in this contribution a paradigm change: moving from a concept of state-centred solidarity to a concept of solidarity centred on the individual. I will demonstrate how the application of the principle of mutual recognition in the field of positive asylum decisions can play a key part in achieving this paradigm change. I will argue in particular that positive mutual recognition – if accompanied by full equality and access to the labour market for refugees across the European Union – is key towards addressing the lack of effectiveness in the current system. I will end this contribution by looking boldly to the future, and exploring how refugee-centred solidarity can be achieved by moving from a system of inter-state cooperation based on national asylum determination to a common, EU asylum procedure and status.

State-Centred Solidarity in European Asylum Law – A Constitutional Perspective

An examination of European constitutional law reveals a concept of asylum solidarity, which is state-centred, securitised and exclusionary (Mitsilegas 2014). This view of solidarity has been prominent in the debates on allocation of responsibility for asylum seekers across the EU way before the entry into force of the Lisbon Treaty, with the use of the term 'burden' to describe increased pressures imposed upon the state – with asylum seekers thus vie-wed implicitly as a burden to national systems. Solidarity here thus takes the form of what has been deemed and analysed as 'burden-sharing' (Betts 2003; Boswell 2003; Noll 2003; Thielemann 2003a and 2003b) and in particular from a legal perspective, the sharing of the responsibility for increased flows of asylum seekers. The logic of burden-sharing in effect securitises asylum flows by viewing asylum seekers and asylum-seeking in a negative light (Noll 2003). While the term 'burden-sharing' does not appear in EU constitutional law, one could argue that it has been replaced in the Treaties of the European Union[1] by a state-centred, securitised and exclusionary concept of solidarity. The emphasis on the interests of the state is confirmed by the provisions of the Lisbon Treaty on solidarity in the Area of Freedom, Security and Justice. According to Article 67(2) of the Treaty on the Functioning of the European Union (TFEU), the Union shall ensure the absence of internal border controls for persons and shall frame a common policy on asylum, immigration and external border control, based on solidarity *between Member States*, which is fair towards 'third country' nationals.

Article 80 TFEU further states that the policies of the Union on borders, asylum and immigration will be governed by the principle of solidarity and fair sharing of responsibility, including its financial implications, *between the Member States.* Solidarity is also securitised: as with other areas of European Union law, solidarity in European asylum law reflects a crisis mentality (Borgmann-Prebil and Ross 2010) and has led to the concept being used with the aim of alleviating perceived urgent pressures on Member States. This view of solidarity as an emergency management tool is found elsewhere in the Treaty, in the solidarity clause established in Article 222 according to which the Union and its Member States shall act jointly in a spirit of solidarity if a Member State is the object of a terrorist attack or the victim of a natural or man-made disaster. The concept of solidarity here echoes the political construction of solidarity in European asylum law, in responding to perceived urgent threats. It is framed in a way of protecting the state and requires cooperation not between the state and the individual but between the state

---

[1]   The Treaty on European Union and the Treaty on the Functioning of the European Union.

and the European Union. State-centred securitised solidarity in the field of asylum echoes Ross's assertion that the political power of security can attempt to appropriate solidarity for its own ends (Ross 2010, 39). This view is confirmed by the growing trend towards the securitsation of migration and asylum in EU law and policy (Guild 2009; Mitsilegas 2012a).

Placed within a state-centric and securitised framework, solidarity is also exclusionary. The way in which the concept of solidarity has been theorised and presented in EU constitutional law leaves little, if any space for the application of the principle of solidarity beyond EU citizens or those 'within' the EU and its extension to 'third country' nationals or those on the outside. In a recent thought-provoking analysis on solidarity in EU law, Sangiovanni argues for the development of principles on national solidarity (which define obligations among citizens and residents of Member States), principles of Member State solidarity (which define obligations among Member States) and principles of transnational solidarity (which define obligations among EU citizens as such) (Sangiovanni 2013, 217). 'Third country' nationals are notably absent from this model of solidarity. This exclusionary approach to solidarity appears to be confirmed by the Treaties, with the Preamble to the Treaty on European Union (TEU) expressing the desire of the signatory states 'to deepen the solidarity *between their peoples* while respecting their history, their culture and their traditions' (Preamble, recital 6, emphasis added).

Solidarity functions thus as a key principle of European identity which is addressed to EU Member States and their 'peoples' (see also Art. 167, TFEU on Culture), but the extent to which such European identity based on solidarity also encompasses 'third country' nationals is far from clear (Mitsilegas 1998). This ambiguity remains after the entry into force of the Lisbon Treaty. One of the few provisions of the TEU which may be seen as leaving the door open to a more human-centred concept of solidarity, is Article 2 on the values of the European Union, which states that these values are common to the Member States *in a society in which...solidarity... [must] prevail*. The inclusion of asylum seekers and refugees in this concept of solidarity is unclear. Although asylum law is centred on assessing the protection needs of 'third country' nationals, and in this capacity they must constitute the primary 'recipients' of solidarity in European asylum law, the application of the principle of solidarity in this field appears thus to follow the exclusionary paradigm of solidarity in other fields of EU law where issues of distributive justice arise prominently. Writing on the position of EU social welfare law concerning irregular migrants, Bell has eloquently noted that 'third country' nationals lack the ties of shared citizenship, whilst the extension of social and economic entitlements to them cannot easily be based on a reciprocal view of solidarity (Bell 2010, 151). Asylum seekers seem to be included in a continuum of exclusionary solidarity in this context.

Dublin as the Embodiment of State-Centred Solidarity: The Failure of Negative Mutual Recognition

In order to understand the issues arising from the discussion regarding solidarity in the context of the allocation of asylum seekers and refugees across the European Union, it is essential to point out that the Common European Asylum System currently in place is based on the development and interaction of national asylum systems. The European Union has not developed a unified EU-wide asylum procedure and refugee status. While a key element of the evolution of the European Union into an Area of Freedom, Security and Justice has been the abolition of internal borders between Member States and the creation thus of a single European area where freedom of movement is secured, this single area of movement has not been accompanied by a single area of law. Already in 1999, the European Council Tampere Conclusions stated that 'in the longer term, Community rules should lead to a common asylum procedure and a uniform status for those who are granted asylum throughout the Union.' (European Council Tampere Conclusions, para. 15). While there has been ongoing harmonisation of national rules on asylum procedure, reception conditions and refugee qualifications since Tampere, more than 15 years after this statement, asylum applications in the EU are still examined by individual Member States following a *national* asylum procedure and leading to a national refugee status and ensuing rights. In this context, governance of asylum flows within the European Union and allocation of responsibility for asylum seekers and refugees has been designed within a system of interaction between national legal systems rather than under a system of centralized allocation in a single area. A key mechanism of governance of asylum flows within the European Union has been the application of the principle of mutual recognition in European asylum law.

Mutual recognition creates extraterritoriality (Nicolaidis 2007) and pre-supposes mutual trust (Mitsilegas 2006): in a borderless Area of Freedom, Security and Justice, mutual recognition is designed so that the decision of an authority in one Member State can be enforced beyond its territorial legal borders and across this area speedily and with a minimum of formality. As with other areas of EU law, most notably EU criminal law, in the field of EU asylum law automaticity in the transfer of asylum seekers from one Member State to another is thus justified on the basis of a high level of mutual trust. This high level of mutual trust between the authorities that take part in the system is premised upon the presumption that fundamental rights are respected fully by all EU Member States across the European Union

(Mitsilegas 2009 and 2012b). The presumption of mutual trust is inextricably linked with automaticity in inter-state cooperation. Automaticity in inter-state cooperation means that a *national* decision will be enforced beyond the territory of the issuing Member State by authorities in other EU Member States across the Area of Freedom, Security and Justice without many questions being asked and with the requested authority having at its disposal extremely limited – if any at all – grounds to refuse the request for cooperation.

In the field of EU asylum law, mutual recognition based on automaticity and trust has been introduced by the Dublin Regulation, which sets out a system of automatic inter-state cooperation which has been characterised as a system of negative mutual recognition (Guild 2004). Recognition can be viewed as negative here in that the occurrence of one of the Dublin criteria creates a duty for one Member State to take charge of an asylum seeker and thus recognise the refusal of another Member State (which transfers the asylum seeker in question) to examine the asylum claim. The Dublin Regulation thus introduces a high degree of automaticity in inter-state cooperation. Member States are obliged to take charge of asylum seekers if the Dublin criteria – including notably the criterion of irregular entry via one of the EU Member States – are established to apply, with, at least initially, only limited exceptions (Mitsilegas 2014). In this system of inter-state cooperation based on automaticity and trust, there is little place for the individual situation and rights of asylum seekers to be taken into account. Transfers take place speedily and almost automatically, on the presumption that the receiving state will provide an equivalent human rights protection to asylum seekers as the sending state. Mutual recognition in Dublin thus reflects a model of state-centred, securitised and exclusionary solidarity: Dublin has been designed predominantly with the interests of [certain] states in mind, and is a system that aims to deflect undesirable asylum seekers from Member States' territory.

The Dublin model of automatic mutual recognition has been challenged by the judiciary. Following the finding by the European Court of Human Rights in *M.S.S.* that both the sending and the receiving Member State (in that case Belgium and Greece respectively) were in breach of the European Convention on Human Rights (ECHR) in their implementation of the Dublin system regarding a specific transfer (*M.S.S. v. Belgium and Greece*, judgment of 21 January 2011, Application No. 30696/09), the Court of Justice of the European Union in the cases of *N.S.* and *M.E.* (Joined Cases C411/10 and C493/10) set limits to automaticity in EU law. It did so by finding that an application of the Dublin Regulation on the basis of the conclusive presumption that the asylum seeker's fundamental rights will be observed in the Member State primarily responsible for his application is incompatible with the duty of the Member States to interpret and apply the Regulation in a manner consistent with fundamental rights (para. 99). Such presumption is rebuttable (para. 104). The Court's rejection of the conclusive presumption that Member States will respect the fundamental rights of asylum seekers has been accompanied by the establishment of a high threshold of incompatibility with fundamental rights (Mitsilegas 2012b). A transfer under the Dublin Regulation would be incompatible with fundamental rights if there are substantial grounds for believing that there are systemic flaws in the asylum procedure and reception conditions for asylum applicants in the Member State responsible. This is the case if it results in inhuman or degrading treatment (within the meaning of Article 4 of the Charter on the prohibition of torture and inhuman or degrading treatment or punishment) of asylum seekers transferred to the territory of that Member State (para. 85).

The EU legislator has attempted to incorporate the Court's ruling in the re-casting of the Dublin system in the so-called Dublin III Regulation, adopted in 2013 and currently in force (EU Regulation No. 604/2013 OJ L180/31; for a commentary, see Maiani 2016a). According to Article 3(2) of the Regulation, second and third indent,

> Where it is impossible to transfer an applicant to the Member State primarily designated as responsible because there are substantial grounds for believing that there are systemic flaws in the asylum procedure and in the reception conditions for applicants in the Member State, resulting in a risk of inhuman or degrading treatment within the meaning of Article 4 of the Charter of Fundamental Rights of the European Union, the determining Member State shall continue to examine the criteria set out in Chapter III in order to establish whether another Member State can be designed as responsible.

Where the transfer cannot be made pursuant to this paragraph to any Member State designated on the basis of the criteria set out in Chapter III or to the first Member State with which the application was lodged, the determining Member State shall become the Member State responsible.

Notwithstanding these developments, Dublin III has maintained essentially a state-centred model of solidarity. The Regulation maintains the system of allocation of responsibility for the examination of asylum applications by EU Member States under the same list of hierarchically enumerated criteria set out in its pre-Lisbon predecessor (see Chapter III of the Regulation, Arts. 7–15). Moreover, the Regulation attempts to translate a version of the principle of solidarity into legal terms. Article 33 of the Regulation introduces a so-called mechanism for early warning, preparedness and crisis management in cases where the Commission establishes that the application of the Dublin Regulation may be jeopardised due to either a substantiated risk of particular pressure being placed on a Member States' asylum system and/or to problems in the functioning of the asylum system of a Member State. In these cases the Commission would invite affected Member States to draw up a preventive action plan, without states being bound by the Commission's request (Art. 33(1)). The early warning mechanism established by the Dublin III Regulation is considerably weaker than an earlier Commission version. Under this version this mechanism would be accompanied by an emergency mechanism which would allow the temporary suspension of transfers of asylum seekers to Member States facing disproportionate pressure to their asylum systems. This has not been accepted by Member States (Conclusions of the Justice and Home Affairs Council of 22 September 2011, Council document 14464/11, 8).

The outcome has been a mechanism that again views the asylum process largely from the perspective of the state and not of the affected individuals. The Preamble to Dublin III confirms this view by stating that an early warning process should be established in order to ensure robust cooperation within the framework of this Regulation and to develop mutual trust among Member States with respect to asylum policy. It is further claimed that solidarity, which is a pivotal element in the Common European Asylum System, goes hand in hand with mutual trust and that early warning will enhance trust (Preamble, recital 22). Solidarity and trust are viewed in reality from a traditional 'burden-sharing' perspective involving negotiation of support by the Union to affected Member States (and with the European Asylum Support Office emerging as a key player). Notwithstanding the case-law of the European courts and the findings of United Nations High Commissioner for Refugees (UNHCR) and civil society, the position of the asylum seeker appears to still be considered as an afterthought (Mitsilegas 2014).

Towards a Paradigm Change: Mutual Recognition of Positive Asylum Decisions as Refugee-Centred Solidarity

A way in which the current conceptual and human rights limits of solidarity in the Common European Asylum System can be transcended is to think differently about the application of the mutual recognition principle and focus on the establishment of a system of mutual recognition of positive asylum decisions, which will then carry with them the rights granted to refugees at the national level throughout the European Union. I have advocated the application of the principle of mutual recognition of positive asylum decisions in a Report I prepared for the Open Society Foundation in 2014 (Mitsilegas 2014b), which I presented at the Italian Presidency of the Council of the EU conference on asylum in November 2014 (for the main findings,see Mitsilegas 2015a). My proposal for adopting a model of mutual recognition of positive asylum decisions has since been endorsed by the Council of Europe Parliamentary Assembly (Council of Europe 2015) and reflected in a recent study prepared for the European Parliament Civil Liberties Committee (Guild et al. 2015). I have argued that the application of mutual recognition, in order to achieve the extraterritorial reach of rights, has already been applied in the European criminal justice area by Directive 2011/99/EU of the European Parliament and of the Council of 13 December 2011 on the European Protection Order (OJ L338, 2). The Directive, which was adopted under a legal basis related to judicial cooperation in criminal matters, aims to apply the principle of mutual recognition in criminal matters to orders issued to protect victims in one Member State when these victims find themselves in other EU Member States. In other words, it is aimed that the recognition of a European Protection Order by the authority in the executing Member State will mean that the protection will 'follow' the victim to the Member State they have moved to. (Mitsilegas 2015b and 2016a).

I have argued that the application of the principle of mutual recognition on decisions granting rights to individuals can be applied in the Common European Asylum System (CEAS). The application of the principle of mutual recognition of positive asylum decisions provides five distinct and clear benefits:

1. It will create legal certainty regarding the status and rights of refugees throughout the EU in an AFSJ without internal frontiers.
2. It is consistent with the Treaty aim of establishing a CEAS and a uniform status (TFEU, Art. 78).
3. The necessary harmonisation, which is necessary for the effective operation of mutual recognition, exists at EU level, with the adoption of the second generation CEAS instruments post-Lisbon. There is a need to focus on the implementation of and compliance with these instruments across the EU.
4. Mutual recognition of positive asylum decisions is a corollary to developments examining possibilities for the pooling of reception conditions and join processing of asylum claims. Pooling of reception and procedure must be combined with the pooling of protection. Joint efforts in procedures and reception before the granting of refugee status will create joint ownership and mutual trust which will facilitate the subsequent recognition of positive asylum decisions across the EU.
5. Mutual recognition of positive asylum decisions focuses the discussion on solidarity specifically on the needs and rights of the refugee.

But how can the principle be applied? There are three factors, which must be considered when examining the precise conditions and modalities for the application of the principle of mutual recognition to positive asylum decisions:

1. *Time.* From when will mutual recognition take effect? One option is for mutual recognition to kick in from day one, namely from the date of the judicial decision granting refugee status. This is the preferable option and it could be based on a model granting equal treatment to refugees with citizens of the Union (see also Bast 2016). Another option may be for mutual recognition to take effect after two years of continuous residence in the state that has granted protection in line with the time limits established by the European Agreement of Transfer of Responsibility (see also, with further conditions, Meijers Committee 2015). A third option may be a hybrid model where movement to the second Member State happens immediately but equal treatment with long-term resident 'third country' nationals is granted from day one, whereas equal treatment with nationals of the second state is granted after two years.
2. *Rights.* For mutual recognition to be meaningful, the recognition of status should be accompanied by the recognition of rights. The protection and rights the refugee is granted in the first Member State should follow her in the second Member State. There are different moments in time when this can happen (see no. 1. above).
3. *Quotas.* A possible way forward is to combine mutual recognition with the allocation of responsibility between Member States on the basis of quotas. However, this option faces two challenges: it may disregard the particular situation and wishes of refugees (e.g. in the context of family reunification); and it is difficult to enforce in a Union without internal frontiers.

The application of the principle of mutual recognition of positive asylum decisions was floated by the European Commission some years ago, but the idea seems to have been buried since. Already in 2009, the European Commission, in its Communication on *An Area of Freedom, Security and Justice Serving the Citizen* stated that '[a]s part of a detailed evaluation on the transposal and implementation of second-phase legislative instruments and of progress in aligning practices and supporting measures…by the end of 2014, the EU should formally enshrine the principle of mutual recognition of all individual decisions granting protection status taken by authorities ruling on asylum applications which will mean that protection can be transferred without the adoption of specific mechanisms at the European level' (European Commission (COM) 2009, 262 final, 27–28). In its Communication informing the follow-up to the Stockholm Programme, the Commission noted that relocation of the beneficiaries of international protection, which has been piloted in recent years from Malta, is one form of solidarity that should be enhanced. It further stated that,

> New rules on the mutual recognition of asylum decisions across Member States and a framework for the transfer of protection should be developed in line with the Treaty objective of creating a uniform status valid across the EU. This would reduce obstacles to movement within the EU and facilitate the transfer of protection-related benefits across internal borders (COM 2014, 154 final, 8).

While the principle of mutual recognition has been used thus far in Europe's Area of Freedom, Security and Justice in order to increase and extend the powers of the state, its potential for enhancing fundamental rights and the rights of beneficiaries of international protection is significant. The application of the principle of mutual recognition vis-à-vis positive asylum decisions would help ensure progress towards the policy and Treaty objectives of building a Common European Asylum System including a uniform status, and would be a logical next step in a system that aims at eliminating differences in protection between Member States. Mutual recognition will further focus technical and political efforts upon eliminating the considerable discrepancies regarding asylum determination outcomes in Member States and may help address some of the solidarity-related concerns raised by certain EU Member States. It would, however, need to be designed in a way that would ensure that all Member States would be encouraged to establish and maintain their asylum systems at optimal levels, in order to provide protection beneficiaries with the opportunity to enjoy their rights in the first state that has recognised them.

By focusing on the extraterritorial application and reach of the rights of beneficiaries of international protection, mutual recognition of positive asylum decisions could be seen as an important step towards intra-EU mobility in line with one of the key underlying principles of the EU, providing more flexibility to enable protection holders to use their skills and labour where these could be needed within the Union. It would also ensure legal certainty for both Member States and recipients of international protection vis-a-vis the position of the latter in the borderless Area of Freedom, Security and Justice. It may also act as a first step towards the establishment of a meaningful uniform status for refugees across the European Union, by leading to a centralised EU system of asylum determination and relocation, and by focusing on rights and granting legal certainty in the field – the current failure of the modest EU relocation initiatives. The move to the mutual recognition of positive asylum decisions and ultimately to a uniform status poses fewer challenges than integration on these terms in the field of criminal justice, as European asylum law is marked by a high degree of harmonisation underpinned by a series of detailed human rights standards in European Union and international law (Mitsilegas 2016b). A positive model of mutual recognition would thus empower refugees, and contribute to a paradigm shift from state-centred solidarity towards a model of solidarity centred on the individual.

From Mutual Recognition to Unification: Towards a Uniform Refugee Status in the EU

The application of the principle of mutual recognition to positive asylum decisions pre-supposes the continuation of the current model of the Common European Asylum System, which is based on the interaction of national asylum systems and the existence of national asylum determination procedures. A bold way forward to strengthen refugee-centred solidarity would be to contemplate a move from national to EU asylum determination and refugee status. This idea has been discussed recently and included in the Commission Communication on the reform of the Common European Asylum System published in 2016 (COM 2016, 197 final). One of the options put forward by the Commission was the setting up in the longer term of a new system transferring responsibility for the processing of asylum claims from the national to the EU level. For instance, by transforming European Asylum Support Office (EASO) into an EU-level first-instance decision-making agency with national branches in each Member State, and establishing an EU-level appeal structure (COM 2016, 197 final, 8–9). As seen above in the discussion of Dublin III, this proposal has not been taken forward.

However, the European Union has started examining distributive models – albeit with limited political will by Member States and under a model of solidarity heavily centred on the needs of states, both in its relocation initiatives and in Dublin III. These measures constitute timid but first steps towards rethinking the distribution of asylum seekers and refugees across the European Union. A centralised, EU-wide system is feasible in view of the high level of harmonisation of asylum law in the EU and the international protection roots and needs inherent in the system. Such a centralised system has the potential to achieve the aim of a uniform refugee status across the EU and it can act as a catalyst for the transformation of solidarity under the essential condition that it places the agency and preferences of asylum seekers at its heart.

Conclusion

The development of Europe's Common Asylum System has been based on a concept of solidarity which is predominantly state-centred. This approach has not served EU Member States, or applicants for international protection, well. The Dublin Regulation – notwithstanding its regular revisions – is a highly inefficient mechanism of allocation of responsibility for asylum applications and it poses significant challenges to the rights of asylum seekers without ensuring a high level of compliance with EU asylum law by Member States. The recent revision of the Dublin system by the Commission remains grounded on a state-centred model of solidarity, and therefore it is predicted that it – like its predecessors – will fail if the agency and rights of asylum seekers continue not to be taken into account. This contribution has argued that the way forward to ensure an efficient and rights-compliant asylum system in the European Union is to achieve a paradigm change and move from a concept of solidarity centred on the state to a concept of solidarity centred on the refugee.

This paradigm change can be achieved in two ways. In the short term, by applying the principle of mutual recognition to positive asylum decisions. The contribution has highlighted precedents in the field of criminal justice and has demonstrated the potential that positive mutual recognition has in order to bring the rights and preferences of refugees into the fore. In the longer term, a unified, truly common, European asylum system which will move from national to EU determination and status can be the way forward in reversing the paradigm of solidarity. This paradigm change can only happen if the asylum seeker and the refugee, their agency and choice, are taken into account fully in the development of European asylum law.

References

Bast, Jürgen. 2016. "Deepening Supranational Integration: Interstate Solidarity in EU Migration Law", *European Public Law* 22, no. 2: 289–304.

Bell, Mark. 2010. "Irregular Migrants: Beyond the Limits of Solidarity?." In *Promoting Solidarity in the European Union* edited by Malcolm Ross and Yuri Borgmann-Prebil, 151 – 165. Oxford University Press.

Betts, Alexander. 2003. "Public Goods Theory and the Provision of Refugee Protection: The Role of the Joint-Product Model in Burden-Sharing Theory." *Journal of Refugee Studies* 16: 274–296.

Blake, Nicholas. 2001. "The Dublin Convention and Rights of Asylum Seekers in the European Union." In *Implementing Amsterdam* edited by Elspeth Guild and Carol Harlow, 95–115. Hart Publishing.

Borgmann-Prebil Yuri and Malcom Ross. 2010. "Promoting European Solidarity: Between Rhetoric or Reality?." In *Promoting Solidarity in the European Union* edited by Malcolm Ross and Yuri Borgmann-Prebil, 1–22. Oxford University Press

Boswell, Christina. 2003. "Burden-Sharing in the European Union. Lessons from the German and the UK Experience." *Journal of Refugee Studies* 16: 316–335.

Council of Europe, Parliamentary Assembly. 2015. *After Dublin - the urgent need for a real European asylum system,* Report by Committee on Migration, Refugees and Displaced Persons, doc. 13866, 10 September (rapporteur: Michele Nicoletti).

European Commission (COM). 2009. 262: "Communication from the Commission to the European Parliament and the Council - An area of freedom, security and justice serving the citizen."

European Commission (COM). 2014. 154: "Communication from the Commission to the European Parliament, the Council, the European Economic and Social Committee and the Committee of the regions - An open and secure Europe: making it happen."

European Commission (COM). 2016. 197: "Communication from the Commission to the European Parliament and the Council towards a reform of the common European asylum system and enhancing legal avenues to Europe."

Guild, Elspeth. 2004. "Seeking Asylum: Storm Clouds between International Commitments and EU Legislative Measures." *European Law Review* 29: 198–218.

Guild, Elspeth. 2009. *Migration and Security in the 21st Century*. Cambridge: Polity Press.

Guild, Elspeth, Cathryn Costello, Madeline Garlick and Violeta Moreno-Lax. 2015. *Enhancing the Common European Asylum System and Alternatives to Dublin,* Study for the European Parliament LIBE Committee, July (PE 519.234).

Maiani, Francesco. 2016a. "The Dublin III Regulation: A New Legal Framework for a More Humane System?." In *Reforming the Common*

European Asylum System: The New European Refugee Law edited by Vincent Chetail, Philippe de Bruycker and Francesco Maiani, 101–142. Brill.

Maiani, Francesco. 2106b. *The Reform of the Dublin III Regulation*, Study for the European Parliament LIBE Committee, June.

Meijers Committee. 2015. *Promoting Intra EU Labour Mobility of International Protection Beneficiaries,* CM1511, 18 June.

Mitsilegas, Valsamis. 2016a. *EU Criminal Law After Lisbon: Rights, Trust and the Transformation of Justice in Europe.* Hart.

Mitsilegas, Valsamis. 2016b. *Justice and Trust in the European Legal Order: The Copernicus Lectures*. University of Ferrara and Jovene Editore.

Mitsilegas, Valsamis. 2015a. *Mutual Recognition of Positive Asylum Decisions in the European Union*. FREE Group website, 12 May.

Mitsilegas, Valsamis. 2015b. "The Place of the Victim in Europe's Area of Criminal Justice." In *Protecting Vulnerable Groups* edited by Francesca Ippolito and Sara Iglesias Sanchez, 313–338. Hart.

Mitsilegas, Valsamis. 2014a. "Solidarity and Trust in the Common European Asylum System." *Comparative Migration Studies* 2: 231–253.

Mitsilegas, Valsamis. 2014b. *Mutual Recognition of Positive Asylum Decisions,* Report for the Open Society Foundation, November.

Mitsilegas, Valsamis. 2012a. "Immigration Control in an Era of Globalisation: Deflecting Foreigners, Weakening Citizens, Strengthening the State." *Indiana Journal of Global Legal Studies* 19: 3–60.

Mitsilegas, Valsamis. 2012b. "The Limits of Mutual Trust in Europe's Area of Freedom, Security and Justice: From Automatic Inter-state Cooperation to the Slow Emergence of the Individual." *Yearbook of European Law* 31: 319–372.

Mitsilegas, Valsamis. 2009. *EU Criminal Law*. Oxford/Portland: Hart.

Mitsilegas, Valsamis. 2006. The Constitutional Implications of Mutual Recognition in Criminal Matters in the EU. *Common Market Law Review* 43: 1277–1311.

Mitsilegas, Valsamis. 1998. "Culture in the Evolution of European Law: Panacea in the Quest for Identity?" In *Europe's Other: European Law between Modernity and Postmodernit*y edited by Peter Fitzpatrick and James Henry Bergeron, 111–129. Ashgate-Dartmouth.

Nicolaidis, Kalypso. 2007. "Trusting the Poles? Constructing Europe through Mutual Recognition." *Journal of European Public Policy* 14: 682–698.

Nicolosi, Salvatore Fabio. 2016. "Emerging Challenges of the Temporary Relocation Measures under European Union Asylum Law." In *European Law Review* 41, no. 3: 338 – 361.

Noll, Gregor. 2003. "Risky Games? A Theoretical Approach to Burden-Sharing in the Asylum Field." *Journal of Refugee Studies* 16: 236–252.

Ross, Malcolm. 2010. "Solidarity – A New Constitutional Paradigm for the EU?." In *Promoting Solidarity in the European Union* edited by Malcolm Ross and Yuri Borgmann-Prebil, 23–45. Oxford University Press.

Sangiovanni, Andrea. 2013. "Solidarity in the European Union." *Oxford Journal of Legal Studies* 33: 213–241.

Thielemann, Eiko. 2003a. "Editorial Introduction." *Journal of Refugee Studies* 16: 225–235.

Thielemann, Eiko. 2003b. "Between Interests and Norms: Explaining Burden-Sharing in the European Union." *Journal of Refugee Studies* 16: 253–273.

13

European Union Migration Law and Policy

BENJAMIN HULME & DORA KOSTAKOPOULOU

The creation and implementation of an area free of internal borders is reliant upon three foundations. First, the effective management of the now single European Union (EU) external border and its ability to withstand substantial external pressures fuelled by political instability and conflict in the EU's near neighbourhood. Second, a high degree of solidarity between the Member States, to ensure that those states primarily in the southern Mediterranean receive adequate support to protect their borders. Finally, the creation of a common EU migration and asylum policy, including a distribution mechanism, to ensure that migrants and refugees who enter through the external border receive the same standard of treatment across all the Member States. The recent 'migration crisis', although now abating to a degree, has placed substantial pressure on these foundations, and has necessitated the rapid creation of new EU policies in order to manage the current situation and also prepare for any future large-scale migratory movements. This chapter will first examine a number of the broader historical developments and the lenses through which the EU's migration policy has developed. The focus will then turn to a number of the more recent policy developments, from the creation of a new European Coast Guard to new forms of 'third country' agreements. It will be argued that although these developments are a shift in the right direction, there are still a number of concerns which affect the core of such developments.

The European Union's Area of Freedom, Security and Justice (AFSJ) – formerly known as Justice and Home Affairs Co-operation – has evolved in surprising ways. Its origins lie in the so-called third pillar of the Treaty on European Union (TEU) (in force on 1 November 1993) which was partially communitarised by the Treaty of Amsterdam (in force on 1 May 1999). The new Title IV EC contained provisions on migration, asylum, 'third country' nationals and civic law matters while criminal law matters and police cooperation remained in the third pillar. The latter became part of Community law a decade later when the Lisbon Treaty entered into force on 1 December 2009.

Although the Member States were initially reluctant to 'lose' sovereignty, they realised the importance of cooperation and mutual trust in dealing with transnational issues, such as policing, judicial cooperation in criminal law and migration and asylum policy. But their cooperation was premised on a security paradigm. Organised crime, migration and terrorism were placed on a single security continuum (Bigo 1992) since they were deemed to pose security threats. Therefore, the distinction between these areas was blurred, and required the creation of policies which could encapsulate these previously distinct concerns. Institutional factors, such as the intergovernmental character of the third pillar cooperation and the removal of internal frontiers in the European Union were partly responsible for the prevalence of the security paradigm (Kostakopoulou 1998 and 2001; Geddes 2001). Official discourses in the Member States depicting migration as a threat also played an important role.

Freedom and security became closely aligned following the 9/11 attacks and the Hague Programme, which was agreed upon by the Council in November 2004, and had a strong restrictive and security-based focus. But its successor, the Stockholm Programme (Council of the European Union 2010b) was more 'citizen-oriented' and liberal. In anticipating it, the Commission issued a Communication in 2009 that called for 'a dynamic and comprehensive migration policy which consolidates a global approach to migration' (European Commission 2009, 23–4). The latter was anchored on developing the external dimension of EU migration policy, the promotion of cooperation and dialogue with third countries and the development of an innovative and coherent framework (European Commission 2009, 23–4). An important aspect of the institutional framework was the drafting of an Immigration Code that would incorporate the existing sectoral directives and provide a uniform level of rights. The Commission's and the Stockholm Programme's vision of a 'dynamic and fair migration policy' in the twenty-first century was interrupted by the economic crisis in the Euro-zone, the rise of Eurosceptic and neo-nationalist political parties in Europe and a sudden increase in the number of migrants and refugees seeking admission. According to the Annual Report on Asylum produced by the European Asylum Support Office (2015, 13), more than 660,000 refugees sought protection in the EU in 2014. The war in Syria led to an unprecedented exodus of people and provided a catalyst for wide-ranging reforms and measures in the Area of Freedom, Security and Justice.

The European Union's actions in this field have taken place within the overarching framework of the European Agenda on Migration, which was introduced in May 2015 (European Commission 2015b). The Agenda included both immediate measures and medium-long term measures in order to allow the EU to transition from gaining an effective handle on the migration situation to, in the medium-long term, tackling the root causes and wider issues which are contributing to or causing the movement of so many individuals to the territories of the Member States. The European Commission proposed six different areas in which immediate measures were required, with three of these areas being at the external border or incorporating external dimensions (European Commission 2015b, 3–6). The first set of measures to be introduced immediately are focused on saving lives at sea, including an increase in the number of search and rescue operations in the Mediterranean and a tripling of the budgets for Frontex's Triton and Poseidon joint operations. The second set included measures to combat illegal smuggling into the Member States, including cooperation between Frontex and Europol in order to identify and apprehend smugglers. Third, the EU sought to strengthen its cooperation with third countries of origin and transit, in order to 'intervene upstream' and tackle the 'root causes' of the migration at their source, thereby preventing the need for individuals to migrate. Such measures included regional development and protection programmes to provide support to states with high refugee populations. It is interesting to note that the Commission proposed a linkage between these migration measures and the Union's Common Security and Development Policy (European Commission 2015b, 5), which is emblematic of the increasing blurriness between migration and security in EU policy. It has been argued that such 'blurring' weakens the human rights afforded to those individuals seeking protection in the EU (Amnesty International 2014, 20–25). Such blurring affects the mind-set of Member State governments, as they perceive an increased need to detain migrants, limit access to initial legal advice and ultimately infringe upon basic human dignity by treating all migrants with a heightened degree of suspicion and scrutiny.

In the medium term, the Agenda on Migration was separated into four pillars in order to effectively manage migration, with measures involving either the strengthening of the external borders or cooperation with third countries (European Commission 2015b, 6–17). Measures under the external borders included the strengthening of Frontex (the European Agency for the Management of Operational Cooperation at the External Borders), particularly in light of the need for solidarity between Member States. Concerning the external dimension of the European Union Migration Policy, the Commission highlighted the need to address the root causes of irregular migration. It recognised that the cooperation of countries of origin and of transit would be necessary in order to combat people-smuggling and in order for such states to allow the EU to carry out the effective return of individuals who had no legal right to reside in the territory of the Union. As with many areas of the Common European Asylum System and the Area of Freedom, Security and Justice, more harmonisation would be required in order to make the policies more effective.

Continuing this vein of harmonisation, the EU has sought to establish a European Border and Coast Guard (European Commission 2015a), which received approval from the European Parliament in July 2016 (Council of the European Union 2016a). The new border and coast guard has been created 'in order to ensure a European integrated border management of the EU's external borders, with a view to managing migration effectively and ensuring a high level of security within the Union, while safeguarding the free movement of persons therein' (European Commission 2015a, 77). It is envisaged that the new border agency will create an overall external border management strategy and will cooperate with Member States' border authorities. The border management strategy comprises eight different components, which, in part, go beyond the typical understanding of border management (European Commission 2015a, Art. 4). The key components of the new border control strategy include: fighting trans-border crime; return operations; analysis of security threats and facilitating cooperation between the relevant authorities of the Member States. Although these are all elements within the remit of typical border management, it is also a function of the new coast guard to cooperate directly with the border agencies of third countries of origin and transit. It is important to recognise that the European Border and Coast Guard Agency's activities, known as joint operations (European Commission 2015a, Art. 14–15), require shared responsibility with Member State authorities (European Commission 2015a, Art. 5). Such shared responsibility is reliant on the Member States recognising the need for solidarity, and that the external border is now a single Union border and not 28 separate, distinct borders.

The Agency will further be responsible for establishing a monitoring and risk analysis centre to monitor migration flows, create European Border and Coast Guard and Rapid Intervention Teams, and provide technical and operational assistance to the Member States (European Commission 2015a, Art. 7). The Border and Coast Guard Teams are comprised of Member State officials who are second to the EU (European Commission 2015a, Art. 2(3)). Once deployed, they will receive their instructions from the Member State in question (European Commission 2015a, Art. 20). Rapid Intervention Teams, on the other hand, are drawn from a pool of border guards from Member States and can be deployed within three working days of a request received by a Member State, but only for a limited period of time (European Commission 2015a, Art. 18(5)). These teams may only be requested in the event that a Member State faces 'a situation of specific and disproportionate pressures' (European Commission 2015a, Art.14(2)). The creation of these specific teams is a significant step in addressing the problem at the external borders but risks being undermined by a lack of cooperation from Member States. For many Member States, immigration, particularly from non-EU countries, is an issue of significant political importance which may prevent the diversion of resources to what citizens may perceive as another Member State's problem. Therefore, in order to ensure success, the European Border and Coast Guard must be given the necessary resources and expertise from the Member States, no matter their geographical location. Furthermore, such teams do not operate in isolation, and will rely in the long term on Member States ensuring that their own national border and coast guards are adequately resourced and trained.

In line with the principle of subsidiarity (Treaty on European Union 2010, Art. 5(1)), the role of the new Agency is to intervene when requested by the Member States. To this end, it may undertake vulnerability assessments of the external borders, the results of which will then be passed on to the Member State concerned so that it may introduce corrective measures (European Commission 2015a, Art. 12). If the Member State then fails to implement such measures (European Commission 2015a, Art. 12(6)), the European Commission may intervene and deploy Border Guard or Intervention Teams, or coordinate operations for that Member State (European Commission 2015a, Art. 18).

Operating in conjunction with the new Border and Coast Guard Agency is the EU's hotspot approach, which originates from the Agenda on Migration and involves cooperation among Europol, the European Asylum Support Office (EASO) and the Border and Coast Guard Agency. These bodies will cooperate in Member States to register, identify and fingerprint new migrants (European Commission 2015b, 6), with the aim of providing 'a platform for the agencies to intervene, rapidly and in an integrated manner, in frontline Member States when there is a crisis due to specific and disproportionate migratory pressure at their external borders' (Council of the European Union 2015a, 5). Registering, identifying and fingerprinting new migrants is necessary for the effective application of the Dublin System, in order to definitively establish which Member State should be responsible for an asylum application. EASO will consider the asylum claims of any individuals in these hotspot locations, with the new agency providing support in the return of irregular migrants or those who have not satisfied the criteria for protection in the EU (European Commission 2015b, 6). These teams are known as Migration Management Support Teams (European Commission 2015a, Art. 17). This hotspot approach is currently fully deployed in Leros, Lesbos, Samos and Kos in Greece, and Lampedusa, Pozzallo, Taranto and Trapani in Italy (European Commission 2016a) with significant human rights concerns over reception conditions and access to asylum procedures in the hotspots (ECRE 2016).

The process for the creation of a hotspot begins with the request of a Member State facing disproportionate migratory pressures (Council of the European Union 2015a, 6). The Commission then coordinates the various agencies that are involved, with an EU Regional Task Force coordinating on the ground (Council of the European Union 2015a, 6–7). Due to the differences in the number of migrants arriving in Italy and Greece, Italian hotspots currently have a combined reception capacity of 1600 people, whereas Greek hotspots have capacity for 5,450 people (Council of the European Union 2015a, 1–2). Despite these various measures, the hotspot approach has yet to be effectively implemented, with many areas still not yet completed (European Commission 2016b and 2016c). This is in part due to the need to distribute migrants from these hotspots across the EU, so Greece and Italy are not disproportionally affected. Despite agreements to redistribute 160,000 migrants from Italy and Greece being concluded in September 2015 (Council Decision (EU) 2015/1601 and Council of the European Union 2015b), as of December 2016 only 8,162 people have been resettled (European Commission 2016d).

EASO itself is currently the subject of a number of suggested reforms in order to aid the completion of the Common European Asylum System, with its mandate due to be increased from that given in 2010 (Regulation establishing a European Asylum Support Office, 2010). It is proposed that EASO will become the EU Agency for Asylum, with a focus on the effective implementation and functioning of the Common European Asylum System (European Commission 2016e, Art. 1(1)). Its specific tasks suggest widespread harmonisation between the asylum systems of the Member States, not only on reception, qualification and return, but also on the development of a core curriculum for the training of the judiciary and public authorities, the harmonisation of 'third country' information and of 'third country' cooperation in asylum matters (European Commission 2016e, Art. 2). These are significant developments in the EU's asylum and migration policy, particularly harmonisation of 'third country' information. This is an area where Member States' judicial and political differences come to the fore, with each Member State having different criteria and methods regarding how they decide which sources of information to use when assessing the situation in a 'third country'. The harmonisation of this area could, in theory at least, lead to the overall harmonisation of asylum cases and appeals, and their outcomes, in the Member States. Such an argument rests on the assumption that the new Agency for Asylum itself will conduct its own thorough research using a wide range of sources and subjecting them to the high level of scrutiny that is required. However, in practice it will still be left to the competent Member

State authorities to make the asylum decisions, and they may be affected by the internal political situation in the Member State.

Apart from reforms at the external border and of EU agencies, developments have taken place with respect to the procedures required for the effective return of 'third country' nationals who do not qualify for protection or legal residency in the Member States. One of the most significant, and most controversial, has been the EU – Turkey Statement (Council of the European Union 2016b) for the return of all individuals who have entered the Union irregularly from Turkey and a new 'One-for-One' system, where the EU returns Syrian nationals who entered irregularly from Turkey in exchange for the resettlement of Syrian nationals who qualify for international protection (European Commission 2016f, 2). The legal underpinning of this arrangement is the EU – Turkey Readmission Agreement, which entered into force in 2014 and allows for the return of Turkish nationals and those of third countries who have no legal right of residency in the EU (Agreement between the European Union and the Republic of Turkey, 2014). Typically, EU readmission agreements contain a three-year delay between the return of a state's own nationals and the return of 'third country' nationals and stateless persons who have transited through the 'third country' in question.

However, in the case of Turkey, the 'third country' national element has been brought forward from 2017 to June 2016 (Council of the European Union 2015c). Concerns have been expressed about the ability of individuals to effectively claim refugee/asylum protection in Turkey, and whether Turkey may be classed as a safe country for such individuals (Amnesty International 2016). Furthermore, there are concerns about the effectiveness of the EU-Turkey deal, particularly regarding the reforms, which the agreement requires of Turkish domestic policy (Nielsen 2016). Such concerns are valid in light of the recent political crackdown and allegations of widespread, systematic human rights abuses committed by state officials (Human Rights Watch 2017, 600–607). Most significantly for individuals seeking protection, Turkey still applies its geographical limitation under the Refugee Convention, meaning that non-Europeans are unable to claim refugee status (Protocol Relating to the Status of Refugees, in force on 4 October 1967)

The EU has further deepened its relations with third countries on migration through the new Partnership Frameworks, announced in June 2016 (European Commission 2016f). These frameworks are targeted in the short and long-term at: Lebanon, Jordan, Tunisia, Mali, Niger, Nigeria, Senegal, Libya, Ethiopia, Egypt, Afghanistan, Iran, Morocco and Algeria (European Commission 2016g, 13–16). Like the European Agenda on Migration, the frameworks are comprised of immediate, short- and long-term objectives and measures. In the short term, the aim is to increase the number of successful returns to such states, as well as saving lives in the Mediterranean and taking action to reduce the number of people making the journey to the EU. These aims are to be achieved in the immediate future by improving capacity in border and migration management through increased economic resources and training, as well as offering improved legal routes for migrants to the EU (European Commission 2016g, 5–6).

In the field of return and readmission, the Commission proposed five areas of focus ranging from the identification of irregular migrants, to assisting individuals in voluntary returns and the provision of the appropriate documentation, which is required for an effective return (European Commission 2016g, 7). It may be noted that readmission agreements have not yet been agreed upon with any of the target states, with negotiations currently taking place with Jordan and Nigeria. Concluding a readmission agreement is difficult for the EU due to the inclusion of 'third country' nationals and stateless persons. For example, Morocco is primarily a transit state for migrants from Sub-Saharan Africa. If Morocco assumed legal responsibility for such individuals, and even facilitated their return from the EU, it would come at a significant economic and political cost in terms of reception and processing facilities and relations with neighbouring countries (Carrera et al. 2016, 5–6).

In contrast to these states, the Partnership Framework communication provides a separate list of 16 states including Eritrea, Somalia, Afghanistan, Pakistan, Sudan and Ethiopia, which Member States have discussed for the conclusion of country packages that include cooperation on readmission and return (European Commission 2016g, 8). The human rights situation in many of these states is at best questionable, with many of them receiving particular attention from the United Nations (United Nations Human Rights Council 2015) and the European Court of Human Rights (*Sufi and Elmi v. The United Kingdom* 2012) for state sanctioned torture, inhumane and degrading treatment or punishment of citizens. The human rights situation in such states may operate to prevent the return of nationals where they are able to substantiate a claim that they face a real risk of being subjected to such treatment. The long-term aim of the Partnership Frameworks is to tackle the 'root causes' of migration, with a large focus being placed on financial investment into the third countries in question – €3.1 billion being provided for the period until 2020 under the External Investment Plan (European Commission 2016g, 11).

Aggregating these various policy developments, we can now observe the next stage of a truly Common European Asylum System, at the internal and external levels. The evolution of Frontex into the European Border and Coast Guard, in combination with the mooted reforms of EASO suggest that the EU and Member States are beginning to recognise that 'more Europe' is necessary in order to ensure the functioning of an area free of internal borders. However, in order to ensure the success of such policies the Member States must continue to recognise the importance of solidarity in the area of migration, not only on paper but in practice. These policies will require all the Member States to contribute more resources and expertise to the new agencies. The external dimension is one in which we may observe greater concern. Although we can recognise the political need to do more in order to ensure that irregular migrants who do not qualify for protection in the EU are returned, the shift towards political arrangements with third countries with questionable records on human rights raises concerns as to the EU's own commitment to protecting human rights. External cooperation is further complicated by each 'third country' having its own economic and political concerns to balance with those of the EU. As demonstrated by states such as Morocco, future developments in the policy will rely not only on the political goodwill of the 'third country', but also the EU being able to reconcile the often opposing interests at play in such a politically-sensitive area.

References

Agreement between the European Union and the Republic of Turkey on the readmission of persons residing without authorisation 2014.

Amnesty International. 2014. *The Human Cost of Fortress Europe: Human Rights Violations against Migrants and Refugees at Europe's Borders*. https://www.amnesty.ch/de/themen/asyl-und-migration/festung-europa/dok/2015/die-kampagne-sos-europa/bericht-the-human-cost-of-fortress-Europe

Amnesty International. 2016. *Turkey: No Safe Refugee: Asylum-Seekers and Refugees Denied Effective Protection in Turkey*. https://www.amnesty.org/en/documents/eur44/3825/2016/en/

Carrera, Sergio, Jean-Pierre Cassarino, Nora El Qadim, Mehdi Lahlou and Leonhard den Hertog. 2016. *EU-Morocco Cooperation on Readmission, Borders and Protection: A Model to Follow?* Centre for European Policy Studies, no.87.

Council of the European Union. 2015a. *"Hotspot" Approach – FRONTEX Support to Return of Irregular Migrants – "Safe Countries of Origin."* Brussels.

Council of the European Union. 2015b. *Resolution of the Representatives of the Governments of the Member States meeting within the Council on relocating from Greece and Italy 40,000 persons in clear need of international protection*. Brussels.

Council of the European Union. 2015c. *Meeting of Heads of State or Government with Turkey – EU – Turkey Statement,* 29 November 2015. Brussels.

Council of the European Union. 2016a. *Proposal for a Regulation of the European Parliament and of the Council on the European Borders and Coast Guard and repealing Regulation (EC) No 2007/2004, Regulation (EC) No 863/2007 and Council Decision 2005/267/EC – Outcome of the European Parliament's first reading.* Brussels.

Council of the European Union. 2016b. *EU-Turkey Statement,* 18 March 2016. Brussels.

Council of the European Union. 2005. *The Hague Programme: Strengthening Freedom, Security and Justice in the European Union* [2005] OJ C 53/1, 3 March 2005.

Council of the European Union. 2010a. *Council Regulation (EU) No 439/2010 establishing a European Asylum Support Office*, 19 May 2010.

Council of the European Union. 2010b. *The Stockholm Programme – An Open and Secure Europe Serving and Protecting the Citizens* [2010] OJ C 115/1, 4 May 2010.

Bigo, Didier. 2002. "Border Regimes, Police Cooperation and Security." In *Europe Unbound: Enlarging and Reshaping the Boundaries of the European Union*, edited by Jan Zielonka, 213–239. London and New York: Routledge.

ECRE. 2016. *The Implementation of the Hotspots in Italy and Greece: A Study*. http://www.ecre.org/wp-content/uploads/2016/12/HOTSPOTS-Report-5.12.2016..pdf

European Asylum Support Office. 2015. *Annual Report on the Situation of Asylum in the European Union 2014*, July 2015. http://easo.europa.eu/wp-content/uploads/EASO-Annual-Report-2014.pdf

European Commission. 2009. *Communication on 'An Area of Freedom, Security and Justice serving the citizen: Wider freedom in a safer environment'* COM(2009) 262/4. Brussels.

European Commission. 2015a. *Proposal for a Regulation of the European Parliament and of the Council on the European Border and Coast Guard and repealing Regulation (EC) No 2007/2004, Regulation (EC) No 863/2007 and Council Decision 2005/267/EC*. Strasbourg.

European Commission. 2015b. *Communication from the Commission to the European Parliament, the Council, the European Economic and Social Committee and the Committee of the Regions: A European Agenda on Migration*. Brussels.

European Commission. 2016a. *State of Play of Hotspot Capacity.* Brussels.

European Commission. 2016b. *Annex to the Communication from the Commission to the European Parliament and the Council on the State of Play of Implementation of the Priority Actions under the European Agenda on Migration: Greece – State of Play Report.* Brussels.

European Commission. 2016c. *Annex to the Communication from the Commission to the European Parliament and the Council on the State of Play of Implementation of the Priority Actions under the European Agenda on Migration: Italy – State of Play Report.* Brussels.

European Commission. 2016d. *Relocation and Resettlement – State of Play (6 December 2016).* Brussels.

European Commission. 2016e. *Proposal for a Regulation of the European Parliament and of the Council on the European Union Agency for Asylum and repealing Regulation (EU) No 439/2010.* Brussels.

European Commission. 2016f. *Communication from the Commission to the European Parliament, the European Council and the Council, First Report on the progress made in the implementation of the EU-Turkey Statement.* Brussels.

European Commission. 2016g. *Communication from the Commission to the European Parliament, the European Council, the Council and the European Investment Bank on establishing a new Partnership Framework with third countries under the European Agenda on Migration.* Brussels.

Geddes, Andrew. 2001. *Immigration and European Integration: Towards Fortress Europe?* Manchester: Manchester University Press.

Human Rights Watch. 2017. *World Report 2017* https://www.hrw.org/sites/default/files/world_report_download/wr2017-web.pdf.

Kostakopoulou, Dora. 1998. "Is there an Alternative to 'Schengenland'?." *Political Studies* 46: 337–58.

Kostakopoulou, Dora. 2001. *Citizenship, Identity and Immigration in the European Union.* Manchester University Press.

Kostakopoulou, Dora, Diego Acosta Arcarazo and Tine Munk. 2014. "EU Migration Law: The Opportunities and Challenges Ahead." In *EU Security and Justice Law: After Lisbon and Stockholm*, edited by Diego Acosta Arcarazo and Cian C. Murphy, 129–45. Oxford: Hart.

Moreno-Lax, Violeta. 2014 "Life After Lisbon: EU Asylum Policy as a Factor of Migration Control" In *EU Security and Justice Law: After Lisbon and Stockholm*, edited by Diego Acosta Arcarazo and Cian C. Murphy, 146–167. Oxford: Hart, 2014.

Nielsen, Nikolaj. 2016. "EU-Turkey Readmission Deal in Doubt." *EUObserver*, 6 June 2016. https://euobserver.com/migration/133712

UN General Assembly, Protocol relating to the Status of Refugees, 16 December 1966, A/RES/2198. http://www.refworld.org/docid/3b00f1cc50.html

Sufi and Elmi v. The United Kingdom (2012) 54 EHRR 9. 2012.

Treaty on European Union (Consolidated Version). 2012.

United Nations Human Rights Council. 2015. *Report of the detailed findings of the Commission of Inquiry on Human Rights in Eritrea: Advance Version.* UN Doc. A/HRC/29/CRP.1.

14

Legal Responses to the EU Migrant Crisis: Too Little, Too Late?

JENNY POON

The Syrian war has brought the massive influx of asylum claimants and refugees across the European Union (EU) into sharp relief. Despite the humanitarian crisis, the international and regional EU responses to the migrant crisis have been inadequate and much too late. First, international organisations such as the United Nations High Commissioner for Refugees (UNHCR) have proposed an approach which seems to undermine the original object and purpose of the Refugee Convention by recognising refugees in groups instead of allowing for individualised refugee status determination. Second, the EU approach of trading Syrian refugees one for one from those traveling through Greece to Turkey undermines international protection such as *non-refoulement* for asylum claimants. It is argued that in order to properly safeguard the rights of asylum claimants, proper substantive and procedural safeguards need to be in place, as well as an enlarged role for the regional courts in the EU in adjudicating asylum decisions.

On international legal responses, the UNHCR's attempt to resolve the difficulty of processing massive asylum applications through Guidelines on International Protection, No. 11 (hereafter Guideline) on the '*prima facie* (in Latin means, 'on the face of it') recognition of refugees' is inadequate (UNHCR 2015). The '*prima facie* recognition of refugees' allows states to grant refugee status to a collective group of asylum claimants rather than granting refugee status based on individual assessments of a 'well-founded fear of persecution'. The problem inherent with a system that permits group recognition of refugee status rather than the processing of asylum applications on a case-by-case basis is that it increases the likelihood of abuse of process by claimants. For instance, those undeserving of international protection such as asylum claimants who have committed crimes of mass atrocities, may circumvent the system by claiming for international protection. Group recognition of refugees such as the recognition of those fleeing from the Syrian civil war, it is argued, may potentially undermine the original object and purpose of the Refugee Convention.

On regional legal responses, the EU's attempt has been inadequate and much too late. The recent EU-Turkey Deal (hereafter Deal) reveals the importance of adhering to the principle of *non-refoulement* (Refugee Convention 1951, Art. 33(1)) and the necessity of states to ensure adequate safeguards are accorded to asylum claimants and refugees. *Non-refoulement* is a central tenet in international refugee law and it is the right of the asylum claimant or refugee to not be sent back to his or her country of origin to face persecution (Refugee Convention 1951, Art. 33(1)). As of 20 March 2016, the Deal effectively returns asylum claimants who travel from Turkey to Greece back to Turkey, and for every asylum claimant returned to Turkey, the EU promises to take back one refugee from Syria. Essentially, the Deal swaps one human being for another, treating them as commodities, and promotes violation of *non-refoulement* due to the deficient asylum system in Turkey and the likelihood of subsequent rejected applications (Anderson 2016).

The anticipated finding is that the current international and regional legal responses to the EU migrant crisis are anything but adequate and timely. In order to properly safeguard the rights of asylum claimants and refugees, proper substantive and procedural mechanisms must be in place, including the enlargement of the role of regional courts in the EU and the curtailing of state sovereignty to champion the rights of individual claimants. The examples of the Syrian massive influx of asylum claimants and the Deal will illustrate how these responses are inadequate and much too late.

This chapter will begin by exploring the international and EU law governing refugees and refugee status determination. Then, it will turn to examining the international response from the UNHCR on the EU migrant crisis, and then turn to the regional response from the EU. Next, the importance of adequately addressing the current crisis in a timely manner is explained. It will be demonstrated that the UNHCR and the EU responses to the migrant crisis are too little and too late. Finally, the chapter will end with recommendations and a prediction of what is to come in international and regional responses.

The Law on Refugees and Refugee Status Determination

This section explores, very briefly, the law on refugees and refugee status determination procedures at both the international and the EU level.

International Law

International law provides the bare minimum rules for Refugee Convention contracting parties to follow. It is then up to the contracting parties to transpose the international law requirements to their domestic legislation and establish national procedures to carry out their international law obligations. Under international law, a refugee is defined as someone who is fleeing from a 'well-founded fear of persecution on account of race, religion, nationality, membership of a particular social group or political opinion' (Convention Grounds), who is outside of his or her country of origin, and who is unwilling or unable to avail him or herself to state protection (Refugee Convention 1951, Art. 1A). The asylum claimant has the burden of proof to establish, on the threshold of a 'reasonable likelihood', the above-mentioned elements (UNHCR 1998). The asylum official, in assessing the credibility of the applicant for international protection, should give the applicant the benefit of the doubt (Gorlick 2002). Benefit of the doubt means that the applicant need not prove every part of his or her case as long as the applicant makes a genuine effort to substantiate his or her story (Gorlick 2002). The test is met when the asylum official is satisfied with the applicant's general credibility, and the coherence and plausibility of the applicant's statements, which do not run counter to generally-known facts (Gorlick 2002). In establishing a 'well-founded fear of persecution', both subjective (fear) and objective (well-founded) elements must be proven by the asylum claimant (UNHCR 1998). Factors for the adjudicator to consider when evaluating objective well-foundedness of persecution include: a) factual considerations; b) personal circumstances of the claimant; and c) situation in the country of origin (UNHCR 1998).

It should be noted that the term 'persecution' is not defined under international refugee law or in the Refugee Convention, nor is there a universal definition of 'persecution'. However, the UNHCR, in its commentary, has stated that 'persecution' may comprise of: 'a threat to life or freedom on account of race, religion, nationality, membership of a particular social group or political opinion' or 'serious violations of human rights' (UNHCR 1992). What constitutes 'persecution' is determined on a case-by-case basis (UNHCR 1992). Severe discrimination may also result in 'persecution' if the measures of discrimination lead to consequences of a substantially prejudicial nature for the person concerned, such as: 'serious restrictions on the applicant's right to earn his or her livelihood; or serious restrictions on the applicant's right to practice his or her religion' (UNHCR 1992). Persecution may also occur on cumulative grounds, where various elements, taken together, produce an effect on the mind of the applicant that can reasonably justify a claim of 'well-founded fear of persecution' on cumulative grounds (UNHCR 1992). For example, the combination of adverse factors such as 'general atmosphere of insecurity in the country of origin' may constitute 'well-founded fear of persecution' on cumulative grounds (UNHCR 1992). Whether 'well-founded fear of persecution' is established on cumulative grounds is determined based on the circumstances of the case (UNHCR 1992).

In adjudicating the truthfulness of the asylum claimant, the adjudicator should take into consideration the following: a) the reasonableness of the facts alleged; b) the overall consistency and coherence of the claimant's story; c) the corroborative evidence adduced by the claimant in support of his or her statements; d) the consistency with common knowledge or generally known facts; and e) the known situation in the country of origin (UNHCR 1998).

After a brief overview of the international law governing refugees and refugee status determination, it follows to examine the EU system for processing asylum applications.

EU Law

International law provides the bare minimum rules for Refugee Convention contracting parties to follow. Even though the EU has its own regional interpretation and implementation of international standards, EU Member States nonetheless are bound by international law obligations. In fact, international law obligations prevail over EU obligations (Treaty Establishing the European Community, Art. 307 2002). The EU has established the Common European Asylum System (CEAS), which aims to establish a harmonised, fair and effective asylum procedure to process asylum claims across EU Member States, while complying with international law obligations to protect asylum claimants fleeing persecution (European Commission 2016a). Although the EU is itself not a contracting party to the Refugee Convention, EU law has provided that the CEAS must comply with the Refugee Convention and the 1967 Protocol Relating to the Status of Refugees (Treaty on the Functioning of the European Union 2012, Art. 78). EU Member States are therefore bound by the principle of *non-refoulement*.

The CEAS is comprised of the Dublin System, which consists of the Dublin Convention, Dublin II Regulation and Dublin III Regulation, and which determines the mechanism and criteria for establishing state responsibility with regards to the processing of asylum applications among EU Member States (Dublin Convention 1990; Dublin II Regulation 2003; Dublin III Regulation 2013). Together with key directives including the Qualification

Directive (2011), Asylum Procedures Directive (2013), and Reception Conditions Directive (2013), the Dublin System determines the responsibility and burden-sharing of asylum application processing among EU Member States. The EU Commission has proposed to recast the three key Directives mentioned prior in July 2016, including a proposal for Dublin IV. This chapter will not comment upon these new proposals because they fall outside the scope of this chapter.

Under EU law, a Regulation is a binding legislative act that must be applied in its entirety across the EU (EU 2016). A Directive, on the other hand, is a legislative act that sets out a goal to be achieved by all EU Member States, but is based on the implementation of national law to achieve those objectives (EU 2016). It follows that the provisions found in the Qualification Directive, Asylum Procedures Directive, and Reception Conditions Directive are discretionary and will be dependent upon the Member State in question to transpose into domestic law.

The Qualification Directive gives EU Member States guidance on the standards for qualifying 'third country' nationals or stateless persons for international protection and subsidiary protection and the content of the protection granted. The Asylum Procedures Directive, on the other hand, provides guidance on the procedures utilised by Member States to grant and withdraw international protection. Finally, the Reception Conditions Directive lays down for Member States the standards for the reception condition of applications for international protection.

The Dublin III Regulation is important because it is the current legislation determining which EU Member State is responsible for examining individual asylum applications (European Commission 2016b). If an asylum claimant arrives in a Member State, the asylum official will first determine the category which the applicant for international protection falls under – whether he or she is a minor or has family member(s) in another Member State, for example – in order to determine the Member State responsible for processing the asylum application (Dublin III Regulation 2013, Arts. 8–10). Next, the asylum official will consider whether the applicant is in possession of a visa or residence permit in a Member State, and whether the applicant has entered the EU irregularly or regularly (European Commission 2016b). In processing the asylum application, the asylum official will also determine if the criteria for transferring the applicant to a 'safe third country' apply pursuant to the Asylum Procedures Directive (Dublin III Regulation 2013, Art. 3(3)). If the criteria for 'safe third country' does not apply, and the applicant for international protection does not qualify for refugee status, then the asylum official will consider granting protection under subsidiary protection pursuant to the Qualification Directive (2011, Art. 15). The definitions for 'safe third country' and 'subsidiary protection' are found under the respective instruments describing them.

International and Regional Responses

This section examines the current international and regional responses to the EU migrant crisis and explains why the responses thus far are too little and too late.

The UNHCR Response

The UNHCR exercises a supervisory role over contracting parties' compliance with the Refugee Convention (Statute of the UNHCR 1950, Art. 8(a)). While the commentaries and interpretations by the UNHCR are considered 'soft law' and therefore are non-binding, they are nonetheless considered authoritative and have been interpreted by states as such (UNHCR 2007). Accordingly, UNHCR commentaries should be regarded with the strictest scrutiny given the implications they have on contracting parties' compliance with the Refugee Convention. The UNHCR's response to the EU migrant crisis is, of course, not restricted to the release of the Guideline. Given the limited scope of this chapter and the relevance of this particular Guideline to the EU migrant crisis, an analysis of other actions or commentaries released by the UNHCR will not be made. The purpose of focusing the analysis on the Guideline is twofold. First, the Guideline is current, as of 24 June 2015. Second, the context behind the Guideline is the EU migrant crisis, since the Guideline only applies to situations of massive influx of refugees where individual interviews may not be feasible.

A *prima facie* approach to refugee status determination is not the main focus of this chapter. Rather, this chapter explains the concerns with *group recognition* of refugee status, and discusses how group recognition of refugee status, in contrast with individual status determination, may undermine international protection for asylum claimants and refugees, and potentially contradict the object and purpose of the Refugee Convention. According to the Guideline, *prima facie* recognition of refugees or, a *prima facie* approach, means 'the recognition by a state or the UNHCR of refugee status on the basis of readily apparent, objective circumstances in the country of origin or, in the case of stateless asylum seekers, their country of former habitual residence' (UNHCR 2015). A *prima facie* approach may be applied to individual refugee status determination circumstances, but is most often used in group situations, where 'individual status determination is impractical, impossible or unnecessary in large-scale situations' (UNHCR 2015).

A Brief Overview of the EU Response

This section focuses upon the Deal as one of the many responses utilised by the EU in an attempt to prevent secondary movements, such as smuggling, and to improve on the failed attempts by the Dublin III Regulation to ensure an efficient and fair method of allocating responsibility-sharing among EU Member States in determining the Member State responsible for processing asylum applications. As a result of its currency and implications for asylum claimants moving from the Syrian armed conflict towards Turkey, this section will focus upon the Deal to analyse the EU's response to the migrant crisis. Before moving on to a discussion of the Deal, a brief overview of the concerns related to the Dublin III Regulation will be explored.

The Dublin III Regulation is the current framework legislation used by EU Member States to determine the Member State responsible for processing asylum applications. However, the Dublin III Regulation is not without its own problems. For instance, in the European Court of Human Rights case of *MSS v. Belgium and Greece,* where the court examined the Dublin II Regulation (predecessor to Dublin III) and its compatibility with the European Convention on Human Rights (ECHR), the court held that Belgium cannot send asylum claimants back to Greece under the Dublin transfer procedure because of Greece's deficient asylum system, which may potentially lead to indirect *refoulement* (European Database of Asylum Law 2016). Belgium was held to have violated Article 3 of the ECHR which provided for the prohibition against torture, for sending asylum claimants to Greece, where there were substantial grounds for believing that there would be a real risk that the asylum claimant would be exposed to detention and living conditions in breach of that Article (European Database of Asylum Law 2016; ECHR 1950, Art. 3). This case therefore illustrates that Member States such as Belgium were able to circumvent their *non-refoulement* obligations by using the Dublin transfer procedure to their advantage.

Besides the problems of the Dublin III Regulation, the EU response to the migrant crisis as evidenced by the Deal is also troublesome. The purpose of the Deal is to tackle the issue of irregular migrants as well as to address the migrant crisis (Europa 2016b). The EU and Turkey agreed to a joint action plan on 7 March 2016, where Turkey agreed to 'accept the rapid return of all migrants not in need of international protection crossing from Turkey into Greece and to take back all irregular migrants intercepted in Turkish waters' (Europa 2016b). It should be noted that Turkey is not currently a Member State of the EU, and it is therefore not bound by EU law (Europa 2017). The two main components of the Deal which this chapter will focus on are: 1) all new irregular migrants crossing from Turkey into Greek islands as from 20

March 2016 will be returned to Turkey, 2) for every Syrian being returned to Turkey from Greek islands, another Syrian will be resettled from Turkey to the EU taking into account the UN Vulnerability Criteria (Europa 2016b).

According to the EU-Turkey Statement, 'migrants not applying for asylum or whose application has been found unfounded or inadmissible in accordance with the [Asylum Procedures Directive] will be returned to Turkey', and, priority will be given to those Syrian migrants 'who have not previously entered or tried to enter the EU irregularly' to be resettled from Turkey to the EU (Europa 2016b).

Failures of International and Regional Responses

After a brief overview of the UNHCR and EU responses, this section discusses why the responses are too little and too late.

Failures of the UNHCR Response

The UNHCR response to the EU migrant crisis as suggested by the Guideline through group recognition of refugees may potentially contradict the object and purpose of the Refugee Convention. Pursuant to the *Vienna Convention on the Law of Treaties* (VCLT), 'a treaty shall be interpreted in good faith in accordance with the ordinary meaning to be given to the terms of the treaty in their context and in the light of its object and purpose' (Art. 31(1)). The object and purpose of the Refugee Convention are found in its preamble (Art. 31(2)). The object and purpose of the Refugee Convention, according to a UNHCR 2001 commentary, is 'to ensure the protection of specific rights of refugees, to encourage international cooperation in that regard, including through UNHCR, and to prevent the refugee problem from becoming a cause of tensions between states' (UNHCR 2001). Moreover, the UNHCR itself has stated that, considering the object and purpose of the Refugee Convention, the asylum official 'needs to have both a full picture of the asylum-seeker's personality, background and personal experiences' (UNHCR 2001). It would be difficult to assess an individual applicant's 'personality, background and personal experiences' in the circumstances of group-based recognition. Group-based recognition also takes away the opportunity for the individual applicant to have a right to be heard, whether oral or written, which is a right guaranteed under the Refugee Convention in the case of expulsion orders (Refugee Convention 1951, Art. 32(2)). Having regarded the UNHCR's commentary then, group-based recognition makes individualised assessment of the claimant's 'personality, background and personal experiences' nearly impossible, thus potentially contradicting the object and purpose of the Refugee Convention.

Further, in contrast with individual refugee status determination, which is a common practice among states, where the asylum official needs to assess the subjective fear and objective well-foundedness of that fear of the individual applicant on a case-by-case basis, a *prima facie* approach removes the individual component to that assessment, and applies the assessment uniformly, across the board, to a *group* of individuals on the basis of 'readily apparent, objective circumstances in the country of origin', as reiterated above. It is suggested that a group-based recognition of refugee status, as opposed to individualised assessments takes away the individual applicant's ability to truly demonstrate his or her subjective fear based on the applicable circumstance.

For instance, although the Syrian armed conflict has produced a mass influx of asylum claimants across the EU, it is not necessarily the case that all such asylum claimants are able to meet the threshold of the refugee definition, since not all asylum claimants fleeing from the Syrian armed conflict may experience a 'well-founded fear of persecution' on the basis of the Convention Grounds on both subjective and objective assessments. Further, group-based recognition increases the possibility of asylum claimants who are not legitimately fleeing from a 'well-founded fear of persecution' to circumvent the institution for asylum by not needing to meet the onus of proof to establish subjective fear and objective well-foundedness to the threshold of a 'reasonable likelihood'. The onus of proof requirement is removed from the individual applicant because group-based recognition of refugee status presumes that the individual applicant, as part of a group of applicants, is a refugee *unless there is evidence to the contrary* (UNHCR 2015). A leading academic and practitioner in refugee law agrees that group-based recognition of refugees is problematic, in that it systemically applies discriminatory measures upon a group of asylum claimants, while not every claimant within the group will be able to individually meet the threshold of persecution (Durieux 2008). Moreover, Durieux asserts that group-based recognition of refugees, although efficient in massive influx situations, may nonetheless be detrimental to asylum claimants because efficiency is achieved at the expense of certainty, because of an overly broad definition of groups at risk (Durieux 2008).

While some may argue that the burden of proof for asylum claimants is slightly lower in a group-based recognition system rather than an individualised assessment of refugee status, so that more individuals may be protected as a result, more individuals having an 'easier' time being recognised as refugees does not necessarily conform with the spirit and letter of the Refugee Convention. For instance, the object and purpose of the Refugee Convention, as stated above, is its humanitarian objective – which is to ensure that human beings can enjoy fundamental rights and freedoms free from discrimination (Weis 1990). In order to achieve its humanitarian objectives, it is necessary then, to exclude those who are undeserving of these fundamental rights and freedoms, so that those who *are* deserving of these rights *do* get protected. An example of when an asylum claimant may be deemed undeserving of the rights enumerated under the Refugee Convention occurs when an asylum official deems there to be 'serious reasons for considering' that the asylum claimant has committed 'a crime against peace, a war crime, or a crime against humanity' (Refugee Convention 1951, Art. 1F(a)). In a group-based recognition system, it would be more difficult for the asylum official to determine, on the threshold of 'serious reasons for considering', whether the asylum claimant in question has indeed committed the crimes listed under Article 1F(a). Further, the threshold of 'serious reasons for considering' is necessarily a high one, due to the significant potential impact a rejected application would mean for the asylum claimant having committed the enumerated crimes. It is therefore submitted that, without an individualised assessment, it would be difficult, in some circumstances, to determine whether the asylum claimant in question is indeed deserving of international protection.

Based on these reasons, it is suggested that the UNHCR response to the EU migrant crisis by proposing the group-based recognition approach to determining refugee status is inadequate. The UNHCR proposal for group recognition of refugees is not only inadequate, but also much too late. The Syrian armed conflict began in or about 2011, as a result of anti-government protests (Amnesty International 2016). The Syrian armed conflict in the past five years has produced the displacement of an estimated 4.8 million persons of concern, including asylum claimants, refugees, and internally-displaced persons (UNHCR n.d.). However, despite these statistics, the UNHCR failed to suggest a proposal for group recognition of refugees, or take action, until June 2015. Moreover, group recognition procedures deviate from commonly practised individualised interview procedures, meaning EU Member States will have to make changes to their internal procedures and guidelines, which may increase the overall time required to have an efficient and effective asylum system in place. Under international law, states have an obligation to provide an asylum claimant access to fair and efficient asylum procedures, which is derived from the right to seek and enjoy asylum found under the Universal Declaration of Human Rights (UDHR), an international instrument that is reflective of international custom (1948, Art. 14).

Failures of the EU Response

Next, this chapter turns to the failures of the EU response to the migrant crisis.

The principle of *non-refoulement* is violated when a state sends back the asylum claimant or refugee to massive violations of human rights amounting to persecution, or to death, torture, or other cruel, inhuman or degrading treatment or punishment (International Covenant on Civil and Political Rights 1966, Arts. 6 and 7; Convention Against Torture and Other Cruel, Inhuman or Degrading Treatment or Punishment 1984, Art. 3). The definitions for these enumerated terms can be found in the respective instruments describing them. *Refoulement* may occur directly or indirectly. Direct *refoulement* occurs when a state sends back an asylum claimant or a refugee to his or her country of origin to face persecution (Refugee Convention 1951, Art. 33(1)). Indirect *refoulement* occurs when a sending state sends back the asylum claimant or refugee to a recipient state where the recipient state does not have adequate procedures to process the asylum claimant or refugee (UNHCR 2007). The Deal violates the principle of *non-refoulement* because it proposes to send asylum claimants or refugees back to Turkey, where there will not be adequate asylum procedures to process them. The fact that Turkey has an inadequate asylum processing system and lack of procedural safeguards to ensure adequate protection for asylum claimants and refugees due to a poor human rights record has been recognised by leading academics (Peers 2016). Turkey's poor human rights record makes it more likely for asylum claimants or refugees returned to Turkey to be subjected to death, torture, or other cruel, inhuman or degrading treatment or punishment, or otherwise massive violations of human rights amounting to persecution. Therefore, sending asylum claimants or refugees back to Turkey, where the asylum system is deficient and the human rights record is poor, increase the chances of violations of *non-refoulement* obligations.

Further to the above-mentioned problems, the Deal violates international law because it promotes collective expulsion of asylum claimants or refugees, when massive numbers of asylum claimants or refugees are being returned to Turkey (Refugee Convention 1951, Article 32). Collective expulsion of aliens is also against established EU law (ECHR 1950, Protocol 4, Art. 4). Moreover, the EU presumes Turkey to be a 'safe third country', which, in theory, should permit asylum claimants to access proper asylum procedures after they are sent to Turkey (Poon 2016a). However, in reality, Turkey does not have proper asylum procedures in place to be regarded as a 'safe third country' in the first place (Poon 2016a). These and the above reasons suggest that the EU's response to the migrant crisis is inadequate.

The EU response to the migrant crisis is not only insufficient, but also much too late. The Syrian armed conflict has been ongoing for over five years. Moreover, the failures of the Dublin System in handling the massive influx have been apparent and emphasised by the UNHCR since 2008 (UNHCR 2008). However, the EU's response to the failures of the Dublin System has been slow. The Dublin System has been in place since the inception of the Dublin Convention of 1990; however, the proposal to improve the system did not take place until the Dublin II Regulation of 2003, and the subsequent Dublin III Regulation, ten years later, in 2013. Based on these reasons, the EU response to the migrant crisis has been anything but adequate and timely.

Conclusions and Recommendations

As demonstrated, both the UNHCR and EU responses to the migrant crisis have been anything but adequate and timely. The UNHCR's proposal to establish group-based recognition of refugees appears to be problematic, given that the individualised interview and, therefore, the right to be heard would be curtailed. The EU's proposal to return asylum claimants or refugees back to Turkey where the asylum system is deficient violates *non-refoulement* obligations and the prohibition against collective expulsion.

To properly safeguard the rights of asylum claimants and refugees, it is recommended that regional courts such as the Court of Justice of the European Union (CJEU) and the ECHR play a larger role in the adjudication of asylum decisions and to ensure that proper substantive and procedural safeguards are in place to allow for maximum protection of asylum claimants and refugees. The enlargement of the role of the ECHR, for instance, can be done by defining what constitutes a 'margin of appreciation', which is a creation of the ECHR, to show deference to Council of Europe Member States when they interpret and apply their international law duties such as *non-refoulement* obligations (Shany 2006). A better defined 'margin of appreciation' may strengthen Member States' compliance with *non-refoulement* while at the same time champion the rights of individuals by curtailing state sovereignty (Poon 2016b).

To ensure that international law obligations are adhered to by EU Member States in their asylum application processing, the CJEU may grant the asylum applicants a 'benefit of the doubt' so that well-resourced Member States are not granted discretion, or a 'margin of appreciation', so wide, that they decide asylum applications according to their own state interests, sometimes at the expense of asylum claimants. Further, since the role of the CJEU is primarily to ensure that EU law is interpreted uniformly and applied in the same way across EU Member States, the CJEU has a duty to adjudicate asylum decisions in a way that ensures substantive and procedural safeguards are accorded to asylum claimants across all Member States, such as the right to be heard (CJEU 2016). Now more than ever, the protection against *refoulement* for asylum claimants and refugees must be safeguarded.

*The author wishes to thank Dr. Valerie Oosterveld for her support and guidance throughout the author's PhD research. Any errors are the author's own.

References

Amnesty International. 2016. *Syria 2015/2016* (online). https://www.amnesty. org/en/countries/middle-east-and-north-africa/syria/report-syria/.

Anderson, Bridget. 2016. "Why the EU-Turkey Migrant Deal is a Moral Disaster*." Fortune*. http://fortune.com/2016/03/17/eu-turkey-migrant-crisis-deal-disaster.

Consolidated Version of the Treaty Establishing the European Community (TEU). 2002. OJ C325, 24 December.

Consolidated Version of the Treaty on the Functioning of the European Union (TFEU). 2012. OJ L326/47-326/390, 26 October.

Convention Against Torture and Other Cruel, Inhuman or Degrading Treatment or Punishment (CAT). 1984. (adopted 10 December).

Dublin Convention. 1990. Convention Determining the State Responsible for Examining Applications for Asylum lodged in one of the Member States of the European Communities (adopted 15 June 1990, entered into force 1 September 1997) OJ C254 19 August 1997.

Dublin II Regulation. 2003. Council Regulation (EC) No 343/2003 of 18 February 2003 establishing the criteria and mechanisms for determining the Member State responsible for examining an asylum application lodged in one of the Member States by a third country national OJ L50/1 25 February 2003.

Dublin III Regulation. 2013. Regulation (EU) No 604/2013 of the European Parliament and of the Council of 26 June 2013 establishing the criteria and mechanisms for determining the Member State responsible for examining an application for international protection lodged in one of the Member States by a third country national or a stateless person (recast) OJ L180/31 29 June 2013.

Durieux, Jean-Francois. 2008. *The Many Faces of 'Prima Facie': Group-Based Evidence in Refugee Status Determination*. http://refuge.journals.

yorku.ca/index.php/refuge/article/viewFile/26037/24070.

Asylum Procedures Directive (APD). 2013. Directive 2013/32/EU of the European Parliament and of the Council of 26 June 2013 on common procedures for granting and withdrawing international protection (recast) OJ L180/60 29 June 2013.

EUROPA. 2016a. *Court of Justice of the European Union (CJEU)* (online). https://europa.eu/european-union/about-eu/institutions-bodies/court-justice_ en.

EUROPA. 2016b. *EU-Turkey Statement, 18 March 2016*: http://www. consilium.europa.eu/press-releases-pdf/2016/3/40802210113_en.pdf.

EUROPA. 2017. *EU Member Countries.* https://europa.eu/european-union/ about-eu/countries/member-countries_en.

European Commission (EC). 2016a. *Common European Asylum System*. http://ec.europa.eu/dgs/home-affairs/what-we-do/policies/asylum/index_en. htm.

European Commission (EC). 2016b. *Country Responsible for Asylum Application (Dublin)* (online). http://ec.europa.eu/dgs/home-affairs/what-we-do/policies/asylum/examination-of-applicants/index_en.htm.

European Database of Asylum Law (EDAL). 2016. *ECHR – M.S.S. v Belgium and Greece [GC], Application No. 30696/09.* http://www.asylumlawdatabase. eu/en/content/ecthr-mss-v-belgium-and-greece-gc-application-no-3069609.

European Union (EU). 2016. *Regulations, Directives and Other Acts.* http:// europa.eu/eu-law/decision-making/legal-acts/index_en.htm.

European Convention for the Protection of Human Rights and Fundamental Freedoms (ECHR). 1950. (adopted 4 November 1950, entered into force 3 September 1953).

International Covenant on Civil and Political Rights (ICCPR). 1966. (adopted 16 December 1966, entered into force 23 March 1976).

Gorlick, Brian. 2002. "Common Burdens and Standards: Legal Elements in Assessing Claims to Refugee Status." UNHCR Regional Office for the Baltic and Nordic Countries, Stockholm, October 2002. http://www.uio.no/studier/

emner/jus/jus/JUR5530/v07/undervisningsmateriale/Gorlick%20Burden%20
of%20Proof%20Article.pdf.

Peers, Steve. 2016. "The Final EU/Turkey Refugee Deal: A Legal
Assessment." *EU Law and Analysis*. http://eulawanalysis.blogspot.
ca/2016/03/the-final-euturkey-refugee-deal-legal.html.

Poon, Jenny. 2016a. "EU-Turkey Deal: Violation of, or Consistency with,
International Law?" *European Papers* 1, no. 3, 1195–1203 http://www.
europeanpapers.eu/en/europeanforum/eu-turkey-deal-violation-or-
consistency-with-international-law.

Poon, Jenny. 2016b. "(Re-)inventing the Dublin System: Addressing
Uniformity and Harmonization through Non-Refoulement Obligations."
Working Papers, Paper: 02/2016, Institute of European Law, June 2016.
http://epapers.bham.ac.uk/2183/1/IELWorkingPaper2016No2_(Re)inventing_
the_Dublin_System.pdf.

Qualifying Directive (QD). 2011. Directive 2011/95/EU of the European
Parliament and of the Council of 13 December 2011 on standards for the
qualification of third country nationals or stateless persons as beneficiaries of
international protection, for a uniform status for refugees or for persons
eligible for subsidiary protection, and for the content of the protection granted
(recast) OJ L337/9 20 December 2011.

Reception Conditions Directive (RCD). 2013. Directive 2013/33/EU of the
European Parliament and of the Council of 26 June 2013 laying down
standards for the reception of applicants for international protection (recast)
OJ L180/96 29 June 2013.

Refugee Convention. 1951. *Convention Relating to the Status of Refugees*
(adopted 28 July 1951, entered into force 22 April 1954).

Shany, Yuval. 2006. "Toward a General Margin of Appreciation Doctrine in
International Law?" *The European Journal of International Law* 16, no. 5:
907–940. http://www.ejil.org/pdfs/16/5/330.pdf.

UN General Assembly. 1966. *Protocol relating to the Status of Refugees*. 16
December, A/RES/2198. http://www.refworld.org/docid/3b00f1cc50.html.

United Nations High Commissioner for Refugees (UNHCR). 1950. *Statute of
the Office of the UNHCR* (entered into force 14 December 1950).

UNHCR. n.d. "Syria Regional Refugee Response" *United Nations High Commissioner for Refugees.* http://data.unhcr.org/syrianrefugees/regional. php#_ga=1.175645355.820256109.1444741217.

UNHCR. 1992 [1979]. "Handbook on Procedures and Criteria for Determining Refugee Status under the 1951 Convention and the 1967 Protocol relating to the Status of Refugees." HCR/IP/4/Eng/REV.1 Reedited, Geneva, January 1992. http://www.unhcr.org/4d93528a9.pdf.

UNHCR. 1998. "Note on Burden and Standard of Proof in Refugee Claims" *United Nations High Commissioner for Refugees*, 16 December. http://www. refworld.org/docid/3ae6b3338.html.

UNHCR. 2001. *The International Protection of Refugees: Interpreting Article 1 of the 1951 Convention Relating to the Status of Refugees.* http://www. refworld.org/pdfid/3b20a3914.pdf.

UNHCR. 2007. *Advisory Opinion on the Extraterritorial Application of Non-Refoulement Obligations under the 1951 Convention relating to the Status of Refugees and its 1967 Protocol.* http://www.unhcr.org/4d9486929.pdf.

UNHCR. 2008. "The Dublin Regulation: Asylum in Europe." *United Nations High Commissioner for Refugees.* http://www.unhcr.org/4a9d13d59.pdf.

UNHCR. 2015. *Guidelines on International Protection No. 11: Prima Facie Recognition of Refugee Status.* http://www.unhcr.org/558a62299.html.

Universal Declaration of Human Rights (UDHR). 1948. 10 December.

Vienna Convention on the Law of Treaties (VCLT). 1969. (adopted 23 May 1969, entered into force 27 January 1980).

Weis, Paul. 1990. "The Refugee Convention, 1951: The Travaux Preparatories Analysed with a Commentary by Dr. Paul Weis." *United Nations High Commissioner for Refugees.* http://www.refworld.org/docid/53e1dd114. html.

Conclusion

Observations on Migration in the Twenty-First Century: Where to from Here?

MARIANNA KARAKOULAKI, LAURA SOUTHGATE
& JAKOB STEINER

Migration studies is an incredibly wide field, with multiple strains of research associated with a number of different research fields, from Anthropology and Sociology to International Relations and Development. Jorgen Carling (2017) recently compiled a list of 36 different nexuses between migration and other topics found in academic literature. A list that is likely to expand in the future, it showcases the way different fields of study interconnect and intersect with migration studies. This makes compiling a collection that explores migration a challenging task, and it results in many aspects being left uncovered. This is no less true for this book and it should be kept in mind when assessing the book's scope.

Migration is trapped in the triangle between controversial scholarly, popular and political debate, with decisions affecting the lives of thousands directly and often immediately. Peter Scholten, Han Entzinger and Rinus Penninx (2015) note how the field of migration studies has fragmented increasingly in recent years. They hypothesise that its politicisation has played an important role in that. They also find that while the number of studies has mushroomed, this has not translated into more evidence-based policies being implemented on the ground at the European level. In the same book, Ann Singleton (2015) frames it even more starkly, stating that academic research commissioned by governments or government related institutions is used as a justification for certain pre-ordained policies or 'policy-based evidence making'. Mired in this web of controversy, scholars must ask themselves how their work affects and is affected by the two remaining corners of the triangle – media coverage and popular perception, as well as policy and political decisions. What is missing from the current scholarly debate on migration? Is research shaping narratives, and are they helpful? Can research better inform popular opinion and policy approaches, and if so, how? While data driven research on migration is still undeniably important, these questions ask for critical reflections on migration on a number of levels beyond numerical data.

In an attempt to address these questions, we sought chapters from scholars and practitioners from different fields of study, in order to give a more critical and interdisciplinary overview of migration in the twenty-first century. Influenced by our own work in the field, as well as coverage of what has been dubbed 'the migration crisis', we wanted to create something that provides and explores a variety of aspects so that readers of this book can see migration from different perspectives. The book therefore connects migration to political and social theory, security and critical security studies, human rights and legal studies, criminology and media studies, with anthropological and sociological notions.

At the very root of these reflections sits the migrant. As highlighted in the introduction, the terminology to address this topic still remains an unresolved issue. Nando Sigona (2017) argues that the way we categorise the migrant or the refugee has important legal and political implications. Michael Collyer, Franck Düvell, and Hein de Haas (2012), note that terminology relating to migrants has often been used to mean what is politically desirable, rather than represent an actual state of affairs. And while the importance of the inclusion of civil society in the development of policies and narratives has been emphasised here and elsewhere (Singleton 2015; Banulescu-Bogdan 2011), migrants themselves, as part of civil society, should also be involved – in public discourse as well as academia. Dimitris Papadopoulos, Niamh Stephenson and Vassilis Tsianos (2008, 202–221) discuss the centrality of the migrant in political and public discourse in their development of the notion of the autonomy of migration. They argue that contrary to popular belief of the invisibility of the migrant, the migrant actually has a role in the formation of sovereignty, as they form a variety of activities and realities while they are on the move, despite their lack of papers. If we consider the migrant as a politically active subject, then those voices within the migrant community currently prevented from being heard need special attention.

Although it is only partly accounted for in the current volume, migration is quickly equated with what is currently framed as a 'crisis' in Europe. This includes refugees and migrants moving towards Australia, which is often used in European policy debates as an example. Other migrations and their associated drivers, motivations and narratives, including movements within the African continent without Europe as the final target (de Haas 2008), migration between Central Asia and Russia (Marat 2009) or migration of Chinese migrants abroad and internally (Mallee and Pieke 2013), remain largely side-lined. This makes it easier to frame the current 'migration crisis' as a singular event that can be dealt with, detached from a larger context.

This book is published at a time when migration still dominates our media headlines. The exodus of Rohyngya from Myanmar, the deaths in the Mediterranean and the ordeal of refugees stranded on its islands, as well as a US president who has vowed to build a wall to keep migrants out, are just a few stark examples. A critical debate on migration will therefore need to be sustained. At the same time, we need to consider that with migration comes integration, and a strong impact on a country's social structure, economy and relations between home and host countries. This has been dealt with in literature before, especially for the case of migrants from Turkey to Germany (Oestergaard-Nielsen 2003), and less so for migrants from Pakistan to the UK (Shaw 2000). What was regarded as a brief influx of 'foreigners' then turned into something that changed the social fabric and history of – among other regions – the two largest cities of Western Europe. What is discussed as an imminent 'crisis' today for Europe will eventually be seen through the lens of a long lasting process of change.

Exemplified by the many questions arisen here, this book also remains a first step towards different pathways of critical approaches towards migration. As such, for the time being, it is effectively without conclusion. We hope instead that it will be the beginning of a fruitful debate.

References

Banulescu-Bogdan, Natalia. 2011. "The Role of Civil Society in EU Migration Policy: Perspectives on the European Union's Engagement in Its Neighbourhood." Washington D.C.

Carling, Jorgen. 2017. "Thirty-six migration nexuses, and counting." 31 July 2017. https://jorgencarling.org/2017/07/31/thirty-six-migration-nexuses-and-counting/.

Collyer, Michael, Franck Düvell and Hein de Haas. 2012. "Critical Approaches to Transit Migration." Population, Space and Place 18 (4). John Wiley & Sons, Ltd: 407–14.

de Haas, Hein. 2008. "The Myth of Invasion: The Inconvenient Realities of African Migration to Europe." *Third World Quarterly* 29 (7): 1305–22.

Mallee, Hein and Frank N. Pieke, eds. 2013. *Internal and International Migration: Chinese Perspectives*. New York: Routledge.

Marat, Erica. 2009. "Labor Migration in Central Asia: Implications of the Global Economic Crisis." Silk Road Paper Series. Washington D.C. http://isdp.eu/content/uploads/images/stories/isdp-main-pdf/2009_marat_labor-migration-in-central-asia.pdf.

Oestergaard-Nielsen, Eva. 2003. *Transnational Politics: The Case of Turks and Kurds in Germany*. London: Routledge.

Papadopoulos, Dimitris, Niamh Stephenson and Vassilis Tsianos. 2008. *Escape Routes*. London: Pluto Press

Scholten, Peter, Han Entzinger and Rinus Penninx. 2015. "Research-Policy Dialogues on Migrant Integration in Europe: A Conceptual Framework and Key Questions." In *Integrating Immigrants in Europe*, edited by Peter Scholten, Han Entzinger, Rinus Penninx and Stijn Verbeek, 1–16. Springer.

Shaw, Alison. 2000. *Kinship and Continuity: Pakistani Families in Britain*. New York: Routledge.

Sigona, Nando. 2017. "The Contested Politics of Naming in Europe's 'refugee crisis'." *Ethnic and Racial Studies*: 1–5.

Singleton, Ann. 2015. "Speaking Truth to Power? Why Civil Society, beyond Academia, Remains Marginal in EU Migration Policy." In *Integrating Immigrants in Europe*, edited by Peter Scholten, Han Entzinger, Rinus Penninx and Stijn Verbeek, 131–40. Springer.

Note on Indexing

E-IR's publications do not feature indexes. If you are reading this book in paperback and want to find a particular word or phrase you can do so by downloading a free PDF version of this book from the E-International Relations website.

View the e-book in any standard PDF reader such as Adobe Acrobat Reader (pc) or Preview (mac) and enter your search terms in the search box. You can then navigate through the search results and find what you are looking for. In practice, this method can prove much more effective than consulting an index.

If you are using apps (or devices) to read our e-books, you should also find word search functionality in those.

You can find all of our e-books at: http://www.e-ir.info/publications

www.ingramcontent.com/pod-product-compliance
Lightning Source LLC
Chambersburg PA
CBHW060315030426
42336CB00011B/1051